INTERNATIONAL ACTORS AND TRADITIONAL JUSTICE
IN SUB-SAHARAN AFRICA

INTERNATIONAL ACTORS AND TRADITIONAL JUSTICE IN SUB-SAHARAN AFRICA

Policies and Interventions in Transitional Justice and Justice Sector Aid

Edited by
Eva Brems
Giselle Corradi
Martien Schotsmans

intersentia
Cambridge – Antwerp – Portland

Intersentia Ltd
Sheraton House | Castle Park
Cambridge | CB3 0AX | United Kingdom
Tel.: +44 1223 370 170 | Email: mail@intersentia.co.uk

Distribution for the UK:
NBN International
Airport Business Centre, 10 Thornbury Road
Plymouth, PL6 7PP
United Kingdom
Tel: +44 1752 202 301 | Fax: +44 1752 202 331
Email: orders@nbninternational.com

Distribution for the USA and Canada:
International Specialized Book Services
920 NE 58th Ave Suite 300
Portland, OR 97213
USA
Tel.: +1 800 944 6190 (toll free)
Email: info@isbs.com

Distribution for Austria:
Neuer Wissenschaftlicher Verlag
Argentinierstraße 42/6
1040 Wien
Austria
Tel.: +43 1 535 61 03 24
Email: office@nwv.at

Distribution for other countries:
Intersentia Publishing nv
Groenstraat 31
2640 Mortsel
Belgium
Tel.: +32 3 680 15 50
Email: mail@intersentia.be

International Actors and Traditional Justice in Sub-Saharan Africa. Policies and Interventions in Transitional Justice and Justice Sector Aid
Eva Brems, Giselle Corradi and Martien Schotsmans (eds.)

ISBN: 978-1-78068-287-7
Depot no.: D/2015/7849/5
NUR 828

British Library Cataloguing in Publication Data. A catalogue record for this book is available from the British Library.

PREFACE

This book originates in a research project conducted by the Human Rights Centre of Ghent University (UG) in partnership with the University of Cape Town (UCT). The project 'Addressing Traditional Law in Post-Conflict Judicial and Legal Development Aid in Sub-Sahara Africa' (AFTRALAW) was funded by the Belgian Science Policy Office (BELSPO) from April 2008 to March 2011, and was carried out under the supervision of Professor Eva Brems (UG) and Professors Thomas Bennett and Christina Murray (UCT), with Martien Schotsmans as a researcher for the component on transitional justice (UG) and Giselle Corradi (UG) and Lia Nijzink (UCT) as researchers for the component on justice sector aid. An initial version of the results of this three-year policy-supportive research was published in Dutch in Bennett, Brems, Corradi, Nijzink and Schotsmans' *Internationale Actoren en Traditioneel Recht in Sub-Sahara Afrika: Beleid en Interventies op het Vlak van Transitional Justice en Ontwikkelingshulp aan de Justitiesector* (Academia Press).

ACKNOWLEDGEMENTS

The editors of this book wish to thank the Belgian Science Policy Office for funding the AFTRALAW research project (Addressing Traditional Law in Legal and Judicial Development Aid in Sub-Saharan Africa) that gave rise to this book, and in particular Mrs Margarida Freire and her predecessor, Mrs Zakia Khattabi, for their enthusiasm and support throughout the course of the research. We are also grateful to the scientific committee that followed up the project from beginning to end for providing their input and advice: Mrs Lara Deramaix, Prof. Marie-Claire Foblets, Mr Renaud Galand, Prof. Em. Luc Huyse, Mr Robert Olbrechts, Prof. Barbara Oomen, Mr Dick Oosting, Prof. Stephan Parmentier, Prof. Filip Reyntjens, Dr Heidy Rombouts, Dr Stef Vandeginste, Mr Marc Van Wymeersch and Mr Pierre Vincke. We are also much indebted to Dr Marleen Renders who played a key role in the design of the AFTRALAW project and the acquisition of the funding that made the research possible, as well as to our South African partners, Prof. Tom Bennett, Prof. Christina Murray and Mrs Lia Nijzink from the University of Cape Town with whom we collaborated in the course of the research. Our thanks are also due to all the interviewees who dedicated their time and shared their views with us during the fieldwork. A word of thanks also goes out to the keynote speakers and participants in the focus group discussions held during the 'Traditional Justice and the Role of External Actors in Africa' international forum organised in Cape Town from 23 to 25 March 2010: Mrs Jane Frances Adongo, Prof. Joe Alie, Mr Littleton Braima, Mr Abdul Carimo, Mr Jacob Chibwe, Mr Peter Chinoko, Prof. Danwood Chirwa, Dr Aninka Claassens, Mrs Olayinka Creighton-Randall, Mr Custodio Dumas, Mrs Charlotte Duncan, Mr Gratien Dusingizimana, Mr Christian Eldon, Mr Anastase Gakire, Prof. Chuma Himonga, Mrs Urusaro Alice Karekezi, Mr Fergus Kerrigan, Mr Daniel Komakech, Mr Sheku A. Koroma, Mr Kenan Manda, Mr Greg Moran, Dr Sindiso Msisi, Mr Daniel Muwolobi, Mr Freddy Mutanguha, Mrs Annette Nhekairo, Mrs Frieda Nicolai, Mr Lino Owor Ogara, Mr Kenneth Akena Oketta, Mr Robert Olbrechts, Mr Benedict Sannoh, Mr Monfred Sesay, Ms Emily Sikazwe, Mrs Yasmin Sooka, Mrs Katja Taela, Mr Hugo Van der Merwe and Mr Charles Villa-Vicencio, as well as the keynote speakers and panel participants of the 'International Actors and Traditional Justice in Sub-Sahara Africa: Policies and Practices in Justice Sector Aid and Transitional Justice' international seminar held in Brussels on 14 February 2011: Dr Phil Clark, Dr Tanja Chopra, Mrs Jacky Devis, Mr Mark Freeman, Prof. Anne Griffiths, Mr Fergus Kerrigan, Mrs Kersty McCourt, Mr Robert Olbrechts, Mr Mark Salter, Mr Albrecht Stockmayer and

Dr Stef Vandeginste. Finally, we wish to thank Ms Martine Dewulf for her administrative support in the course of the project and her assistance with setting up the bibliography for this book.

CONTENTS

LIST OF ABBREVIATIONS

ASF	Avocats Sans Frontières
BTC	Belgische Technische Coöperatie
CDDH	Centre Danois des Droits de l'Homme
CFJJ	Centro de Formação Juridica e Judiciaria
DANIDA	Danish International Development Agency
DFID	Department for International Development
DPKO	Department for Peace Keeping Operations
EU	European Union
FAO	Food and Agriculture Organization
GTZ	Gesellschaft für Technische Zusammenarbeit
ICC	International Criminal Court
ICTJ	International Center for Transitional Justice
ICTR	International Criminal Tribunal for Rwanda
ICTY	International Criminal Tribunal for the former Yugoslavia
INGO	international non-governmental organisation
IRCSL	Inter-Religious Council of Sierra Leone
NGO	non-governmental organisation
OECD	Organisation for Economic Cooperation and Development
OECD-DAC	Organisation for Economic Cooperation and Development – Development Assistance Committee
PRI	Penal Reform International
RCN Justice & Démocratie	Réseau des Citoyens – Citizens' Network for Justice & Democracy
RPF	Rwandan Patriotic Front
SCSL	Special Court for Sierra Leone
TRC	truth and reconciliation commission
UNDP	United Nations Development Programme
UNICEF	United Nations Children's Fund
UNIFEM	United Nations Development Fund for Women
UNOHCHR	United Nations Office of the High Commissioner for Human Rights
USAID	United States Agency for International Development
UN	United Nations
WLSA	Women and Law in Southern Africa

PART I

GENERAL INTRODUCTION

CHAPTER 1

INTERNATIONAL ACTORS AND TRADITIONAL JUSTICE IN AFRICA

Giselle Corradi and Martien Schotsmans

1. INTRODUCTION

International actors, such as multilateral, bilateral and non-governmental donors and organisations, play an important role in the legal landscapes of Sub-Saharan Africa. On the one hand, they support transitional justice initiatives in the framework of post-conflict reconstruction efforts. On the other hand, they provide assistance for interventions in the context of justice sector aid. While international support for transitional justice and justice sector aid is not unique to the African continent, in this region, international actors' involvement in these domains is noteworthy. This can be explained by a range of factors, such as the prevalence of armed conflict and the emergency of democratic regimes in the aftermath of the Cold War (Piron, 2005: 1, 2). Concerned with the promotion of peace- and statebuilding, the rule of law and human rights, these interventions are not neutral. They have significant political consequences in as much as they can 'directly or indirectly influence existing legal relations and change the conditions under which people are able to use their rights' (Weilenmann, 2009: 156). Not surprisingly, in the past, academics and practitioners have produced a number of critical studies of international actors' legal and judicial interventions in this region (Piron, 2006; Barnett et al., 2007; ICTJ, 2007; Samset, Peterson and Wang, 2007; Uvin, 2009; Lekha Sriram et al., 2011). One of the topics that has recently gained momentum within studies of the role of international actors in the field of transitional justice and justice sector aid in Africa – and beyond – is the interest these actors have started to show in legal pluralism and local normative orders, which in this book we refer to by the umbrella term 'traditional justice'.[1] In both

---

1 The terms 'traditional law' and 'traditional justice' are used as umbrella terms throughout this book in order to denote a range of local normative orders, legal processes and actors, the authority and legitimacy of which does not stem from the state. See Chapters 2 and 8 respectively regarding the terminological choices specific to Part II of this book dealing with transitional justice and Part III dealing with justice sector aid.

areas, international actors are confronted with the fact that 'the law' in Africa differs from Western concepts and ideals. African legal orders are composed of a combination of formal legislation rooted in legal transplants from former colonial powers, co-opted and transformed structures of customary authority with judicial functions, and a multi-layered range of local dispute resolution mechanisms, the legitimacy of which derives from local socio-historical processes (Obarrio, 2011). All these normative orders are constantly interacting with each other, constituting a highly challenging backdrop for any intervention. Independently from the particular stance that international actors take towards this complex reality, the interventions they finance and support are inevitably impacted by and have an impact on these legal configurations.

Nevertheless, international actors have rarely taken 'the whole picture' into account. Despite their partial relevance, international actors have traditionally focused almost exclusively on formal justice institutions and legal processes, while neglecting the rest (Sriram et al., 2011: 7). There are a number of reasons for this. On the one hand, international actors have long regarded traditional justice institutions as backward.[2] On the other hand, international actors tend to over-rely on technical and legalistic approaches, including a narrow view on international law standards and human rights, which are not always easily compatible with traditional justice (McEvoy, 2008; Isser, 2011). International actors' concern that engaging in traditional justice would amount to institutionalising poor justice for poor people (Harper, 2011), and that those living in post-conflict countries are entitled to 'the same kind of conventional legal mechanisms as everyone else living in modern states' (Allen, 2006), can be read against these two issues. In addition, 'statebuilding' is approached from a centralistic and Westphalian perspective so that engagement with other sources of power is regarded as posing a threat to political stability and sovereignty (Chopra, 2009; Clarcke, 2011; Isser, 2011; Kyed, 2011). In the case of post-conflict and so-called fragile states (i.e. states that are no longer capable of providing their core functions – OECD, 2010), the reasoning is that they present a greater risk of new conflict, and therefore, that peacebuilding needs to focus on statebuilding, i.e. the reinforcement of state structures and institutions. This also applies to justice, considering the monopoly of the central state on the use of coercion and thus its primary role in the provision of security and justice (Albrecht and Buur, 2009; Baker and Scheye, 2007). Hence, there is no place for traditional justice in this view. This position became increasingly questioned by a second school of thought that points out that the Western-style Weberian state 'hardly exists in reality outside the OECD' (Boege et al., 2009; Scheye, 2009). Indeed, in many developing countries, alongside or even in the absence of functioning centralist state institutions, authority has always been situated among various actors. In such 'hybrid political orders' the state shares

[2] For an overview of international actors' perceptions of traditional justice in the context of evolving development paradigms see Corradi and Schotsmans, 2012.

its authority and legitimacy, including its capacity to provide security and justice, with other structures, and thus differs fundamentally from our Western state model (Boege et al., 2009). This is also called the 'rule of the intermediaries' or 'the second state', i.e. 'a series of networks and politics that substitute and compensate for the lack of authority of the central state and its inability to deliver essential public goods and services' (Scheye, 2009). These networks – customary courts, secret societies, traditional structures such as tribal headmen, traditional leaders, village communities, clan elders, religious brotherhoods – provide public goods and services such as justice to those who adhere to them (Scheye, 2009). Though the particular rationales provided by the literature on transitional justice and justice sector aid for explaining the need to move beyond state centric approaches to justice in Africa may differ in some regards, it is possible to identify a common denominator: working with non-state actors starts from the reality on the ground, i.e. the plurality of actors providing justice and security (Albrecht and Buur, 2009; Baines, 2010), not from an ideal that was never a reality in most African countries (e.g. Englebert and Tull, 2008). In addition, some authors emphasise the link between legal institutional arrangements and the paradigms of order that lay at the basis of different world views. According to this line of argument, in many African countries, it is necessary to engage in a plurality of justice institutions since a diversity of world views coexist at different scales (Kuyu and Le Roy, 1997). In addition, some authors highlight the fact that it is necessary to look at how different law institutions are suitable to handle issues emerging from different kinds of social relations (Penal Reform International, 2000). This resulted in the compelling argument that focusing on the state while leaving out traditional justice from the equation is exclusionary (Chirayath et al., 2005). Consequently, international actors started to react to these arguments by showing an increased concern with 'the local', including local forms of justice such as traditional justice.[3]

In transitional justice, the idea grew around the millennium that each transitional justice strategy needs to identify the most appropriate combination of complementary approaches and mechanisms considering the specific context of the post-conflict country, as a reaction to the one-size-fits-all solutions and externally imposed models used until the early nineties, and to the fact that more transitions occurred after internal conflicts that involved large groups of citizens as perpetrators, victims or both (Shaw and Waldorf, 2010; McEvoy and McGregor, 2008; Huyse and Salter, 2008; Roht-Arriaza and Mariezcurrena, 2006; among others). It is now generally accepted that, in order to be effective transitional justice strategies must be 'localised', i.e. contextually and culturally appropriate (Lutz, 2006: 333), 'place-based' (Shaw and Waldorf, 2010: 5), coming 'from below' (McEvoy and McGregor, 2008: 3) or be 'home-grown' (Lundy, 2009: 323). The call for the 'localisation' of transitional justice implied a call to increase 'local

3 See for example, DANIDA, 2010; UNDP, 2005, 2004; UN Secretary-General, 2004; OECD-DAC, 2007; World Bank, 2006, 2003; DFID, 2004; GMECD, 2002.

ownership', a concept borrowed from development and peacebuilding (Accra Agenda, 2008; Paris Declaration, 2005; OECD, 2001). It has meanwhile been integrated in various official documents on transitional justice (United Nations, 2011; United Nations, 2010; United Nations, 2004; Peace Building Commission, 2009). The United Nations acknowledge the value of traditional mechanisms in the framework of post-conflict justice: 'For the United Nations, justice is an ideal of accountability and fairness in the protection and vindication of rights and the prevention and punishment of wrongs. Justice implies regard for the rights of the accused, for the interests of victims and for the well-being of society at large. It is a concept rooted in all national cultures and traditions and, while its administration usually implies formal judicial mechanisms, traditional dispute resolution mechanisms are equally relevant' (United Nations, 2004). In the field of justice sector aid, the emphasis on poverty reduction that characterises the current development paradigm is often translated into interventions that aim at improving 'access to justice for the poor'.[4] As the argument goes, poverty is not just a matter of material deprivation, but it also entails powerlessness, vulnerability, lawlessness and fear for crime (Narayan, 2000). In the African context, this has led to the acknowledgement that most people have very limited access to formal justice, while an estimated 80 percent of disputes are handled by traditional justice institutions (Piron, 2005: 9). Hence, the need to include these institutions within access to justice interventions.

This seems to be leading to a progressive shift in the position of international actors towards traditional justice in Africa and other parts of the world, which can potentially provide some room for looking beyond formal justice – although for now this is more the case in the field of justice sector aid than in transitional justice, where international actors take a more reluctant approach.[5] It is unclear whether international actors start to give positive value to different justice institutions or whether they merely accept legal pluralism as a matter of pragmatism and simply attempt to 'manage' it (Kyed, 2011). In any case, we seem to witness the emergency of a new paradigm where international actors start to perceive traditional justice as a Janus-faced phenomenon. On the one hand, it can potentially contribute to the relevance of their interventions, but on the other hand, engaging traditional justice goes hand in hand with numerous challenges.[6] First of all, there seems to be a lack of clear theory guiding international actors' interventions (Chirayath et al., 2005). Secondly, working with these institutions remains problematic from the point of view of the various kinds of management systems that international actors apply (Harper, 2011). Third, these legal orders are often problematic from a human rights perspective (ICHRP, 2009; UNDP, UN Women, UNICEF and UNDP, 2012). Last but not least, there are serious political

---

4 See for example the 'Justice for the Poor' initiative of the World Bank and the 'Legal Empowerment of the Poor Initiative' of the United Nations Development Programme.

5 With an exception for donor support to Rwanda's Gacaca justice (Schotsmans, 2011).

6 This perception of traditional justice is visible in all the documents mentioned in supra note 3.

issues to be considered, both at the local and at the national levels (Clarcke, 2011). Against this backdrop, studies of international actors' involvement with traditional justice and legal pluralism have increased considerably. Though their regional focus is not always Africa in particular, the sheer relevance of traditional justice in this part of the world entails that in practice, a considerable share of these studies draw on examples from this region. Varied in nature and scope, these studies range from scholarly publications to guidelines prepared for international agencies.[7] As this body of knowledge grows some recurrent threads become evident, such as the need to understand the socio-historic-political and cultural context and devise tailored interventions that respond to it, the importance of taking the political dimensions of legal pluralism into account and enhancing the downwards accountability of local actors, the necessity to 'base' interventions on the experiences of justice users, the idea that international actors need to look at justice in a holistic way and engage all stakeholders, and the recognition that all these processes take time and require a long term commitment.

While also concerned with the work of international actors, this book links theory and practice moving back and forth between the empirical and the normative. In other words, this book studies the role of international actors in the areas of transitional justice and justice sector aid with respect to traditional justice in Africa with the aim of identifying current trends in policies and interventions and analysing this empirical material from the perspective of existing normative insights. On the one hand, the different chapters interrogate how international actors deal with traditional justice in a number of case study countries. They describe the kinds of policies and interventions that are actually supported and financed with special attention for the kinds of strategies that are deployed in order to address areas of tension between traditional justice and human rights. On the other hand, the book explores the relationship between international actors' interventions and the body of knowledge that exists in these domains, as well as a general socio legal theory. The different chapters are guided by the following questions: do the international actors that are active in transitional justice and justice sector aid in Africa have any policy or view regarding traditional justice? If so, what are the main features of these policies? What kinds of interventions do international actors support regarding traditional justice? Are there identifiable trends and/or gaps? What are the strategies that international actors follow in relation to possible areas of tension between traditional justice and human rights? How can these trends feed into the debate about the role of international actors in

7 For transitional justice related publications see Huyse and Salter, 2008, among others. For further publications see Chapter 2. For justice sector aid related publications see Le Roy and Kuyu, 1997; Penal Reform International, 2000; Nyamu-Musembi, 2003; DFID, 2004; Odinkalu, 2005; Kimati, 2005; Chirayath et al., 2005; Wojkowska, 2006; Weilenmann, 2007; ICHRP, 2009; DANIDA, 2009; Toomey, 2010; Wojkowska and Cunningham, 2010; Albrecht et al., 2011; Obarrio, 2011; HAKI, 2011; Kyed, 2011; Isser, 2011; Harper, 2011a, 2011b; Clarcke, 2011; Ubink and Van Rooij, 2011.

transitional justice and justice sector aid in Africa? The volume does not attempt to provide an evaluation of international actors' interventions nor an exhaustive inventory covering all countries of the region. Rather, it offers empirical data drawn from examples of who is doing what in a series of case studies. Thereby, this contribution identifies regional trends and links them to the existing literature by examining the extent to which the insights generated so far by scholars and practitioners is reflected in the work of international actors. Based on this, the book formulates a number of hypotheses that may explain current trends and proposes additional issues that need to be considered in future research agendas. Finally, the volume links two fields of intervention that have so far evolved in rather parallel ways and explores the commonalities and differences that can be found in the areas of transitional justice and justice sector aid.

2. METHODOLOGICAL CHOICES

The material presented in this book is based on a combination of research methods that in some regards overlap and in others differ for the sections on transitional justice and justice sector aid. This section presents the methodological choices that were made in general, while the introductory chapters in Part II on transitional justice and Part III on justice sector aid outline the methodological choices that differ.

Due to the nature of the research questions, this book relies heavily on the case study method. This entails an empirical enquiry that investigates a contemporary phenomenon in depth and within its real-life context, especially when the boundaries between phenomenon and context are not clearly evident (Yin, 2009). The case study is the preferred method when 'how' or 'why' are the core questions of the research, the investigator has little control over events and the focus is on a contemporary phenomenon (Yin, 2009). It relies on multiple sources of evidence and the triangulation of data while benefiting from the prior development of theoretical propositions to guide data collection and analysis (Yin, 2009).

Both for the sections on transitional justice and justice sector aid, a first exploratory phase consisted in a systematic review of grey literature produced by international actors. During this exercise, the focus was on identifying which actors had produced documents discussing their views on traditional justice and legal pluralism. At the same time, this phase was dedicated to mapping interventions related to traditional justice in Sub-Saharan Africa. Though this mapping was not exhaustive, it provided the basis for the identification of interesting case studies. The latter were selected on the basis that in those countries a number of international actors were found to be active in the field of traditional justice and legal pluralism. In addition, they were selected because different actors were involved in each case, so that a broader range of actors could be studied. Based on this, three countries were selected for research in the area of transitional justice and another four in the area of justice sector aid. The former included Rwanda, Sierra Leone and Uganda, whereas the latter researched the cases of Malawi, Mozambique, Sierra Leone and Zambia. At the same time, this phase included an extensive review of academic sources, on the basis of which a status question was drafted and which provided the foundations for the development of a first analytical framework against which the empirical data would be analysed.

The second phase of the research consisted in fieldwork in the above-mentioned case studies.[8] The methods of data collection included semi-structured interviews with a wide range of stakeholders, such as government representatives, representatives of international actors' country offices, representatives of civil society, formal and traditional justice providers and justice users. One of the main objectives of the fieldwork was to be able to deepen on the information that was available in the grey literature. Particular attention was paid to discussions with international donors that were active in this area so that their specific country discourses on traditional justice became clear. In addition, the fieldwork provided an excellent opportunity to discuss the topic with international actors that were not active in the area of traditional justice and explore their reasons for dismissing it. Interviews at governmental and civil society level revealed yet another series of issues in relation to local strategies of implementation. Based on this, it was possible to produce country mappings of interventions directly or indirectly related to traditional justice. In most cases, a number of upcountry projects were visited in situ.[9] Finally, interviews with formal and traditional justice providers and users were geared towards uncovering local perspectives on the relevance of interventions.

Once the empirical data had been collected, the findings from the different case studies were analysed in a systematic way in order to assess whether similar trends were identifiable, both within the fields of transitional justice and justice sector aid and across them. At this point, the research moved into a third phase where preliminary findings were presented and discussed with stakeholders from the case study countries. An International Forum was organised in Cape Town from 23 to 25 March 2010, which brought together representatives of stakeholders identified during the field research. The Forum served as a platform to discuss the

[8] For the case studies on transitional justice, the fieldwork in Sierra Leone took place from 05/04/09 to 17/04/09, including 52 interviews, in Rwanda from 10/07/09 to 03/08/09 (including a few interviews in Burundi) and from 10/07/10 to 24/07/10, including a total of 115 interviews, and in Uganda from 04/08/09 to 22/08/09, including 46 interviews. For the case studies on justice sector aid, the fieldwork in Malawi took place from 27/08/09 to 10/09/09, including 25 interviews; in Mozambique from 11/08/09 to 25/09/09 and from 13/09/10 to 10/10/10, including 102 interviews; in Sierra Leone from 05/04/09 to 17/04/09, including 52 interviews and in Zambia from 26/11/09 to 05/12/09, including 13 interviews.

[9] In Sierra Leone the researchers conducted interviews with local stakeholders in Makeni, Bo and Moyamba. In Mozambique, the researchers conducted interviews with local stakeholders in Morrumbene, Massinga, Maxixe and Pemba.

findings and explore further questions with these actors. Invited representatives from the selected countries were asked to present their views and reflect on their experiences with regard to international actor's engagement with traditional law. For this purpose, a series of structured focus group discussions were organised during the forum, which aimed at collectively exploring a range of relevant topics so that the analytical framework could be refined. In the area of transitional justice, considering the important differences between the transitional justice landscape in the countries under study, the emphasis of the discussions was on the need for localisation, hence for consideration of traditional values and mechanisms – which are constantly evolving – and the dilemmas donors are confronted with when invited to support such mechanisms, especially when these are not part of the state's transitional framework or when they do not respect international human rights or when traditional actors have lost their legitimacy. In the domain of justice sector aid, the focus group discussions explored the role of institutional frameworks for legal pluralism and reform proposals dealing with state recognition and regulation of customary law and traditional justice, the role of international actors active in justice sector aid and their current approaches to traditional justice in general and the perspectives of traditional justice users and providers and the way processes of change unfold at the grassroots level. Finally, a more refined version of the results was presented at an international seminar, which took place in Brussels on 2 February 2011. The seminar was attended by a mixed public of academics and practitioners and it was divided into two parts, one focusing on justice sector aid and the other on transitional justice. In both cases, the presentation of the research results was preceded by a keynote address and followed by a discussion with a panel of experts. Consequently, this book results from a process of systematic involvement and consultation of relevant stakeholders.

The usual ethical principles guiding qualitative social science research applied during the research, namely informed consent, respect regarding confidentiality requested by interviewees and access to research results for all actors involved in the process.

3. STRUCTURE OF THE BOOK

This book is divided into four parts. In addition to this general introduction, which constitutes Part I, Part II is dedicated to transitional justice and Part III to justice sector aid. Finally, Part IV deals with a number of common conclusions and recommendations.

In Part II, Chapter 2 introduces the research regarding transitional justice and develops the conceptual difference between traditional justice mechanisms and tradition-based justice mechanisms in transitional justice. Chapter 3 frames the policies and interventions of international actors in the historical evolutions on development thinking, international criminal justice, peacebuilding and the concepts of ownership and localisation. Chapters 4, 5 and 6 present the empirical data from the case studies in Rwanda, Northern Uganda and Sierra Leone respectively. Chapter 7 analyses the data and presents a number of conclusions and recommendations for transitional justice.

In Part III, Chapter 8 introduces the aim and scope of the section dealing with justice sector aid. The chapter clarifies a number of specific terminological and methodological choices that apply only to this section and situates the study within the existing literature on the topic. Chapter 9 provides the general background to the empirical data presented in the case studies by outlining a series of common features running across the legal landscapes of Africa as well as the way in which justice sector aid has so far engaged with them. Chapter 10 explores how socio-legal theory on legal pluralism relates to the practice of development actors and discusses its implications. Chapters 11, 12, 13 and 14 present and discuss the empirical data from the case studies in Malawi, Mozambique, Sierra Leone and Zambia respectively, while Chapter 15 analyses how the latter relates to the insights presented in Chapters 9 and 10.

Finally, Chapter 16 explores the differences and commonalities between international actors' engagement with traditional law in the context of transitional justice and justice sector aid and proposes some recommendations.

BIBLIOGRAPHY

Albrecht, P., Kyed, H.M., Isser, D. and Harper, E. (eds.) (2011) *Perspectives on Involving Non-State and Customary Actors in Justice and Security Reform*. Rome: International Law and Development Organization.

Albrecht, P. and Buur, L. (2009) An uneasy marriage: non-state actors and police reform, *Policing and Society: an International Journal of Research and Policy*, 19:4, 390–405.

Allen, T. (2006) *Trial Justice. The International Criminal Court and the Lord's Resistance Army*. London/New York: Zed Books.

Baines, E. (2010) Spirits and Social Reconstruction after Mass Violence: Rethinking Transitional Justice, *African Affairs*, 109/436, 409–430.

Baker, B. and Scheye, E. (2007) Multi-layered justice and security delivery in post-conflict and fragile states, *Conflict, Security & Development*, 7(4), 503–528.

Barnett, M., Kim, H., O'Donnell, M. and Sitea, L. (2007) Peacebuilding: What Is in a Name?, *Global Governance*, 13, 35–58.

Boege, V., Brown, A., Clements, K. and Nolan, N. (2009) On Hybrid Political Orders and Emerging States: State Formation in the Context of 'Fragility'. In *Building Peace in the Absence of States: Challenging the Discourse on State Failure*. Berghof Handbook Dialogue Series No. 8, Berghof Research Center for Constructive Conflict Management, 15–35.

Chirayath, L., Sage, C. and Woolock, M. (2005) Customary Law and Policy Reform: Engaging with the Plurality of Justice Systems [online] http://siteresources.worldbank.org/INTWDR2006/Resources/477383-1118673432908/Customary_Law_and_Policy_Reform.pdf (10/07/12).

Chopra, T. (2009) When Peacebuilding Contradicts Statebuilding: Notes from the Arid Lands of Kenya, *International Peacekeeping*, 16:4, 531–545.

Clarcke, R. (2011) Customary Legal Empowerment: Towards a More Critical Approach. In Ubink, J. (ed.) *Customary Justice: Perspectives on Legal Empowerment*. Rome: International Legal Development Organization.

Corradi, G. and Schotsmans, M. (2012) Introduction. In Bennett, T., Brems, E., Corradi, G., Nijzink, L. and Schotsmans, M. (eds.) *African Perspectives on Tradition and Justice*. Antwerp: Intersentia.

DANIDA (2010) Informal Justice Systems. How to Note. Ministry of Foreign Affairs of Denmark [online] http://www.danidadevforum.um.dk.

DFID – UK Department for International Development (2004) Non-State Justice and Security Systems [online] http://www.gsdrc.org/docs/open/SSAJ101.pdf (30/03/12).

Donais, T. (2009) Empowerment or Imposition? Dilemmas of Local Ownership in Post-Conflict Peacebuilding Processes, *Peace & Change*, 34:1, 3–26.

German Federal Ministry for Economic Cooperation and Development (2002) Paper 405, Division of Development Education and Information.

HAKI Legal Empowerment Network (2011) Engaging Customary Justice Systems, White Paper [online] http://www.hakinetwork.org/resource-center/ (11/07/12).

Harper, E. (2011a) *Customary Justice: From Program Design to Impact Evaluation*. Rome: International Law and Development Organization.

Harper, E. (ed.) (2011b) *Working With Customary Justice Systems: Post-Conflict and Fragile States*. Rome: International Law and Development Organization.

Huyse, L. and Salter, M. (eds.) (2008) *Traditional Justice after Violent Conflict. Learning from African Experiences*. IDEA: Stockholm, Sweden.

ICHRP – International Council on Human Rights Policy (2009) When Legal Worlds Overlap: Human Rights, State and Non-State Law. Versoix: International Council on Human Rights Policy.

Isser, D. (ed.) (2011) *Customary Justice and the Rule of Law in War-Torn Societies*. Washington DC: United States Institute of Peace Press.

Kimati, L.W. (2005) Non-State Institutions as a Basis of State Reconstruction: The Case of Justice Systems in Africa. Paper presented for CODESRIA's 11th General Assembly, Maputo, 6–10 December 2005.

Kuyu, C. and Le Roy, E. (1997) La Politique Française de Coopération Judiciaire: Bilan et Perspectives. Observatoire de la Coopération Française, Rapport 1997, 36–65. Paris: Karthala.

Kyed, H.M. (2011) Introduction to the Special Issue: Legal Pluralism and International Development Interventions. *Journal of Legal Pluralism*, 63, 1–23.

LAWRENCE, M. (2012) Towards a Non-State Security Sector Reform Strategy. SSR-Issue Papers no. 8, May 2012, The Centre for International Governance Innovation, Canada. www.ciginonline.org.

LEKHA SRIRAM, C., MARTIN-ORTEGA, O., and HERMAN, J. (2011) *Peacebuilding and Rule of Law in Africa. Just Peace?* London/New York: Routledge.

LUNDY, P. (2009) Exploring Home-Grown Transitional Justice and Its Dilemmas: A Case Study of the Historical Enquiries Team, Northern Ireland, *The International Journal of Transitional Justice*, 3, 321–340.

LUTZ, E. (2006) Transitional Justice: Lessons learned and the road ahead. In: Roht-Arriaza, N. and Mariezcurrena, J., *Transitional Justice in the Twenty-First Century. Beyond truth versus justice.* Cambridge: Cambridge University Press, 325–341.

MCEVOY, K. (2008) Letting go of Legalism: Developing a 'Thicker' Version of Transitional Justice. In McEvoy, K. and McGregor, L. (eds.) *Transitional Justice from Below. Grassroots Activism and the Struggle for Change.* Oxford/Portland, OR: Hart Publishing.

MCEVOY, K. and MCGREGOR, L. (eds.) (2008) *Transitional Justice from Below. Grassroots Activism and the Struggle for Change.* Oxford/Portland, OR: Hart Publishing.

NARAYAN, D. (2000) *Voices of the Poor. Can Anyone Hear Us?*, The World Bank Group

NYAMU-MUSEMBI, C. (2003) Review of Experience in Engaging with 'Non-State' Justice Systems in East-Africa [online] http://www.gsdrc.org/docs/open/DS37.pdf (10/07/12).

OBARRIO, J. (2011) Traditional justice as rule of law in Africa: an anthropological perspective. In Lekha-Sriram, C., Martin-Ortega, O. and Herman, J. (eds.) *Peace Building and Rule of Law in Africa. Just Peace?*, 21–43. London/New York: Routledge.

ODINKALU C.A. (2005) Poor Justice or Justice for the Poor? A Policy Framework for Reform of Customary and Informal Justice Systems in Africa. In Sage and Woolcock (eds.) *The World Bank Legal Review, Law, Equity and Development Vol. 2*, 141–165. Washington DC: Martinus Nijhoff.

OECD (2001) *Helping Prevent Violent Conflict. The DAC Guidelines.* International Development. www.oecd.org.

OECD (2010) *The State's Legitimacy in Fragile Situations: Unpacking complexity.* www.oecd.org.

OECD-DAC (Organization for Economic Cooperation and Development) (2007) Handbook on Security System Reform, Supporting Security and Justice [online] http://www.oecd.org/dataoecd/43/25/38406485.pdf (08/05/12).

PEACEBUILDING COMMISSION (2009) Working Group on Lessons Learned. Lessons Learned from National Dialogue in Post Conflict Situations. Chair's Summary.

PENAL REFORM INTERNATIONAL (2000) *Access to Justice in Sub-Saharan Africa. The Role of Traditional and Informal Justice Systems.* London: Astron Printers.

PIRON, L.H. (2005) Donor assistance to justice sector reform in Africa: living up to the new agenda? In Open Society Justice Initiative (ed.) *Human Rights and Justice Sector Reform in Africa: Contemporary Issues and Responses.* Governance and Social Development Resource Centre.

Piron, L.H. (2006) Time to Learn, Time to Act in Africa. In Carothers, T. (ed.) *Promoting the Rule of Law Abroad: Search of Knowledge*, 275–299. Washington DC: Carnegie Endowment for International Peace.

Roth-Arriaza, N. and Mariezcurrena, J. (2006) *Transitional Justice in the Twenty-First Century. Beyond truth versus justice*. Cambridge: Cambridge University Press.

Samset, I., Peterson, S. and Wang, V. (2007) Maintaining the process? Aid to Transitional Justice in Rwanda and Guatemala. 1995–2005, The Working Group on Development and Peace (FriEnt), Bonn, November 2007.

Scheye, E. (2009) *State-Provided Service, Contracting Out, and Non-State Networks: Justice and Security as Public and Private Goods and Services*, The International Network on Conflict and Fragility (INCAF), OECD.

Schotsmans, M. (2011) 'But we also support monitoring': INGO monitoring and donor support to *gacaca* justice in Rwanda. *International Journal of Transitional Justice*, 5, 390–411.

Shaw, R. and Waldorf, L. (2010), *Localizing transitional justice. Interventions and priorities after mass violence*. Stanford, CA: Stanford University Press.

Toomey, L. (2010) A Delicate Balance: Building Complementary Customary and Sate Legal Systems, *The Law and Development Review*, 3(1), 156–208.

Ubink, J. and Van Rooij, B. (2011) Towards Customary Legal Empowerment: An Introduction. In Ubink, J. (ed.) *Customary Justice: Perspectives on Legal Empowerment*. Rome: International Legal Development Organization.

Ubink J. (ed.) (2011) *Customary Justice: Perspectives on Legal Empowerment*. Rome: International Law and Development Organization.

UN Women, UNICEF and UNDP (2012) Informal Justice Systems. Charting a Course for Human Rights Based Engagement [online] (15/10/12).

UNDP – United Nations Development Programme (2004) Access to Justice: Practice Note [online] http://www.undp.org/governance/docs/Justice_PN_English.pdf (08/05/12).

UNDP – United Nations Development Programme (2005) Programming for Justice: Access for All [online] http://regionalcentrebangkok.undp.or.th/practices/governance/a2j/tools/index1.html (30/03/12).

United Nations (2004) *The Rule of Law and Transitional Justice in Conflict and Post-Conflict Societies*, Report of the Secretary-General, 23 August 2004, S/2004/616.

United Nations (2010) *United Nations Approach to Transitional Justice*, Guidance Note of the Secretary-General.

United Nations, Office of the High Commissioner for Human Rights (2009) *National Consultations on Transitional Justice, Rule-of-Law Tools for Post-conflict States*. New York and Geneva, HR/PUB/09/2.

Uvin, P. (2009) The development/peacebuilding nexus: a typology and history of changing paradigms. *Journal for Peacebuilding and Development*, 5–24.

Weilenmann, M. (2007) Legal Pluralism: A New Challenge for Development Agencies. In Penal Reform International and Bluhm Legal Clinic of the Northwestern University School of Law (eds.) *Access to Justice in Africa and Beyond: Making the*

Rule of Law a Reality [online] http://www.penalreform.org/files/rep-2007-access-africa-and-beyond-en.pdf (06/07/12).

Weilenmann, M. (2009) Project Law – a Power Instrument of Development Agencies: A Case Study from Burundi. In von Benda-Beckmann, F., von Benda-Beckmann, K. and Griffiths, A. (eds.) *The Power of Law in a Transnational World*. New York/Oxford: Berghahn Books.

Wojkowska, E. and Cunningham, J. (2010) Justice Reform's New Frontier: Engaging with Customary Systems to Legally Empower the Poor. In Golub (ed.) *Legal Empowerment: Practitioners' Perspectives*. Rome: International Law and Development Organization.

Wojkowska, E. (2006) Doing justice: how informal justice systems can contribute [online] http://www.democraciaejustica.org/cienciapolitica3/sites/default/files/doingjusticeewawojkowska130307.pdf (08/05/12).

World Bank (2003) *Legal and Judicial Reform: Strategic Directions*. Washington DC: The World Bank.

World Bank (2006) World Development Report, Equity and Development [online] http://siteresources.worldbank.org/INTWDR2006/Resources/477383-1127230817535/082136412X.pdf (08/05/12).

Yin, R. (2009) *Case Study Research. Design and Methods*. Los Angeles: Sage.

PART II

INTERNATIONAL ACTORS AND TRADITIONAL JUSTICE IN TRANSITIONAL JUSTICE

CHAPTER 2
THE ROLE OF TRADITION IN TRANSITIONAL JUSTICE

Martien SCHOTSMANS

1. AIM AND SCOPE OF THE RESEARCH

Over the past two decades, more than 15 countries in Sub-Saharan Africa have put an end to armed conflict or an authoritarian regime.[1] Most of these were intra-state conflicts, i.e. conflicts within a single state, between the government and one or more armed groups, or between two or more armed groups.[2] These conflicts caused large numbers of casualties (over 1 million in Sudan, DRC and Mozambique, and between 99,000 to 1 million in Rwanda, Angola, Ethiopia, Burundi and Liberia).[3] During many of these conflicts massive human rights violations were committed against civilians and often by civilians.

As a consequence, donors developed strategies to deal with post-conflict reconstruction in these countries, with a view to enhance sustainable peace as a precondition to the further development of the countries involved. Dealing with crimes committed during the conflict, in other words transitional justice, was added to the agenda. In this regard, donors have supported internationally created tribunals and truth commissions. Given the strong involvement of civilians in these conflicts, there was a need for mechanisms to pursue justice and reconciliation at a local level, including mechanisms based on traditional values.

In the framework of this evolution, this book looks into to the following research questions. First, have international actors involved in transitional justice developed a policy in relation to traditional justice and what are the main features? Second, what projects, programmes and interventions in the field of traditional

1 Angola, Burundi, CAR, Congo Brazzaville, DRC, Ethiopia, Eritrea, Ivory Coast, Liberia, Mozambique, Nigeria, Uganda, Rwanda, Sierra Leone, Sudan, Chad, Togo and South Africa. Source: Uppsala University, UPCD-PRIO dataset, www.pcr.uu.se.

2 www.pcr.uu.se/database/definitions_all.htm.

3 Source: Political Economy Research Institute, University of Massachusetts, www.peri.umass.edu.

justice are supported by international actors? And third, how do international actors deal with possible tensions between traditional justice and human rights?

2. METHODOLOGY

As mentioned in the introduction to this book, the research methodology comprised three steps: a literature review, a series of case studies and the submission and discussion of the findings with stakeholders and academics during two international seminars. Specifically for the transitional justice part of this research, three types of literature were analysed: the literature on transitional justice, on peacebuilding and on development. Additionally, some literature on legal anthropology, legal pluralism and international criminal law was consulted. As to 'grey' literature, policy documents of donors, international non-governmental organisations (INGOs) and other international actors were studied.

Subsequently, three case studies were selected for this part of the research, instead of two as planned in the research project, thus allowing further comparison. The selection criteria are explained below (section 2.3.1). For each of the three cases a literature study was conducted on the country and conflict background, in order to map the transitional justice landscape and provide an overview of traditional views and mechanisms in the country. Based on this research, hypotheses, and questionnaires were developed to conduct semi-structured interviews during the field research. The field research in Sierra Leone took place in April 2009, in Rwanda (and Burundi) in July 2009 and July 2010 and in Uganda in August 2009. The research was not limited to the capital of the country, but always included one or more regions in which tradition-based activities had taken place (for Sierra Leone: the Makeni, Bo and Moyamba district; for Rwanda: various locations in the Huye district, in Rwamagana and around Kigali; in Uganda: various locations in and around Gulu). In each country a wide range of stakeholders was interviewed: from government to donors, international and local non-governmental organisations (NGOs), traditional and religious leaders, academics, people involved in policy making and persons who had participated in the respective tradition-based mechanisms, either as judge or mediator, as perpetrators or victims, or as members of the public. Furthermore, some donors were interviewed by telephone or in Belgium and various information exchanges took place via e-mail. A total of 212 persons were interviewed (including eight persons who were interviewed twice). Focus group discussions were organised when considered useful. Furthermore, some tradition-based activities were observed (*gacaca* hearings and an *itorero* session in Rwanda, and a *wang oo* meeting in Uganda).

After an initial mapping of post-conflict countries in Sub-Saharan Africa, the selection was narrowed down to those countries where traditional mechanisms were in one way or another used to deal with past crimes or violations (thus excluding Burundi, among others), then again narrowed down to those countries where such mechanisms had been supported by international actors (thus excluding Mozambique, among others). This led to the selection of Sierra Leone, Rwanda and Northern Uganda as case studies, leaving aside some other countries where the peace process was still more recent at the time the research started and where no lessons were to be learned yet (such as Liberia and Kenya).

The selection of these countries has several advantages.

First, comparison is possible since all three countries have known a proximity conflict, i.e. a conflict where civilians were the main targets of the crimes committed and where civilians were also among the perpetrators: they joined the armed forces or an armed opposition movement in committing these crimes, after forceful or voluntary conscription or as a result of hate campaigns. This means that victims and perpetrators, even if they did not know each other directly, were often from the same village or region and have to live together again after the conflict. It is therefore interesting to compare how in the three countries tradition-based mechanisms are being used to address problems of post-conflict coexistence at an individual and community-level, or even at a national level.

Second, the three countries have ended their respective conflicts in a chronological order (Rwanda in 1994, Sierra Leone in 1999 and Northern Uganda in 2007, at least according to the dates of the peace agreements for the latter two). This timeframe coincides with important shifts in both transitional justice and peacebuilding strategies. The study of the three countries and donors' agency therein will illustrate these developments.

Third, a body of literature and research on the use of tradition is available on the three countries (although to a lesser extent for Sierra Leone). Since this research project did not comprise empirical sociological field studies it will not present a final analysis of the use of tradition-based mechanisms dealing with past crimes, nor an assessment of their impact. Where appropriate, relevant literature will be referred to.

After analysing the obtained data, the preliminary findings were then reviewed during the already mentioned Forum in Cape Town, to which five key stakeholders from each country were invited (government, donors, NGOs and academics). During this Forum, three academics, one from Sierra Leone, one from Rwanda and one from Uganda, gave a presentation on an aspect of tradition-based mechanisms in their countries. This was followed by three focus group discussions. The first concerned the donor perspective and dealt with motives, challenges and the responsibility of donors in making the choice whether or not to support activities based on tradition. The second looked at the official government policy on the use of traditional mechanisms and explored the contradiction between the posted and the underlying motives thereof, as well as the problem of the lack of political will and how this can be tackled. The third discussion examined the issue from the local perspective and looked into the legitimacy of tradition-based mechanisms, and questioned the importance of knowing whether they are (re)invented or based on local values. Each participant was asked to make a presentation depending on his personal view, followed by a debate. The Forum concluded with the presentation and adoption of the findings of the participants.

During the final seminar in Brussels, the researchers presented and discussed the main difficulties donors face when deciding whether or not to support tradition-based mechanisms, as well as lessons, to an audience of donors, international NGOs and academics.

3. CONCEPTUAL FRAMEWORK

3.1. TRANSITIONAL JUSTICE

Transitional justice is about how to deal with legacies of abuses committed in the past by previous regimes or during an armed conflict. Transitional justice as a concept first occurred in the early 1990s. However, some mechanisms, which are today labelled as transitional justice mechanisms, were already used much earlier. The war crime tribunals of Nuremberg and Tokyo after World War II, the truth commissions or commissions of inquiry established in several Latin American countries in the eighties and the South African Truth and Reconciliation Commission established in 1995 are all transitional justice mechanisms.

But it is only since some 25 years that transitional justice emerged as a specific field of research and practice. Interestingly, transitional justice is being studied by various disciplines: law (mainly human rights and criminal law), political science, sociology, anthropology, psychology and peace and conflict studies (Kritz, 2002). Criminology is only recently starting to gain interest in the topic, through studies on political crimes and restorative justice (Parmentier, Vanspauwen and Weitekamp, 2008). This multidisciplinary approach is linked to the fact that transitional justice is a rather policy-oriented field of research. For these reasons, definitions can be found in policy papers, 'grey' literature as well as in academic publications.

With former secretary-general Kofi Annan, the United Nations have fully integrated the concept of transitional justice as part of the UN policy, and defined it as follows (United Nations, 2004):

> 'The notion of "transitional justice" discussed in the present report comprises the full range of processes and mechanisms associated with a society's attempts to come to terms with a legacy of large-scale past abuses, in order to ensure accountability, serve justice and achieve reconciliation. These may include both judicial and non-judicial mechanisms, with differing levels of international involvement (or none at

> all) and individual prosecutions, reparations, truth-seeking, institutional reform, vetting and dismissals, or a combination thereof'.

The United Nations Development Programme (UNDP, 2006) developed its own position on transitional justice that it sees as a growing realm within the field of human rights. UNDP adopts the following definition:

> 'Transitional justice covers the ways in which societies in transition from authoritarian rule to democracy, or from armed conflict to peace, address legacies of gross and systematic human rights abuses and other violations such as large-scale corruption'.

The International Centre for Transitional Justice (ICTJ), a leading NGO in this field, defines the concept as follows:[4]

> 'Transitional justice refers to a range of approaches that societies undertake to reckon with legacies of widespread or systematic human rights abuse as they move from a period of violent conflict or oppression towards peace, democracy, the rule of law, and respect for individual and collective rights. In making such a transition, societies must confront the painful legacy, or burden, of the past in order to achieve a holistic sense of justice for all citizens, to establish or renew civic trust, to reconcile people and communities, and to prevent future abuses.'

Whereas there is a common understanding of what transitional justice is about, opinions differ slightly on what kind of abuses should be looked into: Kofi Annan uses a broad concept of 'abuses', whereas ICTJ clearly limits this to widespread or systematic human rights abuses, while UNDP mentions gross and systematic human rights abuses, meanwhile adding 'corruption' as a separate category of abuses to be addressed. It is clear that transitional justice does not just refer to any kind of abuse, nor to individual or ad hoc abuses. There needs to be a legacy of widespread violence or repression, of mass abuses (Freeman, 2006). For the purposes of this research, the focus is on international crimes and gross and massive human rights violations, as explained further.

Generally, scholars and practitioners agree on accountability, truth telling, reparations and non-repetition of violence as objectives of transitional justice. Another objective added by many, although not unanimously, is reconciliation (Huyse and Salter, 2008). The objective of institutional reform seems to cover a broad, not clearly defined area of activities, going from vetting programmes (ICTJ) to anything needed to prevent the conflict from reoccurring (UNDP). One can wonder if such institutional reform is not too broad a category to be considered as a transitional justice mechanism (Roth-Arriaza, 2006). Others,

4 International Centre for Transitional Justice, www.ictj.org, 16/05/08.

however, see institutional reform as the correspondent of the state's obligation to prevent serious human rights violations in the future (Freeman, 2006).

This research examines where traditional justice mechanisms fit into these objectives. Whereas the first idea probably is that traditional justice mechanisms are essentially focused on social healing and reconciliation, the challenge will be to verify to which extent they also meet the objectives of accountability, truth telling and reparations, and what implications that has. The research will not focus on institutional reform in the part of the research regarding transitional justice, since this is the object of the chapter on justice sector aid (Chapter 3).[5]

In conclusion, the research uses the following definition of transitional justice: 'that set of practices, mechanisms and concerns that arise following a period of conflict, civil strife or repression, and that are aimed directly at confronting and dealing with past violations of human rights and humanitarian law' (Roht-Arriaza, 2006).

3.2. TRADITIONAL AND TRADITION-BASED MECHANISMS IN TRANSITIONAL JUSTICE

During the 1990s, transitional justice was perceived as a kind of 'tool box', with criminal prosecution, truth finding, reconciliation processes, vetting and institutional reform as its main instruments, from which countries emerging from conflict could select the most appropriate ones for as far as the international community had not already made a choice for them.

Around the year 2000, the limitations of such one-size-fits-all solutions began to become clear, and the importance of context-specific solutions was slowly being recognised, both by local actors (see for example the criticism regarding the distant character of the International Criminal Tribunals for the former Yugoslavia and for Rwanda) and by international organisations. In 2004, UN Secretary-General Kofi Annan said: 'We must learn as well to eschew one-size-fits-all formulas and the importation of foreign models, and, instead, base our support on national assessments, national participation and national needs and aspirations' (UN, 2004).

A consequence of the move away from the one-size-fits-all solutions and the models imposed from the outside was the flaring up of a debate within transitional justice about the need for localisation (Huyse and Salter, 2008; Orentlicher, 2007; Roth-Arriaza and Mariezcurrena, 2006; Gready, 2005; Kritz, 2002). In this debate, transitional justice is understood to be the search for the best combination from the wide array of available mechanisms and instruments to serve the situation in the country involved. In this spectrum, local mechanisms

[5] Although the possibility to implement transitional justice measures often depends on the prior existence of functioning state institutions (Bossire, 2006).

to deal with crimes from the past are increasingly emphasised during the past few years. These vary from informal to formal, and some are completely new or modern. In this context, 'local' does not necessarily refer to their applicability in a limited geographical area, but more acutely to the source of the mechanisms, that emerge from a bottom-up approach, instead of being imposed from above. It comprises more traditional mechanisms for conflict resolution, meaning 'non-state justice systems which have existed, although not without change, since pre-colonial times and are generally found in rural areas' (Penal Reform International, 2000). Tradition is not a static whole of frozen norms and practices, but is, on the contrary, flexible, continually in development and constantly adapting to the changed reality.

With the already-quoted report by Kofi Annan, the UN consider the concept of justice as being rooted in all national cultures and traditions, recognising the specific value of traditional mechanisms: 'For the United Nations, justice is an ideal of accountability and fairness in the protection and vindication of rights and the prevention and punishment of wrongs. Justice implies regard for the rights of the accused, for the interests of victims and for the well-being of society at large. It is a concept rooted in all national cultures and traditions and, while its administration usually implies formal judicial mechanisms, traditional dispute resolution mechanisms are equally relevant' (UN, 2004).

Colonial rule gradually replaced informal justice systems by more or less formalised native or customary courts, composed of laypersons, who were often appointed by the colonial authorities. They would deal with civil matters and minor crimes among natives, applying customary law, while more serious crimes had to be dealt with by formal courts applying colonial legislation. In many African countries, such semi-formalised customary courts continue to co-exist with formal justice, leading to a variety of challenges, further analysed in Chapter 3 of this book. Under the surface of formal justice, informal justice mechanisms continue to play an important role in the settlement of day-to-day conflicts. Today, the coexistence and simultaneous operation of a variety of formal and informal justice mechanisms in the debate on justice sector aid, is acknowledged as the inevitable reality of legal pluralism. However, it is also a reality in transitional justice, though it is rarely acknowledged as such (Nagy, 2009; Berman, 2007; see further in section 2.4.3).

In addition to these day-to-day conflicts, some traditional mechanisms informally deal with serious crimes that would normally fall under the jurisdiction of the formal courts, thus replacing or complementing formal justice. In Northern Uganda for instance, a person who has been convicted for murder and served a prison sentence, may still be subjected to *mato oput* – a process comprising confessions, mediation, reparations and ritual reconciliation among Acholi clans – in order to be fully accepted again in his community (see case study on Uganda, section 2.3.4). In Sierra Leone, some acts of wilful revenge killing of returning ex-combatants took place after the war, following decisions of the secret societies and implemented by these societies. In Rwanda, a kind of informal *gacaca* – a way of dispute settlement among relatives or neighbours at grassroot level – re-emerged in some communities soon after the genocide, mainly to settle property disputes related to the genocide without entering into the crimes committed.

The transitional justice part of the research distinguishes between two levels – the official and the unofficial. Local lay courts applying customary law will not be considered, since they usually only have jurisdiction over minor conflicts and do not deal with crimes of the past.

It is clear however, as many scholars have pointed out, that these old practices have not been conceived to deal with the consequences of serious crimes committed at a large scale, across ethnic boundaries, by large numbers of perpetrators against large numbers of victims, sometimes even with interchanging roles (Huyse and Salter, 2008). In addition, the social context may have been disrupted: people have been displaced or lived in camps for many years (as in Northern Uganda), traditional leaders have not always been neutral in the conflict (as in Sierra Leone), many generation conflicts occur between the elders and the youth and poverty is overwhelming, thus making compensation by the perpetrators an illusion in all three countries. Finally, even people in rural areas in Africa are not living disconnected from the outside world anymore: sensitisation campaigns, primary school education, radio and mobile phones and mobility in general have made them aware of human rights standards.

Not surprisingly, as tradition is not static but flexible and dynamic, post-conflict societies adjust traditional mechanisms to this reality: they create new, tradition-based mechanisms, inspired both by the underlying traditional justice and reconciliation values of old mechanisms and by modern standards such as gender and children's rights, while being considerate of the enormous post-conflict constraints, such as the high numbers of perpetrators, the trauma of both victims and perpetrators and the need for peaceful coexistence of victims and perpetrators belonging to the same communities.

This leads to a great variety of mechanisms, situated on a spectrum from traditional over tradition-based mechanisms, to real hybrids of traditional and modern justice, having in common that each of them is based on the living values of a community regarding justice and reconciliation.

3.3. TRADITIONAL VALUES

This research has tried to look beyond both the romanticised, idealised promotion of tradition and the legal centralist rejection of tradition, and to adopt a more pragmatic position based on what happens on the ground and on how donors and other external actors deal with that. Indeed, the polarisation of the debate around the intrinsic value of tradition versus its invented character, compared to the universal nature versus externally imposed human rights standards, is not helpful to the debate and does not facilitate the choices donors inevitably have to make.

Whether such mechanisms are traditional as such, and therefore legitimate, or invented and therefore illegitimate, is in fact a false debate (that one could also apply to formal court-based justice mechanisms in these countries, which are equally alien to a large apart of the population). The basic point is that they are deeply rooted in a people's culture and based on existing local values regarding appropriate responses to serious crime.

Even where traditional practices have fallen into oblivion or where traditional leaders have lost legitimacy, people's concepts on how best to respond to serious crime are deeply rooted in their cosmovision or world view, of which traditional values are an undeniable part. In the three countries studied in this research the underlying traditional justice and reconciliation values of response to serious crimes are: the need for acknowledgment of wrong-doing by the perpetrator, but also of the context in which the crime occurred, the offering of apologies and the possibility to accept these (to be distinguished from forgiveness), a commitment not to repeat the past, compensation, reconciliation, full reintegration and the restoration of social harmony. The community is an active participant, being an important stakeholder considering the need for social harmony.

Unsurprisingly, there are differences as well: whereas ritual reconciliation with the ancestors is very important in Sierra Leone, this is not the case in Rwanda, where traditional rituals seem to have disappeared. On the contrary, finding the bodies of one's relatives and honouring them with a Christian funeral is crucial in Rwanda, while people in Sierra Leone do not really bother about bones and rather emphasise the spiritual dimension. In contrast, in Northern Uganda, a parcel of land on which people have been killed or skeletons have been found can only be cultivated again after purification. Also, whereas the need for the perpetrator to acknowledge his responsibility seems crucial in the three countries, the extent to which public truth telling is a requirement, or something that may just be useful or in contrast, entirely inappropriate is the object of controversy (among anthropological scholars).

However, none of these common values sound awkward to a Western public, nor do they seem to be in contradiction with human rights. Indeed, they resonate to restorative justice values, as practiced in Western countries too, be it not for such grave crimes. The way some of the values are materialised in traditional justice practices may seem repugnant – such as animal sacrifices – or unusual – such as the direct participation of the population in the debates, without being unacceptable.

This recent tendency to create hybrid mechanisms, trying to marry international standards and local practices, will become more important in the future and presents important challenges to donors (see section 2.4.3).

Such hybridisation – puzzling different pieces together – is not an easy task and does not provide a perfect picture from either perspective. In fact, when we call such hybrid, tradition-based mechanisms 'traditional', traditional leaders in these countries may very well call them 'human-rights based' or 'Western-based'. Thus, each emphasises the alien aspect of the new mechanism and criticises it, depending on his or her perspective.

Looking for inspiration in a society's (former) traditional practices can have the advantage of calling upon an existing normative framework. Their tradition-based character enhances the chances for local ownership and therefore their effectiveness and sustainability. As we will see, the argument of local ownership has been one of main motives for donors to support these unfamiliar tradition-based mechanisms. Problems occur, however, where the existing local values are in conflict with international standards. In such instances, donors hesitate to support such mechanisms, since they are in contradiction with the principles of the donors' own policy, and supporting them is opposed by international human rights organisations.

BIBLIOGRAPHY

Berman, P.S. (2007) Global Legal Pluralism, *Southern California Law Review*, 80, 1155–1237.

Freeman, M. (2006) *Truth Commissions and Procedural Fairness*. Cambridge: Cambridge University Press.

Gready, P. (2005) Analysis: Reconceptualising transitional justice, embedded and distanced justice, *Conflict, Security and Development*, 5(1), 3–21.

Huyse, L. and Salter, M. (eds.) (2008) *Traditional Justice after Violent Conflict. Learning from African Experiences*. Stockholm, Sweden: IDEA

Kritz, N. (2002) Where We Are and How We Got Here: An Overview of Developments in the Search for Justice and Reconciliation. In Henkin, A.H. (ed.) *The Legacy of Abuse: Confronting the Past, Facing the Future*, 21–45. Aspen Institute, New York University School of Law.

Nagy, R. (2009) Traditional justice and legal pluralism in transitional context: the case of Rwanda's gacaca courts. In Quinn, J.R. *Reconciliation(s). Transitional justice in post-conflict societies*, 86–115. Montréal: McGill-Queen's University Press.

Orentlicher, D. (2007) Settling accounts revisited: reconciling global norms with local agency, *International Journal for Transitional Justice*, 1, 10–22.

Parmentier, P., Vanspauwen, K. and Weitekamp, E. (2008) Dealing with the legacy of mass violence. Changing lenses to restorative justice. In Smeulers, A. and Haveman, R. (eds.) *Supranational Criminology: Towards a Criminology of International Crimes*, 335–356. Antwerp: Intersentia.

Penal Reform International (2000) Access to Justice in Sub-Saharan Africa, The Role of Traditional and Informal Justice Systems. London.

Roht-Arriaza, N. (2006) The new landscape of transitional justice. In Roht-Arriaza, N. and Mariezcurrena, J. (eds.) *Transitional Justice in the Twenty-First Century. Beyond truth versus justice*, Cambridge: Cambridge University Press.

Roht-Arriaza, N. and Mariezcurrena, J. (2006) *Transitional Justice in the Twenty-First Century. Beyond truth versus justice*, Cambridge: Cambridge University Press.

United Nations (2004) The Rule of Law and Transitional Justice in Conflict and Post-Conflict Societies, Report of the Secretary-General, 23 August 2004, S/2004/616.

CHAPTER 3

THE POLICY OF INTERNATIONAL ACTORS ON TRADITIONAL JUSTICE IN TRANSITIONAL JUSTICE

Martien SCHOTSMANS

1. THE CONTEXT OF POLICY DEVELOPMENT

The fact that this research project started in 2008 is not a coincidence at all, as it finds itself at the crossroads of the trend towards globalisation that started in the nineties and the gradually increasing attention for localisation that came up around the millennium. Where these two trends intersect, we found the challenge of providing substance to localisation without throwing global standards over board. This led to the creation of hybrid solutions – and their criticism, as we will see. These are obviously complex developments, which this book can only sketch in broad lines, with the risk of lack of nuance that any simplification entails.

1.1. GLOBALISATION IN INTERNATIONAL CRIMINAL LAW, PEACEBUILDING AND HUMAN RIGHTS

In the nineties, the importance of international criminal law gradually increased: first with the establishment of the International Criminal Tribunals for the former Yugoslavia in 1993 and for Rwanda in 1994 and following the adoption of the Rome Statute in 1998 and the establishment of the International Criminal Court (ICC) in 2002. In addition, the obligation to prosecute and the prohibition of amnesty for international crimes developed to become an emerging rule of international customary law, some aspects of which were already implied in various international conventions (like the Geneva Conventions of 1949, the Convention for the Prevention of Genocide of 1952, the Convention against Torture in 1987). These standards were reflected in various UN instruments such as the (Updated) Principles for the Protection and Promotion of Human Rights through the Fight against Impunity of 2005. This is illustrated by the fact that ruling authoritarian elites were able to proclaim self-amnesties during the 1980s, which became increasingly excluded in the last two decades, due to pressure by local and international human rights organisations, drawing 'the net of transitional justice tighter' (Call, 2007).

With regard to our research, illustrations of this evolution can be found in the UN disclaimer in the Lomé Peace Agreement of 1999 relating to Sierra Leone – which excluded amnesty for international crimes – and the increasing number of trials based on universal jurisdiction (including the prosecution of Rwandan suspects, among others, in Lausanne in 1999 and in Belgium since 2001), and of course the debate about whether the Ugandan traditional mechanisms meet the international obligation to prosecute.

With the end of the Cold War and of a number of armed conflicts and authoritarian regimes in Africa, donors started to gain interest for peacebuilding in post-conflict countries as a separate policy area between emergency relief and development. Considering the high risk of a renewed outbreak of violence within five years after the end of an armed conflict (between 20 and 50%, see: Collier and Hoeffler, 2004) programmes for peacebuilding tried to find ways to create positive peace (Galtung, 1985) as a condition for sustainable development. This means that post-conflict countries require a transitional period of peace before they can be incorporated into development programmes. Over the years, the initial linear distinction between preventive diplomacy, peace negotiations, peacekeeping and peacebuilding (see: United Nations, 1992) was replaced by the view that peacebuilding is a complex process for which a more integrated and coordinated strategy of the various actors and a wide range of measures are needed (see: United Nations, 2000). The conviction grew that such strategies are only successful if they focus on the root causes of the conflict. Hence the importance attached to democracy, good governance, the rule of law, combating corruption and finally the need for justice for past crimes increased. (Chetail, 2009; OECD, 1997; UN Secretary-General, 1998).

This coincided with the fact that in the nineties respect for human rights also became an important principle in development (Carey, 2007; UN Secretary-General, 2005; Uvin, 2002; UN Millennium Declaration, 2000; OECD-DAC, 1993; European Community, 1991), and peacebuilding (Uvin, 2009; OECD-DAC, 2001). This comprised the 'do no harm' principle, which means that all aid has an impact beyond its intended goal and that any unintended negative impacts should be avoided wherever possible (OECD-DAC, 2007a). Donors should therefore ensure that their intervention is not perceived as a complicity to human rights abuses (OECD-DAC, 2007b). Even Kofi Annan stressed in his 2004 report the importance of respecting human rights and international standards in developing a transitional justice strategy (UN Secretary-General, 2004).

This recognition of the need to address past crimes as part of peacebuilding and the increasing importance attached to the criminal prosecution of international crimes brought transitional justice automatically on the agenda of peace negotiators (as in Sierra Leone, Northern Uganda, the DRC, Burundi, Liberia, among many others).

1.2. LOCALISATION IN TRANSITIONAL JUSTICE

As explained above, around the same time an evolution took place in transitional justice, from the use of standard solutions to more attention for the specific context and for local solutions, including tradition-based mechanisms. This coincided with the shift in the nature of armed conflicts (more intra-state then interstate), which implied that – either voluntarily or under coercion – more civilians were involved in the conflict, as perpetrators and as victims, often with interchanging roles. Inevitably perpetrators and victims had to learn to live together again after the conflict, creating a need for mechanisms to establish sustainable peace at a local level, in addition to mechanisms operating at a national or international level. Moreover, experience (in Rwanda) had learned that the retributive justice system could not provide this solution because of the massive scale of the crimes.

1.3. LOCAL OWNERSHIP AND HARMONISATION IN DEVELOPMENT COOPERATION

This development went parallel with a shift within the development paradigm, which caused an increased attention for traditional law in justice sector aid as well. As explained in Chapter 9, development aid only gained interest in the justice sector in the 1990s and in traditional law only since the late twentieth century. Justice sector aid was initially focused on the state and on institution-building based on the international model, but evolved into more interest in an accessible, local justice in the context of the fight against poverty. This shift was reflected in the Paris Declaration on Aid Effectiveness (2005) which contains the principles for reform of international aid, and indicators to monitor progress. The Declaration stresses the importance of ownership by the partner country and requires donors to align their interventions to the policies and development strategies of partner countries and provide mutual accountability. The principle of local ownership was later retained by the UN Peacebuilding Commission.[1] In addition, the Paris Declaration found that there was a need for greater harmonisation on the donor side. In 2008, the Accra Agenda for Action adopted, aiming at accelerating and deepening the implementation of the Paris Principles – including an emphasis

1 Peacebuilding Commission, Emerging lessons and practices in Peacebuilding 2007–2009, Working Group on Lessons Learned of the Peacebuilding Commission, May 2010.

on national ownership – effective and inclusive partnerships and a results-based approach.[2]

Not only were donors under the Paris Declaration encouraged to harmonise their policies and interventions with other donors and to align them to the development policy of the partner country, they also had to harmonise the policies and practices of various ministries or departments within their own country in dealing with partner countries.

Where donors initially left the conduct of peace negotiations with their diplomatic services, while the defence department participated in peacekeeping efforts, followed by the development agencies which then started the long term work, the development of peacebuilding as a separate phase, and as a complex of various political, military and humanitarian measures, lead to a need for internal donor harmonisation. This meant that the different departments within a donor country could no longer implement their own policies in the post-conflict countries, sometimes with contradictory agendas and interests, with only some attempts for coordination. The whole-of-government concept was born, also known as the '3 Ds policy', i.e. diplomacy, defence and development as an integrated strategy. In light of this development and especially for post conflict countries, some multilateral and bilateral donors created inter-departmental units, while some others established entirely new departments or organisations for peacebuilding.[3] Such agencies have the advantage that their procedures are often smoother and faster, require no long term planning and allow funds from different donors to be grouped and managed through for example UNDP (Uvin, 2009). An analysis of such agencies from 24 countries has, however, indicated that they use very different definitions of peacebuilding and that the mandate of these agencies, their priorities and activities vary considerably (Barnett et al., 2007). Hence, the authors of this analysis state that interventions are often based on the supply of these agencies, rather than on a demand by the post-conflict country. In addition, this complicates an effective coordination between donors that goes beyond agreements on the division of labour. Finally, the establishment of these agencies as such does not fulfil the need for more substantive harmonisation

2 Accra Agenda for Action (2008) Third High Level Forum on Aid Effectiveness, Accra.

3 Some examples: The Office of Transition Initiatives in the United States; the Africa Conflict Prevention Pool and the Global Conflict Prevention Pool in the UK established in 2002, the Postconflict Reconstruction Unit in the UK established in 2004 and transformed into the Stabilization Unit in 2007; the Inter-ministerial Steering Group for Civilian Crisis Prevention in Germany. The UN have created the Peacebuilding Commission and the Peacebuilding Fund, while UNDP established the Bureau for Conflict Prevention and Recovery. In the field, integrated UN offices have been established in various countries, in which temporary UN missions (DPKO) cooperate with UNDP, UNOHCR, etc. The European Commission created a Conflict Prevention and Crisis Management Unit. The Netherlands have a Section for Peacebuilding and Fragility within the Ministry of Foreign Affairs. Belgium did the same with the Service for Peacebuilding.

between the various aspects of peacebuilding programmes, such as between demobilisation programmes and transitional justice.[4]

2. POLICIES REGARDING TRADITIONAL MECHANISMS IN TRANSITIONAL JUSTICE

To see to what degree the context described above influences donor policy regarding traditional justice as transitional justice mechanism, the policy of donors on transitional justice has to be dissected first.

2.1. POLICIES REGARDING TRANSITIONAL JUSTICE

With exception of the United Nations (UN Secretary-General, 2004), it would appear that not a single donor (multilateral or bilateral) has formulated a comprehensive approach specifically regarding transitional justice. The already cited report by Kofi Annan premises a number of definitions (see Chapter 3, point 3.1), sketches the role of the UN in this context and recommends certain guidelines and methods. Additional guidelines were proposed in 2010 (UN Secretary-General, 2010). The point of departure of this policy is the notion that sustainable peace is only feasible if there are legitimate mechanisms for conflict resolution. This requires the establishment of the Rule of Law on the one hand and transitional justice on the other, which must include dealing with the causes of the conflict. The guidelines refer to the importance of including transitional justice in peace agreements, excluding amnesty and capital punishment, respecting international norms and human rights, and paying special attention to women, children, minorities, refugees and prisoners. Additional attention is drawn to the importance of adjusting every transitional justice strategy to the specific context and local needs, involving all stakeholders in the process, among others through consultations, capacity building, defining the most appropriate combination of mechanisms and the necessary coordination between UN agencies among themselves and with other actors.

Other donors mention the importance of democratisation, good governance, (re)establishing the Rule of Law, respect for human rights and the fight against impunity as their general goals, both in their foreign policy (including peacebuilding) and in their development policy. Furthermore, one often finds an enumeration of currently supported and future activities, without a comprehensive policy. Support for the various mechanisms used in transitional justice – criminal prosecution by international, mixed or national tribunals and

4 For example: DDR and Transitional Justice, Issue paper, Second International conference on DDR and Stability in Africa, Kinshasa, DRC, 12–14 June 2007.

courts, truth mechanisms, rehabilitation programmes, reconciliation activities and institutional reform – is spread out over several policy domains, strategies and budget lines. For example, the aforementioned agencies for peacebuilding often state that they support transitional justice, referring *in concreto* mostly to support for the International Criminal Court, ad hoc tribunals and sometimes a truth commission in the context of their goal to fight against impunity. Supporting national criminal justice reform often holds a prominent place on the post-conflict reconstruction agenda, since it is a necessary requirement to prosecute past crimes and prevent new violence, but it can also be found in development aid. Support for reparations is quite rare, unless it involves rehabilitation, which can be found either in post-conflict reconstruction programmes, or as part of the development aid to the respective sectors. Examples can be found in the health sector (e.g. trauma counselling, prosthetics, retroviral medication, removal of scars) and in the education sector (e.g. programmes for the education of former child soldiers). Bilateral support by donors for programmes aimed at direct financial compensation of victims is uncommon, unless it occurs through multilateral organisations such as the Peacebuilding Fund. Support for reconciliation activities usually falls under programmes for peacebuilding and conflict prevention. In fact, reconciliation turns out to be an umbrella term under which all kinds of local activities are grouped, ranging from training on conflict mediation, counselling programmes, support for the reintegration of persons in their community, to microcredit, infrastructure projects and support for farming projects, of which the link with reconciliation is not always clear. As Daly and Sarkin state, there are 'literally thousands of groups that at any given moment work on reconciliation all around the world.' The authors claim that it is impossible to ascertain exactly how many groups are involved, partly because new groups are created and old groups disappear or merge into collective organisations (Daly and Sarkin, 2007). Institutional reform as part of a transitional justice strategy to deal with the causes of the conflict can comprise a wide range of activities that are usually labelled as Security Sector Reform (SSR), which includes justice reform and vetting programmes. In reality, SSR, in the context of peacebuilding, often concerns reform of police and the military. Justice sector reform other than criminal justice reform usually follows later and is then part of development cooperation.

This overview shows that most donors not only lack a comprehensive policy on transitional justice, but that interventions that can be seen as transitional justice support are spread out over several programmes and budget lines, and often even over several services or agencies of the same donor. Moreover, many bilateral donors support peacebuilding through multilateral organisations, such as the diverse UN agencies,[5] that support transitional justice mechanisms. This

5 Regarding transitional justice these are mainly: UNOHCHR, UNDP, UN Peacebuilding Fund, and, to a certain degree, Unicef, Unifem (now UN Women).

lack of policies on transitional justice does not prevent donors from becoming more and more interested in the development of such policy (International Centre for Transitional Justice, 2007). Several donors have recently supported policy-preparing research on transitional justice.[6] It furthermore turns out that in their interventions these donors *de facto* apply most guidelines formulated by the UN.

2.2. POLICIES REGARDING TRADITIONAL MECHANISMS

Donors who in one way or the other support transitional justice also support traditional mechanisms in that context. Since few donors have a policy on transitional justice, they *a priori* lack such policy regarding the use of traditional mechanisms in the framework of transitional justice. As the case studies and their analyses will show, donor support for such mechanisms is largely prompted by the requirement of local ownership, as expressed in the Paris Declaration of 2005 and further elaborated upon in the Accra Agenda for Action of 2008. This development also had an impact on the debate surrounding the localisation of transitional justice, as already referred to above.

The application of the concept of local ownership in transitional justice led to the following developments. First came an acknowledgment of the need to adjust strategies and mechanisms to the local context: the toolbox mechanisms were maintained, but more or less adjusted to the context, while the most appropriate combination of mechanisms was identified considering the specific situation of the post-conflict country. This remained a top-down approach from the international to the national level. At the level of international justice, this is when mixed mechanisms emerged, such as the Special Court in Sierra Leone (2000), the Serious Crimes Panels in Timor (2000), the Extraordinary Chambers in the Courts of Cambodia (2001) and the War Crimes Chambers in Bosnia-Herzegovina (2005).

This was later followed by an increasing acknowledgment of the value and even prime responsibility of national mechanisms in addition to international ones, if consistent with international standards: e.g. the prosecution of international crimes by domestic courts and donors' investment therein (e.g. Rwanda and Burundi). The ICC itself, established in 2002, is an illustration of this evolution since it emphasises that the prime responsibility for prosecution rests with the

6 Some examples: for the European Union, the report 'the European Union and Transitional justice' by Laura Davis for the Initiative for Peacebuilding Mediation Cluster, June 2010; for the Netherlands the report 'Transitional justice. Justice and peace in transitional situations' of the Advisory Council on International Affairs and the Advisory Committee on Issues of Public International Law, Advise no. 65, AIV/n°19 CAVV, April 2009; for Germany: 'Transitional justice & Dealing with the past' by Natascha Zupan and Sylvia Servaes for FriEnt (Working Group on Development and Peace), June 2007.

country where the crimes occurred, while the ICC serves as a complement in case the country is unable or unwilling to prosecute.[7]

The Paris Declaration emphasised the need for country ownership, which initially was understood as mainly government ownership (the fact that *gacaca* justice was in the first place a 'Rwandan' solution was very attractive to donors around the millennium) – while the legitimacy in the eyes of the population was not verified. At the level of international criminal justice, this is when discussion on the legacy (transfer of capacity and cases) of international and mixed courts towards domestic courts occurred.

The concept of country ownership gradually expanded to national ownership, hence the involvement of non-state actors as stakeholders in the peacebuilding process (Accra Agenda for Action 2008). This was not an obvious evolution since peacebuilding strategies initially focused on statebuilding and the fear was that working with local structures would undermine this process (Chopra, 2009).

Thus, non-state actors – civil society organisations, religious and traditional leaders – became important participants in both peace processes (conferences, negotiations) and in transitional justice mechanisms (monitoring, participation). Hence, donor support that allowed these organisations to participate in preliminary conferences (as in Sierra Leone between 1996 and 1999) and even in peace negotiations (in Lomé for Sierra Leone and in Juba for Northern Uganda) primarily aimed at creating local ownership.

At the same time, international guidelines for peacebuilding emphasised the importance of supporting civil society as watchdogs of government policy, protectors of human rights, advisors and peace negotiators (OECD-DAC, 2001). That is why donors supported capacity building of local NGOs (through international organisations such as the International Center for Transitional Justice) and activities of transitional justice coalitions of civil society stakeholder organisations of a particular country. The restoration of traditional leaders in Sierra Leone and Northern Uganda was also inspired by the importance of local involvement in peace negotiations and transitional justice mechanisms. Regarding criminal justice, the importance of outreach by international, hybrid or mixed courts started to be emphasised. One step further was the involvement of the population as such. Hence, the importance of consultations was added. Apart from asking the input of civil society organisations, popular consultations (by NGOs and INGOs, the UNOHCHR, the government) became a current practice. Most of them were conducted post-decision, i.e. when the transitional justice strategy had already been established (as in Rwanda, where people's opinion was asked when the decision to establish *gacaca* courts had already been taken at a political level). In Burundi, the government supported by the UN has held real national consultations, but only years after the framework of the transitional justice strategy had been adopted in the Arusha Peace Agreement of

7 Rome Statute of the International Criminal Court, 17 July 1998, preamble and art. 17.

2000. The Guidance note of the Secretary General of the United Nations of March 2010 promotes national ownership either 'to shape the design of an overarching transitional justice strategy' or 'within the context of a specific mechanism'. However, real popular involvement in the decision process *ab initio* is rare (UN Secretary-General, 2010).

The fact that top-down planning in transitional justice has been replaced by a process in which the national governments and later civil society stakeholders are included has opened the door to traditional and other local views on justice and reconciliation, which led the Secretary-General of the United Nations to acknowledge the value of traditional justice within a rule of law and transitional justice framework in his 2004 report.[8]

Because donors attach great importance to local ownership, aiming for this is an important motive in decisions concerning specific interventions. While in the past donors decided to support or refrain from supporting certain mechanisms once these were established, we now observe a move to additional donor interventions during preparation processes. These aim to identify the local needs and to create ownership. The increased attention for human rights and the 'do no harm' principle subsequently gave rise to more donor interventions related to monitoring and supervision of the mechanisms.

Hence, donor interventions regarding the use of traditional mechanisms in the framework of transitional justice can be classified into four categories. First, support for preliminary processes. These include, among others: (i) facilitating the participation of traditional leaders in negotiations, conferences and consultations (including the preceding restoration of traditional leadership or traditional bodies and training on transitional justice and human rights); (ii) the promotion of traditional values, directly by traditional leaders or by other civil society actors; and (iii) support for processes that create hybrid, tradition-based mechanisms through policy-oriented research and consultations. Second, support for tradition-based mechanisms as an element of peacebuilding and the official transitional justice policy. Third, support for tradition-based mechanisms outside of the official transitional justice policy. And fourth, support for monitoring/supervising tradition-based mechanisms, especially in view of respect for human rights.

3. CONCLUSION

The above shows that traditional mechanisms for justice and reconciliation have not come to the attention of donors because of their intrinsic values, but mainly because the concept of local ownership generated attention for local, tradition-

8 See also the Nuremberg Declaration on Peace and Justice, 2007. Peacebuilding Commission Lessons Learned Working Group, 2008.

based solutions. These were proposed as part of transitional justice either by the government of the partner country (such as the *gacaca* courts in Rwanda), or by civil society actors consulted and supported by donors (such as in Uganda). The fact that traditional mechanisms were not integrated in the official transitional justice policy in Sierra Leone is also a result of this evolution, since state ownership was decisive at that moment (1999).

It subsequently shows that the increased importance of peacebuilding and the search for mechanisms to create sustainable justice on a local level also play a role, while donors engage themselves to respect international standards with regards to the duty to prosecute international crimes and to ensure respect for human rights.

The convergence of these different developments and the dilemmas that emanate from them show that the support for tradition-based mechanisms is not obvious for donors and implies quite some challenges. This will be illustrated by the case studies presented in Chapters 4 to 6.

BIBLIOGRAPHY

BARNETT, M., KIM, H., O'DONNELL, M. and SITEA, L. (2007) Peacebuilding: What Is in a Name?, *Global Governance*, 13, 35–58.

CALL, C. (ed.) (2007) *Constructing justice and security after war.* United States Institute of Peace Press, Washington.

CAREY, S.C. (2007) European Aid: Human Rights versus Bureaucratic Inertia ?, *Journal of Peace Research*, 44(4), Special Issue on Protecting Human Rights, July 2007, 447–464.

CHETAIL, V. (ed.) (2009) *Post-conflict peacebuilding. A lexicon*, Oxford: Oxford University Press.

CHOPRA, T. (2009) When Peacebuilding Contradicts Statebuilding: Notes from the Arid Lands of Kenya, *International Peacekeeping*, 16:4, 531–545.

COLLIER, P. and HOEFFLER, A. (2004) Greed and grievance in civil war, *Oxford Economic Papers* 56, 563–595.

DALY, E. and SARKIN, J. (2007), *Reconciliation in divided societies. Finding common ground.* Philadelphia: University of Pennsylvania Press.

EUROPEAN COMMUNITY (1991) Declaration on Human Rights and Foreign Policy.

GALTUNG, J. (1985) Twenty-five years of peace research: ten challenges and some responses, *Journal of Peace Research*, 22(2), 141–158.

INTERNATIONAL CENTER FOR TRANSITIONAL JUSTICE (2007) Donor strategies for transitional justice: tacking stock and moving forward [online] http://www.docstoc.com/docs/29779841/Donor-Strategies-for-Transitional-Justice-Taking-Stock-and-Moving-Forward (15/09/14).

OECD-DAC (1993) Orientations on Participatory Development and Good Governance [online] http://www.acdi-cida.gc.ca/inet/images.nsf/vLUImages/HRDG/$file/Dac-e.pdf (15/09/14).

OECD (1997) Guidelines on Peace, Conflict and Development Cooperation [online] https://www1.umn.edu/humanrts/instree/OECDdev.htm (15/09/14).

OECD-DAC (2001) The DAC Guidelines. Helping Prevent Violent Conflict [online] http://www.oecd.org/dac/incaf/1886146.pdf (15/09/14).

OECD-DAC (2007a) Principles for good international engagement in fragile states & situations [online] http://www.oecd.org/development/incaf/38368714.pdf (15/09/14).

OECD-DAC (2007b) Action-oriented policy paper on human rights and development [online] http://www.oecd.org/development/governance-development/39350774.pdf (15/0914).

UN Secretary-General (2004) The rule of law and transitional justice in conflict and post-conflict societies [online] http://www.unrol.org/files/2004%20report.pdf (15/09/14).

UN Secretary-General (2005) In Larger Freedom: Towards Development, Security and Human Rights for All [online] http://www.ohchr.org/Documents/Publications/A.59.2005.Add.3.pdf (15/09/14).

UN Secretary-General (2010) Guidance note of the secretary-general. United Nations Approach to Transitional Justice [online] http://www.unrol.org/files/TJ_Guidance_Note_March_2010FINAL.pdf (15/09/14).

United Nations (1992) An Agenda for Peace, preventive diplomacy, peacemaking and peace-keeping, Report of the Secretary-General pursuant to the statement adopted by the Summit Meeting of the Security Council on 31 January 1992, 17 June 1992, A/47/277–S/24111 [online] http://www.un-documents.net/a47-277.htm (15/09/14).

United Nations (2000) Report of the Panel on United Nations Peace Operations, A/55/305, S/2000/809 [online] http://www.un.org/documents/ga/docs/55/a55305.pdf (15/09/14).

Uvin, P. (2002) On High Moral Ground: The incorporation of Human Rights by the development enterprise, *The Fletcher Journal of Development Studies*, XVII, 1–11.

Uvin, P. (2009) The development/peacebuilding nexus: a typology and history of changing paradigms, *Journal for Peacebuilding and Development*, 5–24.

CHAPTER 4

NON-OFFICIAL USE OF TRADITION: A CASE STUDY ON SIERRA LEONE

Martien SCHOTSMANS

1. BACKGROUND TO THE CONFLICT

Sierra Leone gained independence from the United Kingdom in 1961. Before then, the country was divided into two parts: the Freetown peninsula, i.e. the current Western area, which was a British colony. It was considered a part of the British Empire and was directly ruled by the British administration. It was mainly populated by freed slaves who spoke Krio. Here common law was applied. The rest of the country was a protectorate, inhabited by 'natives', ruled indirectly and under a mixed system of common and customary law. The British divided the protectorate into 400 chiefdoms that were indirectly ruled by traditional chiefs who now became the representatives of the British and were called 'Paramount Chiefs'. This undermined their legitimacy and abolished their downward accountability.

The 1947 Constitution united the country to prepare it for independence. After independence, any government in power relied on the traditional chiefs as their local representatives, as did the colonial power before. Bad governance, the submission of all state institutions (army, police, parliament, judiciary, civil service, chieftaincies, etc.) and non-state oversight bodies (media, civil society, etc.) to party control, the imposition of a one-party system in 1978, corruption, nepotism, the plundering of state assets and the lack of respect for any human rights of the citizens, led to a strong feeling of alienation: the central government became almost irrelevant to people's everyday lives and they rather turned to local, traditional leaders and secret societies instead (traditional organisations of persons who have been initiated together and who share a number of secrets).[1] However, even at this level, the bad governance practices of the central government had trickled down to the chiefs, leaving people with no outlet to vent

[1] The most important ones being Poro and Wonde for men, Sande and Bondo for women, but others exist as well.

their grievances. Violence became the only alternative. Poor, disgruntled youth of the rural areas could easily be mobilised by armed groups who opposed the government (TRC report, 2004, Vol. 2 and 3A). Since 1991, Sierra Leone has a constitutional presidential regime based on a multiparty system and periodic elections, which took place even during the conflict.

Sierra Leone experienced a violent conflict from 1991 to 2002. This opposed, on the one hand, the rebels of the Revolutionary United Front (RUF) supported by Liberia, later joined by the military of the Armed Forces Revolutionary Council (AFRC) who overthrew the government in 1997 – and on the other hand the government army (SLA) and local Civil Defence Forces (CDF). Many war crimes and crimes against humanity were committed by all armed factions, be it not to the same extent. During the conflict, over 2 million persons were displaced, an estimated 50,000 to 75,000 people were killed, 50,000 to 64,000 women and girls were victims of sexual violence, approximately 10,000 children participated in the fighting and about 4,000 persons were victim of amputation (Suma and Correa, 2009; Dougherty, 2004; Physicians for Human Rights, 2002; International Crisis Group, 2001).

After the invasion of Freetown on 6 January 1999 and international armed intervention, the Lomé peace agreement was signed on 7 July 1999, providing a blanket amnesty, disarmament, power sharing and new elections. However, in May 2000 the violence resumed and the war was not declared over until 18 January 2002. Bad governance, large-scale corruption, regional discrimination and political polarisation were identified as the causes of the conflict, and not diamonds and other natural resources as often portrayed (Truth and Reconciliation Commission, 2004, Vol. 2 and 3A). Sierra Leone has since known various democratic elections, as well as a peaceful regime change.

2. THE ROLE OF TRADITION IN SOCIETY

In its colonial period, Sierra Leone – like many other African countries (Penal Reform International, 2000) – had a system of traditional justice administered by traditional leaders, sometimes called kings. Sierra Leone knew several systems, varying for all of the 17 ethnic groups, but in most cases the king was not an autocratic ruler, since he ruled together with a council and the secret societies, and partly delegated his power to the traditional chiefs and sub-chiefs. The secret societies still play an important part in settling disputes and in decisions regarding the community, and also act as sources of informal education and social control and cohesion (Manifesto '99, 2001: 8–12; Alie, 1990). The traditional leaders of Sierra Leone have always remained officially recognised (unlike in other countries, such as Uganda and Rwanda, where they were dismissed), but the institution is heavily politicised, and was always manipulated by the government in power (Keen, 2003: 71).

Since many traditional chiefs were killed or died during the conflict, after the war the government, supported by the UK's Department for International Development (DFID), launched a programme to appoint new chiefs and restore the institution (Paramount Chiefs Restoration Programme; Fanthorpe, 2005; Archibald and Richards, 2002). Furthermore, a Council of Paramount Chiefs was established, which advises the government (cf. Statement on Paramount Chiefs by President Kabbah). This was preceded by extensive consultations which showed that, despite their role before and during the conflict, traditional chiefs are still accepted by the people of Sierra Leone, who turn to the chiefs for many of their daily problems (Fanthorpe, 2005; Alterman et al., 2002). The chiefs are regarded as the guardians of traditional heritage, traditional values, the secret societies and local interests (Fanthorpe, 2007). They can, however, no longer act as autocrats, as possible abuse is no longer accepted by the people, who are now, after displacement during the war and after being introduced to human rights through modern media and awareness raising, informed about their rights. The government's decentralisation policy has furthermore placed elected local authorities on level with and above the chiefs (Boersch-Supan, 2009; Keen, 2003; Fanthorpe, 2005). The establishment of the Paramount Chiefs was acknowledged by the Constitution. They have permanent representatives in Parliament.[2] The role and election of the Paramount Chiefs are regulated by law and their tasks are limited to collecting taxes, law enforcement, preservation of cultural heritage and community development.[3] In case of misbehaviour, they can be relieved of their power by the president. In the north of the country, all chiefs are male, while in the southern and eastern regions women are also eligible for the position.

3. TRANSITIONAL JUSTICE LANDSCAPE

The Lomé Peace Agreement[4] granted a blanket amnesty for all crimes committed prior to 6 June 1999 and provided for the establishment of a Truth and Reconciliation Commission (TRC). After a new outbreak of violence in 2000, the United Nations and the government of Sierra Leone established the Special Court for Sierra Leone to prosecute those who bear the greatest responsibility for serious violations of international humanitarian law committed in Sierra Leone since 30 November 1996.[5] It has effectively prosecuted nine persons, eight of whom are now serving their sentences in Rwanda, while Charles Taylor is serving his

2 Constitution 1991, art. 72 and art. 74.
3 Chieftaincy Act 2009, 10 September 2009.
4 Peace Agreement between the Government of Sierra Leone and the Revolutionary United Front of Sierra Leone, 7 July 1999, transmitted to the Security Council on 12 July 1999 (S/1999/777).
5 Agreement between the United Nations and the Government of Sierra Leone on the establishment of a Special Court for Sierra Leone, 16 January 2002. Statute of the Special Court for Sierra Leone, art. 1.1.

sentence in the UK.[6] Both at the Special Court and at national courts, victims can only intervene as witnesses and are not entitled to reparations. At the national level, two trials have taken place convicting 17 low level perpetrators for relatively minor crimes committed after the Lomé Peace agreement (Horovitz, 2009).

The TRC operated from 2002 to 2004 and issued a report, providing a historical record of the conflict, identifying the causes of the conflict and recommending institutional reform, more reconciliation activities and reparations, among others. The TRC heard witnesses in each district during only one week and did not have the opportunity to organise hearings at the lowest administrative levels. Following the TRC's recommendations, the reparations programme has started to be implemented since September 2008, with funding from the United Nations Peacebuilding Fund (Suma and Correa, 2009).

4. THE ROLE OF TRADITION IN TRANSITIONAL JUSTICE

The use of tradition-based mechanisms was not part of the official transitional justice policy in Sierra Leone. In the debates on transitional justice, using traditional justice as an alternative to the formal retributive justice system has never been suggested (unlike Rwanda and Uganda) by either donors, authorities, civil society or the population involved (Hayner, 2007). Most respondents refer to the amnesty provisions in the Lomé peace agreement and consider the Special Court as the only institution with jurisdiction over the international crimes that had been excluded from amnesty in the peace agreement.

The importance of traditional culture was nonetheless recognised within the framework of the transitional justice process, more precisely in the mandate of the TRC. The TRC law determines that the Commission can call on both religious and traditional leaders in the implementation of its activities.[7] The law was co-written by the UNOHCHR after extensive consultations with several organisations from civil society, which included NGOs, the organisation of Paramount Chiefs and the Inter-Religious Council of Sierra Leone (IRCSL). The TRC was a mechanism that would not just operate at the national level, but would also support local reconciliation initiatives. That is why these organisations insisted that both the traditional chiefs and the religious leaders – the latter also played an important role in the peace negotiations – would be involved in the activities of the TRC. The traditional leaders had been consulted earlier as stakeholders during a preparatory conference for the Lomé peace negotiations. Nevertheless, the conference's recommendation not to grant amnesty for serious crimes, but to allow the TRC

6 For more details see the website of the Special Court, www.sc-sl.org.

7 Art. 7(2) of the TRC Act: 'The Commission may seek assistance from traditional and religious leaders to facilitate its public sessions and in resolving local conflicts arising from past violations or abuses or in support of healing and reconciliation.'

to establish accountability, was not taken into account in the peace agreement (Hayner, 2007).

The fact that an official transitional justice body such as the TRC regularly called upon traditional leaders for assistance confirms this recognition, albeit this was not done with the goal of truth finding, as recommended by preliminary research of a local NGO, funded by UNOHCHR (Manifesto '99, 2002), but only for reconciliation purposes, and only to a limited extent. There were several reasons for this: the variety of traditional practices, as identified by Manifesto '99, in addition to the fact that some traditional practices would violate international human rights (such as certain practices of swearing and oath-taking) and the fact that abuse by traditional leaders in the past was identified as one of the causes of the conflict.

Nevertheless, the TRC did call upon the traditional leaders on various occasions: they were involved during the sensitisation campaign and the statement-taking phase, during the district hearings to participate in the opening ceremonies, attend the hearings and play an active role in the reconciliation ceremonies at the end of each week of hearings, and as participants in the reconciliation workshops, organised by the TRC jointly with the Inter-Religious Council of Sierra Leone (IRCSL).

In certain instances the traditional leaders also testified about their own experiences and played an important exemplary role; this was particularly relevant in the case of a chief testifying that his wife had been raped, and declaring that he did not reject her, which goes against the usual response in Sierra Leone.

However, this remained limited and unilateral: the Commission only called upon the traditional leaders as gatekeepers to the communities to increase the efficiency and legitimacy of its own work as well as its impact (Alie, 2008).

In the same way, traditional leaders, as one of many categories of stakeholders, are being involved in the reparations process of the National Commission for Social Action (NaCSA)[8] and in consultations on some of the institutional reform (such as the restatement of customary law in Moyamba district, see Chapter 3). The reasons for this are generally the same: their role as gatekeepers to the local community on the one hand, and their role as guardians of traditional values and of the relationship with the ancestors on the other hand.

But traditional justice is not only about the involvement of its institutions, i.e. the traditional leaders, it is also about people's belief in traditional values and in the importance of appeasing the ancestors after the commission of a crime. These beliefs are still very much alive in rural Sierra Leone, which is why any transitional justice mechanism should take them into consideration (also: Alie, 2008). More in particular, our findings show that acknowledgment of wrongdoing, apologies and reconciliation have to take place at three levels: at the individual level between the perpetrator and the victim, at the community level between the perpetrator

8 The TRC had recommended that NacCSA implement its proposed reparations programme.

and his community, and at the spiritual level between the community of the perpetrator and the ancestors. After the perpetrator's presentation of apologies and their acceptance by the victim and/or his community, the traditional leaders will offer apologies to the ancestors (and through them to God) on behalf of the community for the bad behaviour of one of their children. Sacrifices will be made and rituals performed to appease the ancestors. Reconciliation is not considered to be complete without such rituals. In contrast, detailed truth revealing does not seem to be so important. While reparations, according to tradition, need to be an integral part of reconciliation, reality makes people at community level accept that these will not be provided for the moment.

To a certain extent, these values have been considered by the TRC during its reconciliation ceremonies, although there was more emphasis on inter-individual and community reconciliation.

Further initiatives were largely left to religious and other civil society organisations. These unofficial activities are often to an even more important extent inspired by traditional values and views. Hence, tradition-based mechanisms were not used for retributive prosecutions at the official level, but as restorative justice mechanisms according to local notions and values at the unofficial, informal level. The *Fambul Tok* project (see below) has taken this approach the furthest, but there are other organisations that base their activities to a greater or lesser degree on traditional values as well.

As mentioned, the TRC jointly with the IRCSL organised a series of reconciliation workshops at district level and set up District Support Committees for reconciliation, with religious and traditional leaders, women and youth representatives, as well as victims and ex-combatants. After the closure of the TRC, the IRCSL conducted activities at chiefdom and section level, based on people's wishes as expressed during the reconciliation workshops. These often comprised traditional as well as religious and communal aspects. One example is the renaming and cleansing ceremonies for abducted and raped girls (previously named after their abductor), through which they became suitable for marriage.[9]

Even before the TRC-IRCSL programme, there had been quite a number of programmes aimed at the reintegration of ex-combatants that used both traditional and religious elements, especially programmes for children. In this context, UNICEF supported several Child Protection Agencies and supplied a complete package, which could include education, skills training, micro-projects and traditional cleansing. The actual rituals differed per community and consistently included elements of purification from negative spirits, and of reconciliation with the community and ancestors (Alie, 2008; Zack-Williams, 2006; Stark, 2006). These are supposed to have had a significant positive impact

9 These were supported by the BCPR of UNDP.

on further co-existence (Ginifer, 2003).[10] They were not linked to the actual role during the conflict of the individual involved and thus did not provide accountability, although general apologies were sometimes expressed. Even though the cleansing rituals provided a first step in that direction, they did not entail an actual initiation into the secret societies – still a requirement for one to be considered a full member of a local community in Sierra Leone (Fanthorpe, 2007) (for a more detailed account: see section 2.4.2).

Other NGO initiatives were taken regarding peacebuilding and conflict prevention, such as the Bo Peace and Reconciliation Movement (BPRM) (Hanson-Ap, 2007; Baker, 2005). This organisation started working in 1996 with a coalition of local NGOs and worked with both professionally trained and voluntary peace monitors, the latter selected by the communities and working in Chiefdom Peace and Reconciliation Committees. The methodology for conflict resolution applied by the peace monitors is a mixture of traditional and modern methods, focusing on the restoration of the broken relationship behind the conflict and using traditional ceremonies such as the pouring of libation and sacrifices to pacify the ancestors, as well as religious prayers, social activities and 'modern' conflict mediation techniques, respecting human rights. They deal with contemporary conflicts, as well as conflicts that existed before the war, which are often related. These reconciliation sessions are followed up by the peace monitors. Many other projects for peacebuilding and conflict prevention exist, some of which also involve traditional elements (e.g. Park, 2007).

Fambul Tok[11] is a tradition-based mechanism, which uses traditional methods and values, although adjusting them to some extent. The methodology involves several steps, starting with consultations and training (on traditional reconciliation values, mediation, PTSD and human rights), preliminary mediation of cases presented by either victim or perpetrator to a Reconciliation Committee, concluded by a reconciliation ceremony. The latter comprises a bonfire in the evening where victims and perpetrators share their experiences, perpetrators apologise and ask for forgiveness and are embraced by victims and community leaders. In this regard, forgiving was described as accepting apologies, while 'forgiveness of the heart' could come later. The following day, traditional ceremonies are performed to achieve reconciliation between perpetrator and victim, between perpetrator and community and between community and ancestors. Rituals to appease the ancestors may include prayers, sacrifices, the pouring of libation or purification and cleansing (Manifesto '99, 2002). Although many respondents viewed reparations as a condition for reconciliation – reality forces victims to accept apologies anyhow since most perpetrators lack the

[10] According to UNAMSIL 75,490 combatants were demobilised after the conflict, 6,845 of whom were children. United Nations Mission in Sierra Leone, *Fact Sheet 1: Disarmament, Demobilization and Reintegration*, www.un.org/Depts/dpko/missions/unamsil, December 2005.

[11] Krio for Family Talk, referring to the traditional way of conflict resolution through palaver.

necessary means. Afterwards, a peace tree is identified under which benches are constructed for people to gather at regular times to solve more disputes. In addition, community farming projects are set up and support groups are established for women (peace mothers), mainly to provide support to victims of sexual violence. Being a civil society initiative, *Fambul Tok* has conducted over 60 reconciliation ceremonies and established 30 projects of community farming since it started in 2008 (Fambul Tok, 2010), and thus remains a small-scale civil society project.

The *Fambul Tok* project uses traditional conflict resolution – the African palaver – the traditional values of mediation and the restoration of relationships and concludes with a traditional ritual of reconciliation with the community and the ancestors. Meanwhile, it integrates modern values: victims, ex-combatants, women and youths participate in the decision and implementation phase, the traditional practices of swearing and oath-taking are replaced by mediation and voluntary confessions and discrimination against women and children is countered by human rights training provided by Forum of Conscience.

Thus, by creating a tradition-based mechanism, *Fambul Tok* manages to create a space for dialogue that goes beyond traditional practices, e.g. the fact that a woman can talk publicly about being raped and ask a man to apologise, or the fact that a small man can ask a big man to apologise.

Nevertheless, not all formal aspects of a traditional mechanism can be changed: regarding reconciliation with the ancestors, for instance, the role of traditional leaders is indispensable, since they are the only ones, through their initiation and position in the secret societies, who can communicate with the ancestors. Thus, where adjustments of tradition-based justice might be possible at the level of inter-personal and community reconciliation, this might not be the case for spiritual reconciliation. In this same regard, where victims and the community can (temporarily) accept that the perpetrator does not pay any reparations, asking the ancestors for forgiveness without offering sacrifices and performing certain ceremonies does not seem to be an option either, which is why external support to conduct such ceremonies will often be required.

Our research has shown that although it is easily said in Sierra Leone that there is no longer a need to talk about the past, people nonetheless have a need to call mid-level commanders and those who committed many atrocities in the communities to account. There is furthermore a need for minimal recognition of guilt and for apologies by low-level executors who wish to reintegrate into their communities (Boersch-Supan, 2008). Hence, the blanket amnesty and the fact that there is no urge to prosecute more perpetrators do not mean that there is no need to establish accountability for what happened. This would allow the perpetrator to relieve his conscience (*to blow his mind*) and to reintegrate into his community (*to be one*), while offering the victim closure (*to have a cool heart*). Several respondents thought that the social climate had become more favourable to such a process, because people felt safer.

This leads us to the conclusion that more interventions regarding transitional justice based on traditional justice values and involving traditional leaders are possible and necessary in Sierra Leone, even with adjustments to a certain extent. Although it is early days to assess the impact of these ongoing initiatives of civil society, transitional justice interventions both at the national and the local level may not be successful in the long run, unless they consider traditional justice and reconciliation values.

5. POLICIES AND INTERVENTIONS OF INTERNATIONAL ACTORS

In Sierra Leone, the government's transitional justice policy was supported by multilateral, bilateral and non-governmental donors. There seemed to be a kind of division of labour: multilateral and bilateral donors principally supported interventions that fit in with the official policy, such as the Special Court and the TRC, while NGOs and foundations seemed more inclined to support informal initiatives, such as the NGO projects mentioned above, aimed at reconciliation.

Since traditional mechanisms as such were not part of the official transitional justice policy, one can only examine the motives of donors to support mechanisms in which traditional elements play a role in one way or another. Interviews with multilateral or bilateral donors have shown that the involvement of traditional leaders in activities, or the use of traditional values or practices in the context of transitional justice interventions, are hardly a sufficient reason to support or decline support for a specific activity. Every donor stated that the role of traditional leaders and the presence of tradition in Sierra Leone are established facts that should be taken into account for an intervention to be successful. With regards to the mention in the TRC mandate of a possible appeal to traditional leaders, the respondents stated that this was an unequivocal request of civil society, i.e. not just of the Paramount Chiefs, but of the NGOs as well. The donors' choice to support activities that contain traditional elements, such as the TRC,[12] seems rather determined by the fact that a mechanism is included in the official government policy. This was also the case in their support for other official programmes in which traditional elements were included, such as their support for the Paramount Chief Restoration Programme and the preceding consultations[13] and the reintegration programmes for children[14] – including ritual cleansing ceremonies. The same applies to the restoration programmes of

---

12 Supported by the United Kingdom, the European Commission, the USA, Canada, France, Germany, Ireland, Luxembourg, the Netherlands, Norway, Sweden and Switzerland. The funds were collected by the UNOHCHR and managed locally by the UNDP. UNIFEM and UNICEF offered the Commission technical assistance.

13 Supported by the Africa Conflict Prevention Pool of the United Kingdom.

14 Supported by UNICEF.

the NaCSA[15] – in which traditional reconciliation activities were also performed as a kind of symbolic reparations, and traditional leaders were called upon to help implement reparation payments – as well as to the TRC-IRCSL programme regarding reconciliation workshops and activities,[16] which was more of an offshoot of the UNDP support to the TRC, despite the fact that the second part, the local (including traditional) reconciliation activities, was executed solely by the IRCSL. In other words, none of these donors had a specific policy regarding the importance of traditional justice in the framework of transitional justice, or supported certain activities specifically because they were based on tradition. The fact that their interventions were largely inspired by government policy has led to a lack of interventions based on traditional values concerning justice and reconciliation, especially at the local level. Despite what donors sometimes think, it is not sufficient to involve traditional leaders or to add some traditional elements to an activity developed on a national scale to make it successful at the community level. To achieve this goal, the activities themselves must be anchored in the population's cosmovision.

At an unofficial level there were some smaller projects, not part of the official traditional justice policy, which were supported by non-governmental donors, such as international NGOs or foundations. These projects are specifically designed to promote the local, traditional values of reconciliation and to acknowledge the important role traditional leaders play in this respect. This goes for projects such as *Fambul Tok*[17] and the – slightly less specifically tradition-oriented – Bo Peace and Reconciliation Movement.[18] The policy of these non-governmental donors to support these projects was inspired by their search for local reconciliation methods which are aligned with the local population's views and which can be used with the assistance of locally anchored structures that can ensure sustainability. In Sierra Leone, this search automatically led to the potential of tradition-based mechanisms, i.e. to the importance of traditional values and the role of traditional leaders in society, besides other local stakeholders. The support for these projects is therefore inspired by the conviction that mechanisms in which traditional values are mixed with modern methods, such as mediation, and respect for human rights, have a better chance of bringing about sustainable justice and reconciliation at the local level.

In general, donors seem to ignore the fact that the recognition of traditional leaders as important actors at the local level will also confirm their authority and legitimacy in the eyes of the population. This means that to prevent novel abuse of power, there is a need for checks and balances. The role of local NGOs in the unofficial tradition-based projects, as initiators and supervisors, and the

15 Supported by the Peacebuilding Fund of the UN.

16 Supported by the Bureau for Conflict Prevention and Recovery (BCPR) of UNDP.

17 Financed by Catalysts for Peace, an American foundation, and substantively supported by the Center for Justice and Peacebuilding of the American Eastern Mennonite University.

18 Supported by the British INGO Conciliation Resources.

integration of respect for human rights in the projects will (hopefully) be sufficient to supply counter-pressure to the power of traditional leaders,[19] although it is still too early to assess their impact.

Finally, the donors' interventions are too restricted in time, meaning that they occur primarily in the first years after the end of a conflict, while people often need longer periods of stability and safety before they feel secure enough to address the past, thereby creating room for reconciliation. The decision of the Peacebuilding Commission to make Sierra Leone one of its first intervention countries runs counter to this trend, but it does not include activities regarding local reconciliation or justice with regard to past crimes.[20]

BIBLIOGRAPHY

ALIE, J.A.D. (1990) *A new history of Sierra Leone*. London: MacMillan Publishers.

ALIE, J.A.D. (2008) Reconciliation and traditional justice: tradition-based practices of the Kpaa Mende. In Huyse, L. and Salter, M. (eds.) *Traditional Justice after Violent Conflict. Learning from African Experiences*, 123–146. Stockholm, Sweden: IDEA.

ALTERMAN, O., BINIENDA, A., RODELLA, S. and KIMYIA, V. (2002) *The Law People See, The Status of Dispute Resolution in the Provinces of Sierra Leone in 2002*. Freetown: National Forum for Human Rights.

ARCHIBALD, S. and RICHARDS, P. (2002) Converts to Human Rights? Popular Debate about War and Justice in Rural Central Sierra Leone, *Africa: Journal of the International African Institute*, 72/3, 339–367.

BAKER, B. (2005) Who Do People Turn to for Policing Sierra Leone?, *Journal of Contemporary African Studies*, 23/3, 371–390.

BOERSCH-SUPAN, J. (2009) *The communities: the crossroads between reintegration and reconciliation. What can be learned from the Sierra Leonean experience?*, Crise Working Paper No. 63.

DOUGHERTY, B.K. (2004) Searching for Answers: Sierra Leone's Truth & Reconciliation Commission, *Africa Studies Quarterly*, 8(1), 40–56.

FAMBUL TOK INTERNATIONAL (2010) *Community Healing in Sierra Leone and The World, Our second year.*

FANTHORPE, R. (2005) On the limits of liberal peace: chiefs and democratic decentralization in post-war Sierra Leone, *African Affairs*, 105(418), 27–49.

FANTHORPE, R. (2007) *Sierra Leone: The Influence of the Secret Societies, with special reference to Female Genital Mutilation*. A Writenet Report Commissioned by the United Nations High Commissioner for Refugees, Status Determination and Protection Information Section (DIPS).

19 Which also already happens through the government's decentralisation policy and the legal regulation of the Chiefs.

20 Republic of Sierra Leone – United Nations Sierra Leone, Priority Plan for Peacebuilding Fund, Sierra Leone, revised October 2008, www.unpbf.org.

GINIFER, J. (2003) Reintegration of ex-combatants. In Malan, M. et al. *Sierra Leone. Building the road to recovery*, Monograph No. 80, 39–52.

HANSON-AP, R. (2007) *Building paths to peace, Bo Peace and Reconciliation Movement Sierra Leone. Bringing together traditional and modern methods of peace building*, Conciliation Resources.

HAYNER, P. (2007) *Negotiating the peace in Sierra Leone: confronting the justice challenge*, Center for Humanitarian Dialogue and International Center for Transitional Justice.

HOROVITZ, S. (2009) *Sierra Leone: interaction between international and national responses to the mass atrocities*, Domac Reports/3.

INTERNATIONAL CRISIS GROUP (2001) *Sierra Leone: Time for a New Military and Political Strategy*, ICG Africa Report No. 28.

KEEN, D. (2003) Greedy Elites, Dwindling Resources, Alienated Youths. The Anatomy of Protracted Violence in Sierra Leone, *Internationale Politiek und Gesellschaft*, 2, 67–94.

MANIFESTO '99 (2002) *Traditional methods of conflict management/resolution of possible complementary value to the proposed Sierra Leone Truth and Reconciliation Commission.*

PARK, A.S.J. (2007) *Restorative approaches to justice: strategies for peace in Sierra Leone*, Center for International Governance and Justice Issues, Australian National University, Paper No. 2, May 2007.

PENAL REFORM INTERNATIONAL (2000) *Access to Justice in Sub-Saharan Africa, The Role of Traditional and Informal Justice Systems.* London.

PHYSICIANS FOR HUMAN RIGHTS (2002) *War-Related Sexual Violence in Sierra Leone. A Population-Based Assessment.* USA.

STARK, L. (2006) Cleansing the wounds of war: an examination of traditional healing, psychosocial health and reintegration in Sierra Leone, *Intervention*, 4(3), 206–218.

SUMA, M. and CORREA, C. (2009) *Report and proposals for the implementation of the reparations in Sierra Leone*, International Center for Transitional justice

TRC – TRUTH AND RECONCILIATION COMMISSION (2004) *Witness to truth*, Report of the Sierra Leone Truth and Reconciliation Commission, Sierra Leone.

ZACK-WILLIAMS, T.B. (2006) Child Soldiers in Sierra Leone and the Problems of Demobilization, Rehabilitation and Reintegration into Society: Some Lessons for Social Workers in war-torn Societies, *Social Work Education*, 25(2), 119–128.

CHAPTER 5

OFFICIAL HYBRIDISATION OF TRADITION: A CASE STUDY ON RWANDA

Martien SCHOTSMANS

1. BACKGROUND TO THE CONFLICT

A former German colony, Rwanda, together with Burundi, became a Belgian mandate after the Second World War, until its independence in 1962. While Belgium applied a system of indirect rule through the *mwami* or king and his chiefs, who were mainly Tutsi (see below), Rwanda's three population groups, the Hutu, the Tutsi and the Twa, have been dominated by a Hutu majority from 1959 until the end of the civil war in 1994.

While crimes of genocide against the Tutsi have been committed and remained unpunished in Rwanda since 1959, the civil war from 1 October 1990 to 4 July 1994, initiated by the Rwandan Patriotic Front (RPF) mainly composed of Tutsi refugees from neighbouring countries, exacerbated the number and intensity of such crimes, culminating in the 100 days of genocide of the Tutsi from 6 April to 4 July 1994. The killings were committed according to a plan developed and implemented by Hutu extremists within the government, who did not agree with the power sharing deals that were being negotiated in Arusha under international pressure. It involved trained militias called Interahamwe as well as large numbers of ordinary citizens, incited by hate campaigns broadcasted over Radio Télévision Libre des Mille Collines (RTLM). The genocide allegedly caused the death of 800,000 to 1,000,000 victims, in addition to victims of crimes against humanity committed against moderate Hutu, and war crimes and other crimes committed by members of the RPF (Des Forges, 1999). Hundreds of thousands of women were allegedly raped (Wells, 2005). In a survey conducted in 2000, 36% of respondents claimed to have lost family members due to the genocide and 23% due to massacres (Gasibirige, 2002).[1] The war ended in a victory of the RPF, which

[1] The survey does not mention whether those crimes were committed in 1994 or before (or after), nor whether there is a possible overlap between both categories.

transformed into a political party that still dominates the political landscape today, following several elections.

2. THE ROLE OF TRADITION IN SOCIETY

In contrast to many African societies, traditional aspects are quite absent from daily life in Rwanda.

Although they were not all Tutsi before colonial times, the Belgian rulers gradually replaced non-Tutsi chiefs by allegedly more loyal Tutsi chiefs. The Second World War and the strife for independence from colonial powers which followed all over in Africa, caused another shift in Belgium's policy, which then started to support the 'oppressed' Hutu against the more independence-minded Tutsi elite. With the so-called 'social revolution' in 1959, over 50% of all Tutsi chiefs were replaced by Hutu chiefs, against the will of the *mwami*, who had the right to nominate chiefs. Later reforms gradually replaced the traditional institutions and chiefs with administrative structures and elected counsellors (Reyntjens, 1985). Rwanda became a republic in 1961. Today, there are no traditional power structures present in Rwanda.

During colonial times, indigenous courts presided over by the chiefs were established by the colonial authorities to replace the traditional *gacaca* system (UNOHCHR, 1996). They had the right to settle disputes according to customary law, with the exception of more important criminal cases, which were handled by established criminal tribunals. Later, the possibility to appeal decisions of indigenous courts at the level of the formal courts was established, while the appointment of judges in the indigenous courts (all Tutsi) had to be approved by the colonial administrator for approval. Thus, indigenous judges gradually lost their legitimacy and moral authority in the eyes of the population (Reyntjens, 1985), while *gacaca* continued to operate as a local mechanism for conflict resolution at the informal level.

3. TRANSITIONAL JUSTICE LANDSCAPE

Immediately after the end of the genocide, Rwanda opted for criminal prosecutions of all those suspected of having committed the crime of genocide and related crimes against humanity. The idea of a blanket amnesty was outright rejected (Republic of Rwanda, 1995). Criminal prosecutions took place at several levels. The United Nations created the International Criminal Tribunal for Rwanda (ICTR) that has tried 75 cases so far.[2]

---

2 UN Resolution S/RES/955, www.ictr.org.

In addition to the ICTR and some trials in third countries using universal jurisdiction powers (Redress, 2008), Rwanda prosecuted about 10,000 accused at the domestic level (Schabas, 2008; Des Forges and Longman, 2004). The 1996 Organic Law[3] provided for reduced sentences in exchange for confessions, which led to almost 30% of accused confessing and offering apologies (Avocats Sans Frontières, 1999). The law also provided for reparations by both the perpetrator and the Rwandan state, but these judgments have never been implemented (Rombouts and Vandeginste, 2005). Meanwhile, a fund[4] provides assistance (housing, medical care, school fees) to survivors. Furthermore, 35 cases of crimes 'of revenge' committed by RPF soldiers have been prosecuted by the military courts at the domestic level,[5] which is generally felt to be disproportionate[6] (Haskell and Waldorf, 2011).

Considering the huge numbers of detainees[7] and the limited capacity of the formal justice system, a new hybrid *gacaca* justice system was created in 2001,[8] involving a mixture of traditional *gacaca* and modern retributive trials. By the end of April 2009 1,138,860 cases had been tried by *gacaca* justice.[9] In July 2010, the process had largely ended, with the exception of some appeal and revision cases.

4. THE ROLE OF TRADITION IN TRANSITIONAL JUSTICE

Despite the fact that most traditional elements from Rwandan society disappeared during the colonial and postcolonial periods, two official transitional justice mechanisms systematically refer to these elements: on the one hand the *gacaca* courts and, on the other hand, the National Unity and Reconciliation Commission (NURC). This concerns mechanisms and activities that to a certain degree are based on traditional values and practices, but are in fact true hybrids, amalgams that adjust traditional elements to contemporary needs and (partly) to modern standards. Both instances are government initiatives that nevertheless relate to

3 Organic Law no. 8/96 of 30/08/1996, J.O. no. 17 of 01/09/1996.
4 Fond d'Assistance aux Rescapés du Génocide.
5 Ministry of Defence, Military Prosecution, RPA soldiers who committed crimes of revenge during and after 1994 genocide and were prosecuted before Rwandan military courts, April 2007.
6 Ministry of Defence, Military Prosecution, RPA soldiers who committed crimes of revenge during and after 1994 genocide and were prosecuted before Rwandan military courts, April 2007.
7 112,000 in 2000 according to Avocats Sans Frontières (2000).
8 Organic Law no. 40/2000 of 26/01/2001, J.O. no. 6 of 15/03/2001. Modified by Organic Law no. 16/2004 of 19/06/2004, J.O. special no. of 19/06/2004, adding the need to try the accused with promptitude. Modified by Organic Law no. 28/2006 of 26/06/2006, Organic Law no. 10/2007 of 01/03/2007 and Organic law no. 13/2008 of 19/05/2008.
9 Information from the National Service of Gacaca Jurisdictions, received in July 2009.

the population's collective memory. This is especially the case with *gacaca* that many people remember from their youth as an informal mechanism to settle minor disputes.

4.1. GACACA COURTS (*INKIKO GACACA*)

Traditional *gacaca* was the lowest informal level of dispute resolution, starting at the household level (*uruko*), going to the level of the extended family (*inzu*) and the level of the lineage or clan (*umuryango).* Women could not participate directly in the process and had to be represented by a man (Wells, 2005). If a dispute could not be settled at this level, the *mwami* could be called upon. He could intervene himself or delegate the case to a lower chief. The primary goal of *gacaca* would be the restoration of social harmony. For capital crimes, however, the restoration of harmony required the killing of a person of equal value of the killer's family, although settlement by gifts or giving a girl for marriage would sometimes, and with time more easily, be possible (Ingelaere, 2008; UNOHCHR, 1996). As mentioned above, colonial authorities withdrew the jurisdiction of capital crimes form traditional authorities. However, *gacaca* as a means of low-level dispute settlement continued to exist. *Gacaca* gradually evolved towards a semi-administrative body, supervised by and composed of local authorities, which tried to settle disputes as a filter to the formal justice system (Reyntjens, 1990). This type of *gacaca* continued to exist even after the genocide (UNOHCHR, 1996).

After the genocide, *gacaca* soon started to revive in a very informal way in some communities at the local level: one type was used mainly to settle property disputes related to the genocide without entering into the crimes committed (Ingelaere, 2008; Vandeginste, 1998). It was acknowledged and sometimes supported by local authorities, and in this regard resembled the semi-administrative *gacaca* mentioned above. Another type of post-genocide *gacaca* focused on reconciliation and was initiated by the Catholic Church (the so-called Christian *gacaca*).[10]

During a conference in Kigali in 1995, the idea to use the traditional *gacaca* as an alternative solution to deal with genocide related property crimes was mentioned (Republic of Rwanda, 1995). In 1996, the outcome of a research, initiated by UNOHCHR, on the potential use of *gacaca* to deal with crimes of genocide was published. The researchers, all Rwandan, found that *gacaca* would be a useful tool for investigation and truth finding, as a kind of truth commission, while the actual trying of crimes should best be left with the formal justice system. In 1998, a series of gatherings and discussions on national unity was initiated by President

---

10 Interview Evèc de Kabga, who mentions that it was practiced in all dioceses in Rwanda during 1999–2000, with a focus on confessions, apologies and reconciliation.

Bizimungu, the so-called *Urugwire village* meetings (Republic of Rwanda, 1999). During these discussions, it was decided to establish modernised *gacaca* courts, not only for truth finding, but also to try crimes. The active participation of the population in this process was deemed indispensable.

Gacaca justice has been extensively described, analysed and assessed (Clark, 2010; Ingelaere, 2008; Haveman, 2008; Clark, 2007; Waldorf, 2006; Schabas, 2005; Stover and Weinstein, 2004), which allows us to mention only those features relevant to the subject of this research.

In contrast to traditional *gacaca*, *gacaca* justice or *inkiko gacaca* is a formalised, state-organised justice mechanism, officially part of the country's transitional justice policy. *Gacaca courts* – following several modifications – deal with almost all crimes of genocide and related crimes against humanity, except for the crime of organising or planning the genocide at a national or prefecture level, which are tried by ordinary courts.

War crimes, such as those committed by RPF military, do not fall under the jurisdiction of *gacaca* justice, nor do revenge crimes committed by either the military or survivors. *Gacaca* jurisdictions were composed of elected honourable persons (*inyangamugayo*) at the lowest administrative levels, each of which had to deal with a specific category of accused: the lowest level conducted investigations, oriented the cases and tried property crimes (3rd category), while the second level dealt with cases of homicide and physical injury (2nd category) and with appeals. Women can participate as judges, witnesses, suspects or in the general public. After a pilot phase in 2002, the legislation was reviewed and *gacaca* trials started all over the country. A number of important adjustments of the system took place during the process.[11]

The discussion surrounding the question whether *gacaca* courts are tradition-based or are in fact a complete new mechanism or a hybrid model (Clark, 2007) is still ongoing. Most donors and INGOs in the field perceive *gacaca* as a modern, newly founded institution that is only vaguely inspired by tradition. Representatives of Rwandan organisations and local NGOs mainly consider popular participation, the lay judges and the objective of reintegration as traditional components, but nevertheless take the view that the traditional character of the *gacaca* courts was primarily used to convince the people to accept the mechanism and actively participate in it.

Gacaca justice has been severely criticised for not respecting fair trial standards and leading to many abuses. Even though all agreed that there had been false accusations (rather made by non-survivors than by survivors in recent

[11] Modified by Organic Law no. 16/2004 of 19/06/2004, J.O. special no. of 19/06/2004, Organic Law no. 28/2006 of 26/06/2006, Organic Law no. 10/2007 of 01/03/2007, Organic Law no. 13/2008 of 19/05/2008. The 2004 laws add the need to try the accused with promptitude. For a detailed description of the system and the various modifications, see: Ingelaere, 2008; Waldorf, 2006; reports by Avocats Sans Frontières, www.asf.be. Penal Reform International, www.pri.org.

years), complots of silence (*ceceka*), 'buying of the hill' (*kugura agasozi*: someone takes the blame on him, in exchange for support to the family) and corruption of both judges and witnesses, many of our respondents felt *gacaca* justice had to a large extent achieved its goal of accountability and allowed the establishment of individual guilt (also: Penal Reform International, 2010; Institut de Recherche et de Dialogue pour la Paix, 2008). Respondents were also positive about the revelation of the factual truth about crimes and the location of bodies of victims, even if the precise role of the perpetrators was not always established (in contrast to: Shaw and Waldorf, 2010; Ingelaere, 2008).

The transfer of authority to try sexual offences from the formal to the *gacaca* courts is more problematic: this led to rape victims having to lay their case before the local *gacaca* court, often comprised of neighbours and acquaintances. Although they could select a confidant(e) from the judges to state their case, and although the *gacaca* hearings took place behind closed doors, dates and locations of these hearings were public knowledge. The *gacaca* courts are said to have handled approximately 8,000 cases, a disproportionally small number, which observers blame on the social stigma regarding rape.

While *gacaca* legislation abolished the possibility to claim compensation from the State, the long promised Victims' Fund was finally established on paper in 2008, but never became operational.[12] Only *gacaca* jurisdictions dealing with property crimes can decide on restitution or compensation for the victims. However, the implementation of these compensation orders was an important concern.

The actual popular participation, i.e. beyond mere physical presence, has been one of the most criticised aspects of *gacaca* justice (Shaw and Waldorf, 2010; Clark, 2010; PRI, 2010; Ingelaere, 2008; Clark, 2008; Avocats Sans Frontières, 2006). Much would depend on the proportion of survivors in the community and in the *gacaca* process, as the presence of only a few victims would allow the community to disregard them more easily (Ingelaere, 2009).

Although in a country where about 15,000 jurisdictions have been operating simultaneously, one can certainly not generalise, what seems to have been lacking in many *gacaca* trials is exactly the feature of traditional justice often promoted for its restorative value: encounter or dialogue (Penal Reform International, 2010; Institut de Recherche et de Dialogue pour la Paix, 2008). As one of the respondents stated: '*Dans gacaca on parle, mais on ne se parle pas*', meaning 'in *gacaca* we talk, but we do not talk with each other'.

As *gacaca* proceedings are not concluded by popular consensus, but by a decision taken by the *inyangamugayo*, the ritual celebration of the agreement to leave the past behind is equally lacking. Even in a country where traditional rites have disappeared from the public landscape, simple rituals such as sharing a beer or a meal are often mentioned as signs of reconciliation. But after a *gacaca* hearing

---

12 Law no. 69/2008 of 30/12/2008, J.O. special no. of 15/04/2009.

everyone just returns home. In other words, there is no closure of the process, and therefore no new beginning. For this reason, many observers I interviewed in 2009 were looking forward to what would come after *gacaca* – the post-*gacaca* – hoping it would bring healing and start a process of reconciliation through sincere dialogue (Penal Reform International, 2010; Republic of Rwanda, 2009; Ingelaere, 2008).

The question is whether encounter[13] as an objective of restorative justice is a realistic expectation for a hybrid mechanism like *gacaca* justice, being a formal procedure guided by the law and by political guidelines of conduct for participants. Perhaps truth finding and accountability through *gacaca* justice – partial as they may be – were preliminary conditions in a long process towards genuine dialogue, of which one can catch a cautious glimpse in Rwanda nowadays. According to a report of the National Unity and Reconciliation Commission (NURC) based on a survey conducted in 2008, the lack of reparations, absence of apologies after *gacaca*, testimonies during *gacaca* and the pressure of government to reconcile are among the main reasons for persisting distrust between survivors and their neighbours[14] (Republic of Rwanda, NURC, 2009).

4.2. NURC: TRADITIONAL VALUES OF UNITY AND RECONCILIATION

During the *Urugwire village* meetings, the need to establish unity and reconciliation among Rwandans was also discussed. Culture was considered to be the needed 'cement for unity' (Republic of Rwanda, 1999). The NURC actively promotes a revival of traditional values for unity and reconciliation purposes and uses them as a justification for certain activities.

The most prominent activities in this regard are the solidarity camps, i.e. residential camps where specific groups are taught civic education for three weeks, and cover topics such as the analysis of Rwanda's problems; history of Rwanda; political and socioeconomic issues in Rwanda and Africa, rights and obligations of citizens and good leadership.[15] Participation is mandatory for both men and women. There are two types of such solidarity camps. *Ingando* camps have been used for the reinsertion of ex-combatants, of released prisoners and for the education of university students of government universities. The cultural origin of these camps is explained as follows: 'In old times, when the country

13 *Encounter* in the framework of *restorative justice* refers to a meeting of offender and victim in a safe and supportive environment where both can play an active role in the discussion, can talk openly and express their emotions and participate in the decision on the problem. (Johnstone and Van Ness, 2007).

14 77.6% of survivors distrust their neighbours, compared to 37% of released prisoners and 53.3% of the general population.

15 www.nurc.gov.rw.

was attacked, there was a retreat of the army commanders, police chiefs and all decision-making groups. If there was a famine, there would be a retreat of another group. If there was a feud among clans: another group. So it was for specific people to solve specific problems. It could be called by the *mwami*, the chief or the head of the military. People of the same level/age/responsibility in society would unite.'[16] *Itorero* camps are more recent and are used for specific professional groups, such as people from the health sector, from veterinary medicine, civil society, teachers, etc. In addition to civic education, these groups also receive professional training. The traditional roots of this mechanism are explained as follows: 'Itorero was a traditional school to pass on life and knowledge. It started at village level: you would learn how to behave at home, how to respect visitors and elders, assignments for boys and girls, etc. It was given to children between 12 and 18 years old. They lived with mentors, not with their family. The children would be given physical training: sports, shooting, wrestling, jumping, ... and literature, philosophy, medicine, veterinary medicine ... the highest level was to graduate into the army. Some people distinguished in other fields, such as veterinary medicine. There were various education fields. Now, we want to use *itorero* to trace those values and to indicate traditional values that got lost. If we revive this, society will be in a better position for coexistence.'[17]

Other tradition-based activities promoted by NURC are *umuganda*, the one day a month communal work obligation, which had continued to exist, but is now combined with meetings during which government policy and problems are discussed; *ubusubane,* during which the community gathers for celebrations; and *ubudehe,* communal work for a specific project, paid by the government in cash or with animals.

In 2005, the NURC held National Unity and Reconciliation consultations in all districts in which several stakeholders participated. This enabled the compilation of an inventory of the numerous local initiatives aimed at reconciliation, without any specific foundation in tradition. The NURC counted approximately 600 initiatives in 2006–2007, but is confessedly unable to update this inventory on a regular basis. In each district, a Unity and Reconciliation Forum was established which involved all stakeholders (local authorities, NGOs, women's organisations, church organisations, etc.). This Forum must present an action plan annually and can obtain funds for activities. In reality, however, the NURC's funds are rather limited and for the funding of local initiatives it depends on the means of other government agencies, such as the Ministry of Local Affairs which enters into performance contracts (*imihigo*, also marked as traditional) with the local authorities, which also include activities concerning *gacaca* and reconciliation. The NURC has attempted to promote local ownership of these activities, aided by volunteers – the *abakangurambaga* – who were recruited in the communities and

16 Interview NURC.
17 Interview NURC.

then received a limited training in peace monitoring. However, our interviews with the local population showed that except for the *ingando* and *itorero* solidarity camps and the monthly *umuganda*, the tradition-based activities promoted by the NURC are rather unknown or are at least not experienced as being based on tradition.

However, it is to be noted that the reading of pre-colonial history is problematic in Rwanda, since the various population groups have a different view of it (Ingelaere, 2008; Des Forges, 1999). While former diaspora, now in power, tend to romanticise the pre-colonial society as peaceful, non-violent and with clear social roles for everyone, only to be distorted by colonial powers, those who lived in the country after 1959 have learned to see this past as one of oppression of the Hutu population by the Tutsi elite. During the *ingando* and *itoreo*, and many other meetings, conferences and debates organised by the NURC, it is the former version of history, as established by the *Urugwire village* meetings, that prevails (Republic of Rwanda, 1999).[18] NURC planned to organise more *ingando* and *itoreo* camps for several hundreds of thousands of Rwandans.[19]

5. POLICIES AND INTERVENTIONS OF INTERNATIONAL ACTORS

Donors have never openly questioned the Rwandan decision to prosecute all perpetrators of genocide and crimes against humanity. The decision was even perceived as a positive one, considering the lack of prosecutions in most post-conflict countries and the fact that it corresponded with the 'fight against impunity' as part of their peacebuilding policies (which is also the reason why international human rights organisations did not reject *gacaca* as such). For the same reason, various donors also supported the ICTR and domestic courts. When it became clear that formal justice would not be able to cope with the huge number of detainees within a reasonable delay and the Rwanda government, following the *Urugwire* village meetings, was proposing *gacaca* justice as a tradition-based alternative,[20] donors were facing a dilemma. On the one hand, the proposed process would make it possible to continue the fight against impunity, in addition to being original and innovative. On the other hand, the proposed mechanism presented serious risks for human rights violations, considering the lack of respect for international fair trial standards, the fear of 'popular' justice

18 Urugwire report, pp. 10–14.

19 NURC, Strategic plan 2009–2011, Kigali, December 2008, p. 28.

20 Republic of Rwanda, Office of the President, Republic of Rwanda, report on the reflection meetings held in the office of the President of the Republic from May 1998 to March 1999, Kigali, August 1999 (hereafter: Urugwire discussion). For a further overview of the creation of *gacaca* justice see: Clark, 2010; Ingelaere, 2008.

too soon after the genocide and the long sentences that could be pronounced.[21] These arguments were also shared by Rwandan lawyers. The decision to create *gacaca* courts was clearly a Rwandan political decision, in which international actors had no voice.

After a period of reflection and discussions with Rwandan authorities, sometimes after advice by an external expert (Uvin, 2001), a number of donors decided to accept the mechanism, on condition that certain observations would be met to reduce the risk of human rights violations (considering the 'do no harm' principle).

Donors especially insisted upon formal aspects. This, for example, included a pilot phase, after which the mechanism could still be adjusted, training for lay judges, sensitisation of the population, independent interim evaluations and monitoring by international and local NGOs. None of the donors considered the presentation of the mechanism as traditional to be a convincing argument, although they were of the opinion that this would increase the potential for local ownership with regards to the population (Samset, Peterson and Wang, 2007). Given that around that time the idea of attaching conditions to developmental aid was considered undesirable and even counterproductive, donors decided to provide their support to realise a result that included respect for human rights (Lenzen, 2009). The Rwandan authorities accepted all these proposals. Moreover, both donors and INGOs[22] were granted access to government bills and amendment bills and could remark upon them. While donors consciously decided not to interfere with the substance of the mechanism, international NGOs did attempt to influence it, with limited success. And although donors furthermore formally pressed for the establishment of a victims' fund and for the criminal prosecution of crimes committed by RPF soldiers, they did not truly insist upon these terms. The only issue in which the donors explicitly interfered was to prevent the *gacaca* courts from pronouncing the death penalty. Upon other issues, such as the transfer of prosecutions for sexual violence to the *gacaca* courts, the donors did not insist, despite the resistance by both international and national NGOs. Neither, finally, did the donors insist that the recommendations of the NGOs monitoring the *gacaca* process be taken into account, which limited the impact of said monitoring.

The donor support concerned a wide range of activities, meaning that the below overview cannot be regarded as an exhaustive one.

---

21 United Nations, Commission on Human Rights, Report on the situation of human rights in Rwanda submitted by the Special Representative, Mr Michel Moussalli, pursuant to Commission resolution 1999/20, 25 February, 2000E/CN.4/2000/41, para. 162. Report of the Informal Seminar on Donor Support for a 'modernised' *gacaca* in Rwanda, Brussels, 27 October 2000.

22 Avocats Sans Frontières, RCN Justice & Démocratie, Penal Reform International, Centre Danois des Droits de l'Homme.

While the main donors supporting *gacaca* justice were the European Commission, Belgium and the Netherlands, additional – sometimes occasional or only initial – funding was provided by UNDP, USAID, Switzerland and Austria. While most donors provided both direct support to the *gacaca* process through the Supreme Court[23] and the Ministry of Justice, and to *gacaca*-related programmes of international and local civil society organisations, some donors (the UK, Canada) only supported civil society.

Other donors, such as the European Commission and Belgium (through its development agency BTC) decided only to support 'neutral' activities, such as paying for certain staff members, the publication of a journal *Inkiko Gacaca*, training coordinators and *gacaca* judges, logistics support and transport, presuming that they would incur less blame should the process fail. Their representatives now admit that this was a mistake, since their position also meant they commanded no expertise to provide technical feedback on the process. The Netherlands, Switzerland and Austria, on the other hand, together founded a Bureau d'Assistance Technique (BAT), which provided both technical and logistical support to the Supreme Court. The Netherlands furthermore funded supplementary education for the *gacaca* judges, as well as activities to sensitise the local authorities and the population in general. Belgium, the Netherlands, the UK, the European Commission, USAID and Switzerland in addition supported monitoring of the process by Avocats Sans Frontières (ASF) and Penal Reform International (PRI), as well as by the National Human Rights Commission and a consortium of local NGOs, united in the *Projet d'Appui de la Société Civile au Processus Gacaca*. The European Commission and the Netherlands also financed the final evaluations of the *gacaca* process.[24] UNDP financed activities according to requests it received from the Rwandan authorities. These activities included the editing of handbooks and forms (implemented by Avocats Sans Frontières), documenting the process by centralising and archiving dossiers and registers, a historical study on the origins and evolution of the *gacaca* process, etc. USAID financed the process only indirectly through NGO activities, such as the training of *gacaca* judges and monitoring (by ASF) and promoting the participation of women in the process, supported by local NGOs. Canada also supported some local NGOs in their promotion of victim participation in the process. The United Kingdom did not offer any direct support to the process, but did provide important budget support to Rwanda. The UK furthermore supported certain NGO activities, such as the PRI's monitoring. The *gacaca* projects of the Rwandan civil society, which received donor support, comprised a wide array of activities,

---

23 The Supreme Court initially housed a 6th Chamber to deal with *gacaca*. It was later replaced by an independent National Service for *Gacaca* Justice.

24 Several donors furthermore offered much more limited support, such as computer systems materials by USAID, other equipment by Norwegian Church Aid, prisoner transport by Trocaire.

including research, sensitisation, monitoring and reporting, media coverage, training and conferences.

Only one donor, Switzerland, decided not to renew its support after an evaluation of the pilot phase. This donor considered the Rwandan authorities to be insufficiently open to the donor's remarks regarding the lack of fair trial, the fact that the investigations were executed by the *inyambakumi* (person responsible for ten houses) instead of during public hearings, and the fact that suspects had too little opportunity to present exonerating evidence. Other donors, such as Belgium and Austria, decided against renewal of their support for more technical reasons. In general the donors – and a number of Rwandan actors – agree that there was not enough willingness on the Rwandan side to enter into a dialogue about possible amendments to the process, except for a few more technical recommendations (such as refraining from the immediate prosecution of witnesses for false testimony), since Rwanda heavily emphasised national ownership.

All in all, donors decided to support the *gacaca* process because it was a component of the official government policy and could therefore boast strong national ownership. This is also why they considered the responsibility for the outcomes of the process to lie with the Rwandan government, and they primarily felt accountable to their home base. They were aware of the risk of human rights violations and did wish to prevent these, but only exercised marginal control over the process. Although the donors' financial support added to the success of the process, both donors and Rwandan actors are convinced that *gacaca* would have taken place without their aid. In hindsight, some donors feel that they could have taken a more critical stance and could have exerted more pressure on the process, but in general they perceive the result of the entire process more positively than negatively and, therefore, still consider their support justified.

The support for tradition-based activities for unity and reconciliation executed or promoted by the NURC is primarily coordinated by UNDP, for which UNDP receives financial support from several donors (among which DFID is the main donor; NURC is part of the 14 national organisations included in the Justice, Reconciliation, Law and Order Sector plan and will therefore enjoy sector support from several donors). An important part of this support consists of logistics for the *ingando* and *itorero* solidarity camps and, formerly, for Peace and Reconciliation Clubs at schools (not tradition-inspired). At donor level, there is concern about the top-down nature of the NURC activities, as well as about the romanticised version of history, which is promoted during *ingando* and *itorero*. Some donors (Belgium and the Netherlands) have explicitly refused to support this.

As said, many local reconciliation initiatives are proposed by local organisations and are later added by the NURC to their database, but these are in fact not tradition-based, although they do aim to restore social harmony. Such local initiatives are usually supported by either international NGOs, such as International Alert or Miserero, or by religiously inspired organisations such as the Commission Paix & Justice, World Vision, Catholic Relief Services and Broederlijk Delen, some of which are supported themselves by bilateral donors such as DFID, GTZ, the Netherlands, USAID or Belgium.

BIBLIOGRAPHY

Avocats Sans Frontieres (1999) *Justice pour tous au Rwanda*, Rapport annuel.

Avocats Sans Frontieres (2006) Monitoring des juridictions *gacaca*. Phase de jugement. Rapport analytique, n° 2, Brussels.

Clark, P. (2007) Hybridity, holism and 'traditional justice': the case of the *gacaca* courts in post-genocide Rwanda, *George Washington International Law Review*, 39(4), 765–832.

Clark, P. (2010) *The Gacaca courts, Post-Genocide Justice and Reconciliation in Rwanda. Justice without Lawyers*. Cambridge: Cambridge University Press.

Des Forges, A. (1999) *Leave none to tell the story. Genocide in Rwanda*. New York/ Paris: Human Rights Watch and Fédération Internationale des Ligues des Droits de l'Homme.

Des Forges, A. and Longman, T. (2004) Legal responses to genocide in Rwanda. In Stover, E. and Weinstein, H.M. (eds.) *My neighbor, my enemy. Justice and community in the aftermath of mass atrocity*, 49–68. Cambridge: Cambridge University Press.

Haskell, L. and Waldorf, L. (2011) The impunity gap of the International Criminal Tribunal for Rwanda: Causes and consequences, *Hastings International and Comparative Law Review*, 34, 49–85.

Haveman, R. (2008) Doing justice to gacaca. In Smeulers, A. and Haveman, R. (eds.) *Supranational Criminology: Towards a Criminology of International Crimes*, 357–398. Antwerp: Intersentia.

Ingelaere, B. (2008) The gacaca courts in Rwanda. In Huyse, L. and Salter, M. (eds.) *Traditional Justice after Violent Conflict. Learning from African experiences*, 25–59. Stockholm, Sweden: IDEA.

Ingelaere, B. (2009) Mille collines, mille gacaca, La vie en marge du processus gacaca. In Marysse, S., Reyntjens, F. and Vandeginste, S., *L'Afrique des Grands Lacs, Annuaire 2008-2009*, 29–42. Paris: L'Harmattan, 2009.

Institut de Recherche et de Dialogue pour la Paix (2008) *Analyse du processus gacaca et de son impact sur la réconciliation et la cohésion sociale au Rwanda*, Note de discussion, Kigali.

Johnstone, G. and Van Ness, D.W. (eds.) (2007) *Handbook of restorative justice*. Willan Publishing.

Lenzen, M. (2009) Roads Less Travelled? Conceptual Pathways (and Stumbling Blocks) for Development and Transitional Justice. In De Greiff, P. and Duthie, R. (eds.) *Transitional Justice and Development. Making Connections*, Chapter 2, 76–109. Advancing Transitional Justice series, International Center for Transitional Justice, Social Science Research Council, New York.

PRI – Penal Reform International (2010) *The contribution of the Gacaca jurisdictions to resolving cases arising from the genocide. Contributions, limitations and expectations of the post-Gacaca phase.* London.

Redress (2008) *Extraditing Genocide Suspects From Europe to Rwanda. Issues and Challenges.* Report of a Conference organised by Redress and African Rights at the Belgian Parliament.

Republic of Rwanda, National Unity and Reconciliation Commission (2009) *Social cohesion in Rwanda. An opinion survey, 2005–2008.*

Republic of Rwanda, Office of the President (1995) *Recommendations of the conference held in Kigali from November 1st to 5th, 1995, on: 'Genocide, Impunity and accountability: dialogue for a national and international response'.*

Republic of Rwanda, Office of the President (1999) *Republic of Rwanda, report on the reflection meetings held in the office of the President of the Republic from May 1998 to March 1999*, Kigali.

Republic of Mozambique (2006), *Poverty Reduction Strategy Paper 2006–2009.*

Reyntjens, F. (1985) *Pouvoir et droit au Rwanda. Droit public et évolution politique*, 1916–1973, Musée Royale de l'Afrique Centrale, Belgium.

Reyntjens, F. (1990) Le gacaca ou la justice du gazon au Rwanda, *Politique Africaine*, no. 40, Le droit et ses pratiques, Karthala, 31–41.

Rombouts, H. and Vandeginste, S. (2005) Reparation for victims in Rwanda: caught between theory and practice. In De Feyter, K., Parmentier, S., Bossuyt, M. and Lemmens, P. (eds) *Out of the Ashes. Reparation for Victims of Gross and Systematic Human Rights Violations*, 309–341. Antwerp/Oxford: Intersentia.

Samset, I., Peterson, S. and Wang, V. (2007) Maintaining the process? Aid to Transitional Justice in Rwanda and Guatemala. 1995–2005, The Working Group on Development and Peace (FriEnt), Bonn, November 2007.

Schabas, W.A. (2008) Post-genocide justice in Rwanda: a spectrum of options. In Clark, P. and Kaufman, Z.D. (eds.) *After genocide: Transitional justice, post-conflict reconstruction and reconciliation in Rwanda and Beyond*, 207–227. London: Hurst & Company.

Shaw, R. and Waldorf, L. (2010) *Localizing transitional justice. Interventions and priorities after mass violence.* Stanford, CA: Stanford University Press.

Stover, E. and Weinstein, H.M. (eds.) (2004) *My neighbor, my enemy. Justice and community in the aftermath of mass atrocity.* Cambridge: Cambridge University Press.

UNOHCHR (1996) *Gacaca. Le droit coutumier au Rwanda.* Rapport final de la première phase d'enquête sur le terrain, Kigali, 31/01/1996. Rapport de la deuxième phase d'enquêtes sur le terrain, Kigali, 30/06/1996.

Uvin, P. (2001) Difficult choices in the new post-conflict agenda: the international community in Rwanda after the genocide. *Third World Quarterly*, 22(2), 177–189

Vandeginste, S. (1998) L'approche 'vérité et réconciliation' du génocide et des crimes contre l'humanité au Rwanda. In Reyntjes, F. and Marysse, S. (eds.) *L'Afrique des Grands-Lacs, Annuaire 1997–1998*, 97–140. Paris: L'Harmattan.

Waldorf, L. (2006) Mass justice for mass atrocity: rethinking local justice as transitional justice. *Temple Law Review*, 79(1), 1–87.

Wells, S. (2005) Gender, sexual violence and the prospects for justice at the gacaca courts in Rwanda. *South California Review of Law & Women's Studies*, 14(2), 167–196.

CHAPTER 6

OFFICIAL COMPLEMENTARITY: A CASE STUDY ON NORTHERN UGANDA

Martien SCHOTSMANS

1. BACKGROUND TO THE CONFLICT

Uganda is a former British colony that became independent in 1962. In previous decennia, the British had applied a divide-and-rule policy. As a consequence of this policy, the more economically and intellectually developed South supported the stuggle for independence that erupted all over Africa after the Second World War. Hence, the South opposed the North, where most military originated from. After independence, the governments of Obote and Amin continued and reinforced this regional opposition.

Although Uganda has known many intra-state conflicts before and after Museveni's takeover in 1986 (Latigo, 2008), the current case study is limited to the conflict in Northern-Uganda between Joseph Kony's Lord Resistance Army (LRA) and the Ugandan army (UPDF), supported by local defence units (LDUs). The reason for this is the fact that discussions regarding the role of traditional justice, as opposed to formal justice, have focused mainly on this conflict, and that external interventions have supported the revival of traditional structures and practices, which makes it an interesting object of analyses.

This conflict in Northern Uganda (mainly the districts of Gulu, Kitgum and Pader) dates from 1986. It has to be understood both in the context of internal politics, including discrimination of the Northern region of Uganda, and the regional conflict, since the government of Sudan was supporting the LRA until the Comprehensive Peace Agreement (CPA) ended the conflict between the then Northern and Southern parts of Sudan in 2005, while Uganda was supporting the South Sudanese secession movement (Latigo, 2008). The LRA has used extreme violence and committed many crimes against the population, the most notorious being the abduction and use of children in the hostilities, estimated between 30,000 and 50,000 (Human Rights Watch, 2003), in addition to sexual violence and other attacks against the civilian population. In order to secure the region, the Ugandan government decided to regroup about 80% of the population, over

1,700,000 persons, in internal displacement camps (IDP camps), where they have spent over 20 years and suffered from many crimes, committed by both the LRA and the UPDF. There are no exact numbers of persons killed, but my respondents estimated they mount up to 15,000. Although a relative security has been established in Northern Uganda,[1] and most people have left the IDP camps, the conflict with the LRA has not officially ended and many people still fear a new outbreak of violence and the return (or even spiritual omnipresence) of Joseph Kony, who since a few years infests the border region between the Democratic Republic of Congo, the Central African Republic and South Sudan.

2. THE ROLE OF TRADITION IN SOCIETY

Before colonial times, what is now called Acholiland was not a centralised kingdom, as existed elsewhere in Uganda (Doom and Vlassenroot, 1999). Communities were governed by traditional chiefs, or *rwodi,* chosen by supernatural powers. Each *rwot* was assisted by a clan tribunal (*kot kwor*) that settled disputes within the clan, set reparations, performed purification rituals, etc. The *rwot* was further assisted by a council of elders, chosen by the clan members. The council members of each clan composed the Grand Council, which, among others, settled disputes between different clans (Latigo, 2008). Under the British colonial rule, traditional leaders were replaced or seconded by appointed, administrative chiefs, who were never fully accepted. The *rwodi* were officially abolished under the Oboti regime in 1966. De facto, the *rwodi* remained the cultural leaders, but without any official recognition. They have been reinstated by Museveni in 1993 and later by the 1995 Constitution, with limited ceremonial and cultural functions and prohibition to participate in party politics or exercise any function in the national or local government (Beke, 2004).[2]

Besides the formal justice system, an administrative system of Local Council Courts is established at five different levels (Beke, 2004). They are composed of laypersons appointed by the Local Council, and have jurisdiction to deal with local civil disputes according to customary law or local byelaws.[3]

---

1 Meanwhile the LRA has moved to Southern Sudan, the Democratic Republic of Congo and the Central African Republic, committing similar atrocities there. See for instance: Human Rights Watch, CAR/DR Congo: LRA Conducts Massive Abduction Campaign, Press release, 11 August 2010. International Crisis Group, LRA: a regional strategy beyond killing Kony, Africa Report no. 157, 28 April 2010.

2 Constitution, Art. 246(e) and (f).

3 Local Council Courts Act, 2006, 24 May 2006.

3. TRANSITIONAL JUSTICE LANDSCAPE

In Northern Uganda, a draft transitional justice framework has been developed, but has not become operational yet. Peace negotiations regarding the conflict have been ongoing for many years (Latigo, 2008). In 2000, at the request of the Acholi population (the ethnic group of Kony and many of his abductees) an Amnesty Act was adopted, granting a blanket amnesty for crimes since 1986 to those who renounce affiliation to a rebel group. This was successful: by August 2009, a total of 23,521 ex-combatants had reported to the Amnesty Commission, of which 53.75% of the LRA, the majority of which was below the age of 18.[4]

In December 2003, President Museveni referred the situation to the International Criminal Court (ICC), which in 2005 issued arrest warrants against Kony and his commanders. The intervention of the ICC concurred with renewed peace negotiations in 2006, which resulted in – among others – an *Agreement on Accountability and Reconciliation* and the *Annexure to the Agreement on Accountability and Reconciliation*. These were signed in 2007 and 2008 respectively, by the Ugandan government and an LRA representative, but not by Joseph Kony, who requested in turn that the ICC arrest warrants be withdrawn first.

The agreements provide three transitional justice mechanisms: the establishment of a War Crimes Division at the High Court of Kampala to deal with 'serious crimes or human rights violations', but not with 'state actors' (including military of the UPDF, who in the view of the Acholi committed many atrocities);[5] the establishment of a truth commission;[6] and the 'adoption and recognition of complementary alternative justice mechanisms' to promote reconciliation,[7] including 'traditional justice processes'.[8] Thus, after a year-long vibrant debate on the choice between the ICC and traditional justice; that divided traditional leaders, the Uganda government, Ugandan and international NGOs, as well as scholars (Baines, 2007; Allen, 2006; Refugee Law Project, 2005, among others), both formal and traditional mechanisms have been officially accepted as part of the transitional justice policy.

Although the agreements have not been signed by Kony, the Ugandan government has engaged to implement them. An International Crimes Division (instead of a War Crimes Division, which was considered too limited) was established in 2008. Only one former LRA commander, Thomas Kwoyelo, has been accused so far. However, Kwoyelo could not be prosecuted, since he had applied for amnesty under the Amnesty Act of 2000, but never received a reply. On

4 Amnesty Commission Kampala, 20 August 2009.
5 Clause 4.1 Agreement and clauses 7–9 Annexure.
6 Clause 2.3 Agreement and clauses 4–6 Annexure.
7 Clause 5.2 Agreement.
8 Clause 5.3 Agreement. Clause 1 of the Agreement refers to the *mato oput* ritual of the Acholi as well as to traditional rituals used by other cultures.

22 September 2011, the Constitutional Court of Uganda ruled that the Amnesty Act should have been applied to Kwoyelo and that the case should be halted.[9] The Amnesty Act has been repeatedly criticised, was abolished, but was reinstated in May 2013. No prosecutions of UPDF military at the level of the military courts have taken place at the time of writing

The government also established a working group on transitional justice within the JLOS (Justice, Law and Order Sector) working group. The purpose was to provide research, conduct consultations and round-table discussions and make proposals on the implementation of the Agreement. After a long process of consultations, the JLOS Transitional Justice working group has prepared a Transitional Justice Policy Draft for the government, which was still under discussion at the time of writing.[10] The Draft recommends the adoption of a Transitional Justice Act that would provide for a truth telling structure, witness and victim protection, the recognition of traditional justice mechanisms as a tool for conflict resolution, a reparations programme and the abolishment of blanket amnesty, among others. The JLOS Working Group section on traditional justice started its work around mid-2009, and has published an extensive study of traditional justice mechanisms (TJMs), based on desk research and consultancies.[11] The study emphasises the restorative components of TJMs and proposes to design a framework for the use of TJMs, but remains vague on issues of jurisdiction, the integration with the formal system and possible conflicts with human rights. Meanwhile, local NGOs, such as the Refugee Law Project, have conducted preliminary studies on the possible hybridisation of traditional mechanisms (Beyond Juba, 2009).

4. THE ROLE OF TRADITION IN TRANSITIONAL JUSTICE

Traditional and religious leaders have undoubtedly played an important role in the peace process in Northern Uganda. Their opposition to the arrest warrants issued by the ICC, which they saw as an obstacle to peace, is well documented (Allen, 2006). Even though the initial objective, i.e. to accept traditional justice as an alternative to prosecution for the LRA leaders, was not achieved, the combined efforts of the traditional and religious leaders and local NGOs, supported by a number of research projects of national and international scholars and by

---

9 Thomas Kwoyelo v. Uganda, Constitutional Court of Uganda, constitutional petition no. 036/11, Judgment, 22 September 2011.

10 The Republic of Uganda, Justice Law & Order Sector, The National Transitional Justice Working Group, 3rd Draft, May 2013.

11 The Republic of Uganda, Justice Law & Order Sector, Traditional Justice and Truth Telling and National Reconciliation. Study Report (Final Draft), July 2012.

international donors have led to the inclusion of provisions on traditional justice in the Agreement.

In Acholi tradition, many ritual procedures exist for various situations. Caritas Gulu Archdiocese has documented an important number of them, pointing out the variety of terminology and practices (Caritas Gulu, 2006). Other ethnic groups have different rituals that are equally mentioned in the Agreement.

Among the Acholi, extensive use has been made of traditional cleansing and welcoming home rituals, such as *nyono tong gweno* (stepping on an egg on a special stick called *laibi*). These are intended to purify the returned persons form any bad spirit (*cen*) they might have attracted while being away, and which otherwise would affect the community. In addition, when people were leaving the IDP camps and returning home, ceremonies to cleanse the land of the bad spirits of people killed or having killed (*tumo cere* or *tumu kir*), have been performed, following the discovery of bodies or the appearance of such spirits.[12]

The main objective of such rituals, mostly applied to formerly abducted children and adults, seems to be purification and reintegration, not accountability for crimes. For this reason, victims in Northern Uganda expressed dissatisfaction with the fact that some LRA commanders had been granted amnesty and even received benefits from the government after a cleansing ceremony, without even acknowledging what they did or offering sincere apologies. To many people, amnesty for high and mid-level commanders should be conditioned by truth telling and compensation, which can be achieved through local practices such as *mato oput* (Conciliation Resources, 2010: 14; UNOHCHR 1996: 54). *Mato oput*, a term sometimes wrongly used to indicate any type of traditional reconciliation (Caritus Gulu, 2006: 79) seems to be the only accountability mechanism for homicide in Acholi culture (in addition to other mechanisms used to establish accountability for minor crimes). It comprises the following steps: the perpetrator, haunted by *cen* (bad spirit), or his family contacts the clan elders and reveals what has happened. He will then be confined to his house and not be allowed to share any meals or drinks with others, since the spirit of the killed person may also affect the community. The same applies to the families and clans of victim and perpetrator, thus preventing the conflict from escalating. Elders representing the chief or *rwot* will start mediation between the clans of victim and perpetrator to decide on the compensation to be paid. When an agreement is reached and implemented, which can even take years, the families will come together and a ceremony will be performed, including spiritual prayers, ritual sacrifices of animals, the drinking of *mato oput* (the juice of the bitter root of a specific tree) and finally the sharing of drinks and a meal. It is important to note that the

12 Traditional elders in the village Kal Centre (a dismantled IDP camp they still preferred to live in at the time of the interview) extensively spoke about a 'talking shoe' that had appeared in a field to several people and explained it had belonged to a killed person. Cleansing ceremonies, involving the sacrifice of a goat, were performed, after which the land could be cultivated in peace again. Interview Village Kal Centre, Parish Kal, Sub-county Ongallo.

ceremonies, which can sometimes be observed by external persons, are only the last step of a lengthy procedure, which involves several previous steps, during which accountability is being established. The rituals confirm the reconciliation between the families and with the ancestors (own research, confirmed by Beyond Juba, 2009; Latigo, 2008; Baines, 2007). The Acholi tradition does not have the death penalty, not even for capital crimes.

Obviously, *mato oput* will not always be possible for LRA crimes, since many ex-combatants do not know whom they have killed. When an individual is haunted by the spirit of such a person, whose identity he does not know, another ceremony can be performed: *lakere ket* (or *moyo kom*). This ritual, however, is merely a ceremony to cleanse an individual from spiritual impurity and does not seem to include an element of accountability or compensation. It involves the killing of several animals, traditional dances and purification rites with water and fire (Caritas Gulu, 2006).[13] Various respondents pointed out that other rituals, even if not directly focusing on accountability, may be steps in a long-term process that can eventually lead to accountability and reconciliation.

To our knowledge, *mato oput* has not been applied to LRA crimes, or only to a very limited extent, while it is more used for non-war related killings, even when a person returns after having served a prison sentence (Beyond Juba, 2009; Baines, 2007; Caritas Gulu, 2006; Allen, 2006). Indeed, ex-combatants have only returned from the LRA in the last few years and are still afraid to talk, while many do not know their victims and have benefited from blanket amnesty without any threat of prosecution. In addition, a huge compensation needs to be paid by the clan of the offender (which sometimes is also the clan of the victim) for which no money is available.[14] These high rates might either lead to the non-use of *mato oput* (Caritas Gulu, 2006) or to the fact that victims accept the absence of compensation, as in other countries. However, since many LRA combatants had formerly been abducted and the government is blamed for not protecting the communities, the idea that the government should provide reparations is widespread (Beyond Juba, 2009).

Some people doubt whether there are useful or adjustable traditional mechanisms for the huge number of sexual offences, since tradition does not state any sanction apart from compensation for the husband or father (Beyond Juba, 2009). Rape victims sometimes experience positive effects from ritual cleansing performed during reintegration ceremonies, but no specific cleansing is performed for rape because of the social stigma. This last reason also explains why girls who were given 'in marriage' to a man in the LRA often do not want

---

13 Interviews traditional chief, Caritas Gulu and one beneficiary of lakere ket ceremony, Gulu, August 2009.

14 The Ker Kwaro Acholi, the cultural institution of the Acholi traditional leaders, issued a Law to declare the Acholi Customary Law, 19 June 2001, which provides the payment of 35 herds of cattle and 3 goats for killing another person, in addition to lodging fees to the traditional leaders, as well animals and other items to perform the ceremony.

formal prosecution (Liu Institute for Global Issues, 2005). They experience social pressure to stay with this man, especially when there are children, even though a majority wishes to leave (Carlson and Mazurana, 2008). In-depth field research shows that victims prefer the restoration of social harmony. Depending on the relationship to the offender, both ritual cleansing (for people they know) and punishment (for strangers) are mentioned as possible responses, but usually neither of these are available in daily practice (Porter, 2012).

In general, the idea is that people need to return to their home villages first, settle all the emerging land disputes, benefit from programmes focusing on economic revival and feel secure, before they will start talking. Once again, the timing of interventions is crucial, since people tend to want peace at any price when the conflict is at its height, but eventually do ask for accountability as well, once the violence has ended.

While it is early days to compare the yet non-operational transitional justice mechanisms in Uganda, clearly the International Crimes Division will not allow for accountability, truth telling or victim participation regarding low level perpetrators, nor regarding UPDF crimes. Whether ordinary courts will play a role in this regard is unlikely, considering the amnesty. With a cautious note on the challenges caused by the generation long displacement of the population, the dire poverty and others, traditional mechanisms such as *mato oput* seem to have the potential of providing more accountability, truth finding, victim participation and dialogue. Compensation might be problematic once again. It remains to be seen if the process of hybridisation of these traditional mechanisms will allow them to safeguard this potential while finding answers to the many challenges.

As stated above, traditional ceremonies have been used to cleanse returning ex-combatants and abducted children, and to purify the land. Considering the costs of both ceremonies, the role of international actors has been a vital one in this context.

5. POLICIES AND INTERVENTIONS OF INTERNATIONAL ACTORS

In Sierra Leone and Rwanda, multilateral and bilateral donors mostly provided support to activities in the context of official government policy concerning transitional justice, while informal activities on a smaller scale and a local level were supported more by international NGOs, foundations and the like. Although the same applies to Northern Uganda, there have been important donor interventions before the official transitional justice policy was developed, including interventions that reinforced traditional leadership, traditional values and traditional practices. There is no doubt that these interventions have contributed to the importance attached to traditional justice during the peace negotiations and in the transitional justice provisions of the peace agreement.

On the other hand, the fact that the supported activities were not part of an official policy might be symptomatic for the lack of political will to implement the part of the peace agreement concerning traditional mechanisms, while most donors (with the exception of USAID) will base their decision for support on the actual policy. In the meantime, they have been supporting preparatory activities, such as consultations during the peace negotiations[15] and the functioning of the JLOS workgroup for transitional justice, which has nevertheless up until now not led to any concrete proposal for implementation.

Regarding donor interventions concerning tradition-based activities before the peace agreement and considering the promotion of traditional practices in Northern Uganda, one could presume that donors support these because they were actually used on a local level. However, this is not the case since many traditions have fallen into oblivion since most Acholi remained in the IDP camps for twenty years, where it was not possible to perform traditional ceremonies. Some authors (Allen, 2006) even suggest that the donors' financial support contributed to the re-invention – or even the invention – of tradition. As mentioned above, this is a false debate, as the underlying values, such as the necessity to acknowledge accountability, the offering and acceptance of apologies, the payment of reparations and the restoration of harmony with the community and the ancestors, are certainly still present among the population (Beyond Juba, 2009). Our interviews with participants of cleansing rituals show that they themselves are very much convinced of the importance and positive impact of the rituals. Belief in the fact that killing a person or committing other crimes summons evil spirits or at least brings bad luck over the involved person, his family and clan is still very much alive, also among young people. Even young people who do not share this world view are willing to submit to the rituals in order to be accepted back into their communities. These world views also cause problems in communities to which ex-combatants return after having been granted amnesty without any acknowledgement of accountability, reparations or cleansing, and feel threatened, stigmatised or discriminated against, for example in the allocation of land or other employment possibilities. Undergoing these rituals is supposed to decrease trauma and stigma. Obviously, such cleansing rituals cannot erase all consequences of the armed conflict, such as the dire economic circumstances, nor can they deal with root causes such as regional discrimination.

Three areas of support by international actors can be distinguished with regards to tradition-based activities implemented before the peace agreement.

First, restoration of the traditional institution. As mentioned earlier, traditional leaders were officially recognised again in Uganda since the 1995 Constitution. A research conducted in 1998–1999 by the NGO ACORD on Acholi chiefs, identified 'traditional leaders', who then were (re)instated in 2000 (Allen, 2006; ACCORD, 2002; Dolan, 2000), after which a Paramount Chief was elected.

15 USAID, Sweden, the Netherlands, Norway, MacArthur Foundation.

Although traditional leadership existed in Acholiland before, appointing a Paramount Chief is a new creation, not a tradition that existed in pre-colonial times, meaning that its legitimacy is limited (Doom and Vlassenroot, 1999). Moreover, the DANIDA, the NUTI programme[16] and the NGO Conciliation Resources[17] supported the cultural organisation of the Acholi traditional leaders, the *Ker Kwaro Acholi* (KKA). This organisation comprises a structure with ministers and a secretariat and is seen as neutral in the conflict. The KKA was also more inspired by structures created by the colonial rulers than by tradition, although the KKA itself claims that the institution has been around since the 1400s (Latigo, 2008). The objective of donor support for these activities was to increase the local leaders' capacity in peace negotiations. This also included human rights training, as well as awareness raising on sexual violence and its consequences. Furthermore, women and young people are part of the council of the wise, which assists the chief or *rwot*, although women are still excluded from the position of chief itself, and they cannot perform traditional ceremonies or intervene in dispute resolution (Beyond Juba, 2009). Several embassies that supported the peace negotiations in Juba financially supported the participation of traditional leaders, and of the *Acholi Religious Leaders Peace Initiative* (ARLPI).

It seems that this financial support was not inspired by the actual role of traditional leaders, but by their assumed potential contribution to reconciliation in the peace process, which they indeed provided. An (at that time) influential report of Dennis Pain, which recommended the anointment of traditional leaders, to restore their credibility in this regard, might very well have influenced donors (Pain, 1997).[18]

Supporting traditional structures involves a risk of reinforcing traditional authority, which might create a power struggle with local administration and local courts. But in Northern Uganda, this is not considered a real risk, since traditional leaders are excluded from all political or administrative functions.

Subsequent studies, on the other hand, show that traditional leaders are respected more because of the role they played in the conflict settlement and the rituals for returned LRA members (Beyond Juba, 2009).

Second, restoration of traditional norms was supported. As mentioned earlier, traditional beliefs on the consequences of crimes are still present among the population. However, since traditional practices have been eroded by the life in IDP camps for two decades, and many elders have died meanwhile, the younger generation is sometimes less familiar with them, nor do they respect traditional leaders as before (Latigo, 2008).[19] Thus, it was deemed important that they would

16 Northern Uganda Transition Initiative, supported by the Office of Transition Initiatives of USAID.

17 Supported by DFID.

18 The importance of supporting traditional leaders was later confirmed by OECD-DAC in the DAC Guidelines. Helping Prevent Violent Conflict, 2001, p. 120.

19 Latigo, Tradition-based practices in Acholi, p. 109.

be sensitised. The Northern Uganda Peace Initiative (NUPI), engaged in a tour of 62 IDP camps in 2005 to make people aware of 'the tradition of reconciliation among the Acholi'. In total, 155,000 people attended the sessions. In addition, radio programmes were broadcast and a documentary on Acholi reconciliation was produced and broadcast.[20] Another forgotten tradition, the *wang oo*, or bonfire where elders would explain tradition to young people through storytelling and traditional dances, has also been revived (Latigo, 2008; NUPI report, 2006).[21]

The criticism that these activities imply a reinvention of tradition is to be rejected. One can also see them as promoting the revival of important traditional values, which have their roots in the Acholi culture that – due to the unwanted circumstances of the conflict – had not been practiced anymore. They are comparable to the outreach and sensitisation activities on the role and mandate of the ICC in Uganda, which – in contrast – is not rooted in local culture or tradition at all. Moreover, the formal justice system was almost absent in Northern Uganda and its rehabilitation will also require sensitisation and training.

The problem is, however, that after the re-instatement of the body of traditional (and religious) leaders, they were perceived as *the* representatives of all Acholi, and their promotion of traditional solutions instead of prosecution by the ICC was seen as *the* Acholi position. In the meantime, surveys and research have shown that most Acholi are not as opposed to the ICC and its arrest warrants or prosecution on a national level as the leaders claimed (Pham and Vinck, 2010; UNOHCHR, 2007; Pham et al., 2007; Pham et al., 2005). Although opinion was divided, many respondents seemed to support a mixed solution, with criminal prosecution of the commanders and a combination of amnesty with confessions, apologies and traditional rituals for the others. These surveys and other investigations have put the legitimacy of traditional norms and values in perspective. The peace agreement, which combines formal prosecution with traditional mechanisms, seems to confirm this perspective.

Third, since the adoption of the Amnesty Act in 2000, restoration of traditional ceremonies has been supported: traditional ceremonies have been performed on thousands of returnees, supported by external actors.[22] The above-mentioned NUPI project claims to have supported the 'stepping on the egg' ceremony for over 12,000 returnees. Caritas claims it has performed such ceremonies for over 3,000 people.

UNICEF has also supported such ceremonies for children returning from the LRA through centres for the sheltering of these children (reception centres). Cleansing and healing were the main objectives of these ceremonies.

---

20 Northern Uganda Peace Initiative (Managing African Conflict), FY2006 Year-End Report. A summary of objectives and Results, 30 October 2006. Supported by USAID/OTI.

21 With the support of USAID-OTI. In practice, the one I attended seemed the reverse, providing a forum to young people to vent out their frustrations and needs to the elders.

22 Mainly by USAID (NUPI and NUTI), the IOM, the NED-US.

Some claim that such ceremonies are not the 'real thing', especially when they are performed collectively (Allen, 2006). Although the effectiveness of such ceremonies is sometimes assumed too easily or overestimated, discussions regarding their real or invented character are based on the assumption that traditional rituals are static and lose their effectiveness if adjusted to post-conflict needs. Donors who support these ceremonies do not seem to be particularly attached to considerations regarding their 'real' nature and support such activities on a demand basis, leaving the assessment of their effectiveness to their local partners. Such (initial) blind support by some donors (mainly USAID) is criticised by other donors, who prefer to support research projects and government consultations before taking a decision.[23]

Finally, various donors present in Uganda do not support any activities regarding traditional practices yet, although they might be inclined to do so in the future, depending on the outcome of the ongoing process to develop a national transitional justice policy, based on the research projects[24] and consultations[25] that they have been supporting.[26] This means they plan to base their decision on official acknowledgement of yet to be created ad hoc mechanisms.

In conclusion, it seems that those donors who supported traditional practices have been led by motifs regarding the potential positive role of traditional leaders in the peace negotiations, as well as the positive impact of purification rituals for returned (abducted) ex-combatants.

Hence, they responded to requests by traditional leaders and local NGOs, while the legitimacy of the traditional leaders was insufficiently investigated. Moreover, the reinforcing impact of the donor interventions on the position of traditional leaders was not taken into account, which meant that – initially – the sometimes deviating opinions of the population were not heard. With regard to supporting tradition in the context of the peace agreement, donors seem to wait for the official transitional justice policy, without having a specific focus on tradition (whereas they do focus on conflict prevention and peacebuilding). However, they did support activities of civil society organisations, such as research, coalition building, consultations, etc. When political will is lacking, such support can be a sensitive issue for the local government since the national government

23 USAID's NUTI programme is more aware of the need for evaluation and verification of the legitimacy of the activities. Interview USAID-OTI, Gulu.

24 Such as, for example, the Liu Institute for Global Issues of the University of British Colombia in collaboration with the Justice and Reconciliation Project of the Gulu District NGO Forum, supported by the Netherlands, the MacArthur Foundation and the Compton Foundation, the research of the Refugee Law project connected with the Makerere University and supported by Sweden, the Ford Foundation and Norway. The Conciliation Resources research was supported by the United Kingdom.

25 Population consultations were supported by, among others, UNOHCHR and the MacArthur Foundation.

26 Mainly donors who also support the JLOS, i.e. the Netherlands, Austria and Irish Aid. To a certain extent Sweden, Norway and DANIDA. The donors also participate in the JLOS Working Group on Transitional Justice.

is the donors' first partner. That is why both political will and adjusting the mechanisms to human rights standards are considered vital. This explains why they choose to support the process instead of the possible outcomes of that process. It is furthermore important to understand that too much attention for the role of traditional leaders and for traditional reconciliation increases the risk of 'localising' the conflict, drawing attention away from its national root causes. Lastly, the momentum for donor support for the transitional justice process in general, and for the use of traditional mechanisms in that process in particular, may be disappearing almost unnoticed.

BIBLIOGRAPHY

ACCORD (2002) *Protracted conflict, elusive peace. Initiatives to end the violence in Northern Uganda*. London.

Allen, T. (2006) *Trial Justice. The International Criminal Court and the Lord's Resistance Army*. London/New York: Zed Books.

Baines, E.K. (2007) The haunting of Alice: local approaches to Justice and reconciliation in Northern Uganda, *The International Journal of Transitional Justice*, 1, 91–114.

Beke, D. (2004) Legislation and decentralisation in Uganda: from Resistance Councils to elected Local Councils with guaranteed representation. In Foblets, M-C. and von Trotha, T. (eds.) *Healing the wounds. Essays on the reconstruction of societies after war*, 145–167. Oxford/Portland: Hart Publishing.

Beyond Juba (2009) A transitional justice project of the Faculty of Law, Makerere University, The Refugee Law Project and the Human Rights & Peace Centre, *Tradition in Transition*, Working Paper No. 1.

Caritas Gulu Archdiocese (2006) *Traditional ways of coping in Acholi. Cultural provisions for reconciliation and healing from war.*

Carlson, K. and Mazurana, D. (2008) *Forced Marriage within the Lord's Resistance Army, Uganda. Strengthening the humanity and dignity of people in crisis through knowledge and practice*, Feinstein International Centre, Tufts University.

Conciliation Resources (2010) *Choosing to return. Challenges faced by the Lord's Resistance Army's middle-ranking commander.* London, October 2010.

Dolan, C. (2000) *Views on the Northern Uganda conflict from inside the war zone.* Report on COPE fieldwork findings, Northern Uganda, ACORD.

Doom, R. and Vlassenroot, K. (1999) Kony's Message: A New Koine? The Lord's Resistance Army in Northern Uganda, *African Affairs*, 98(390), 5–36.

Latigo, J.O. (2008) Northern Uganda: tradition-based practices in the Acholi region. In Huyse, L. and Salter, M. (eds.) *Traditional Justice after Violent Conflict. Learning from African experiences*, 85–120. Stockholm, Sweden: IDEA.

Liu Institute for Global Issues, Gulu District NGO Forum and Ker Kwaro Acholi (2005) *Roco Wat I Acoli. Restoring Relationships in Acholi-land: Traditional Approaches to Justice and Reintegration.*

NUPI – Northern Uganda Peace Initiative (Managing African Conflict) (2006) *FY 2006 Year-End Report. A Summary of Objectives and Results.*

Pain, D. (1997) *The Bending of the Spears. Producing consensus for peace and development in Northern Uganda.* International Alert, London.

Pham, P.N., Vinck, P., Stover, E., Moss, A. and Wierda, M. (2007) *When the War Ends. A Population-Based Survey on Attitudes about Peace, Justice and Social Reconstruction in Northern Uganda.* Human Rights Center, University of California, Berkeley; Payson Center for International Development, Tulane University; International Center for Transitional Justice, New York.

Pham, P.N., Vinck, P., Wierda, M., Stover, E. and Di Giovanni, A. (2005) *Forgotten Voices: A Population-Based Survey of Attitudes about Peace and Justice in Northern Uganda.* International Center for Transitional Justice and the Human Rights Center, University of California, Berkeley.

Pham, P.N. and Vinck, P. (2010) *Transitioning to Peace. A population-based survey on attitudes about social reconstruction and justice in Northern Uganda.* The Human Rights Center, University of California, Berkeley.

Porter, H.E. (2012) Justice and rape on the periphery: the supremacy of social harmony in the space between local solutions and established judicial systems in northern Uganda, *Journal of East African Studies,* 6(1), 81–97.

Refugee Law Project (2005) *Whose justice? Perceptions of Uganda's Amnesty Act 2000: the potential for conflict resolution and long-term reconciliation.*

UNOHCHR (1996) *Gacaca. Le droit coutumier au Rwanda.* Rapport final de la première phase d'enquête sur le terrain, Kigali, 31/01/1996. Rapport de la deuxième phase d'enquêtes sur le terrain, Kigali, 30/06/1996.

UNOHCHR (2007) *Making peace our own. Victims' perceptions of accountability, reconciliation and transitional justice in Northern Uganda.*

CHAPTER 7

TRADITION IN TRANSITIONAL JUSTICE: BETWEEN LOCALISATION AND GLOBALISATION

Martien SCHOTSMANS

1. INTRODUCTION

Everything discussed above shows that donors have no real policy for the use of traditional or tradition-based mechanisms in the framework of transitional justice. Support for such mechanisms is inspired by their peacebuilding policy in which the search for sustainable peace and local ownership come first, as well as respect for international norms, more particularly the duty to prosecute international crimes and respect for human rights.

The analysis below will feature three themes: the evolution of donors' understanding of local ownership; donors' fragmented approach to traditional elements without perceiving these in their context; and a legal pluralistic analysis of donors' quest to deal with the tension between tradition and human rights. For each of these themes the findings of the research are analysed and policy recommendations are made to international actors.

2. LOCAL OWNERSHIP

As explained above, donors are participants in the debate on globalisation and localisation, but they wrestle with the concept and the practical aspects of localisation in the context of transitional justice. Initially, local ownership was understood to be state ownership, which had several consequences. It was later extended to national ownership, which had other consequences. Anyhow, the attention for local ownership led to attention for local – including traditional – mechanisms of conflict resolution.

2.1. STATE OWNERSHIP

Since the risk of conflict is higher in fragile states, peacebuilding used to be primarily aimed at state building, i.e. strengthening the state structures and organisations.[1] In addition, the Paris Declaration of 2005 on aid effectiveness recommends that donor countries align their support with the partner country's policy. It therefore makes sense that multilateral and bilateral donors primarily support the official transitional justice policy. As we have seen, traditional mechanisms are supported as far as they are part of this policy. Initiatives that use tradition-based mechanisms that are not included in the official policy mainly depend on support from non-governmental donors such as foundations or INGOs. The latter group may receive support for this from multilateral or bilateral donors, who prefer to leave the management of such smaller and, in their view, more risky (i.e. sensitive or hard to check) projects to INGOs, which can sometimes lead to tensions between INGOs and local NGOs (Pouligny, 2003), but also to more (substantive and technical) support. This especially applies to projects aimed at reconciliation, cleansing and reintegration of returning soldiers into their community. Post-conflict countries often count dozens, if not hundreds of such projects which may or may not have a loose connection to the conflict and to reconciliation, and which are difficult to inventory (Daly and Sarkin, 2007). Nevertheless, more effort could be made to develop a policy with guidelines to support such initiatives. The tradition-based projects in Northern Uganda, supported by USAID-OTI, are an exception to the above-mentioned and preceded the official transitional justice policy.

As clarified above, traditional views on justice usually comprise the following components: acknowledgement of accountability, offering of apologies and the promise to not relapse into violence, the opportunity to accept apologies, reparations, reconciliation and reintegration into the community. Establishing criminal accountability is, however, considered a state monopoly (unlike reconciliation) and should respect international norms. In post-conflict countries, the formal justice system is usually unable to try all crimes committed on a large scale – let alone according to international norms – or only prosecutes the leaders. Our research has shown that when the offender and the victim are part of the same community, there is most certainly a need for mechanisms that lead to acknowledgement of accountability – even when an official amnesty has been declared – as a condition for reconciliation and social harmony. In such cases, accountability and reconciliation are not separate, isolated activities, and they are sometimes even referred to by the same term (Huyse and Salter, 2008). Absence of such mechanisms leads to tensions, discrimination and stigmatisation (Conciliation Resources, 2010; Boersch-Supan, 2009). We have furthermore shown

[1] OECD-DAC, Principles for good international engagement in fragile states & situations, April 2007.

that tradition-based mechanisms can in fact bring about a full establishment of accountability according to local norms. Nonetheless, donors will not be inclined to support such initiatives unless they are part of the official policy. If this is not the case, a de facto accountability vacuum will emerge at the local level. Although local mechanisms are sometimes spontaneously used without external support, this support is essential to meet the huge demand for such practices considering the scale of the crimes committed. First, such support is needed because many communities are very poor and do not have the means to purchase the animals and goods necessary for the indispensable rituals, even if it is decided to renounce reparations. Second, external support, usually through local organisations, allows for the integration of modern values regarding, among others, gender equality and the prohibition of corporal punishment, through training and consultation, and to counterbalance the power of local leaders through NGO oversight, which is even more important when these leaders are part of the problem. Hence, donors' focus on the official policy may overlook local needs regarding accountability and the subsequent tensions, while the objective of peacebuilding is the search for sustainable solutions.

A further disadvantage of aligning donor interventions with the official transitional justice policy is that interventions will depend on the political will of the authorities. If there is none, donors may put pressure through their diplomatic services, which often leads to agreements just on paper. Furthermore, donors can support all kinds of preparatory actions, such as capacity building for civil society organisations, allowing these organisations to advocate their views with the government, preliminary research to map existing mechanisms or to explore possibilities for hybridisation, popular consultations, participation of traditional or other leaders in negotiations and conferences, or indirect support through local NGOs for projects that may enhance the legitimacy of certain actors or mechanisms. In other words, interventions to support the process that is supposed to lead to the development of the official transitional justice policy or the implementation strategy. Some are not directly aimed at bringing about a transitional justice policy – such as the reinstatement of traditional leaders – but are a part of peacebuilding. Such interventions – even those that require a lot of time – have the advantage of increasing the chances for local ownership of the policy. Although donors have no policy with regards to the added value of tradition in itself, they should be more aware of the fact that the extent to which traditional leaders, values or mechanisms are part of the preliminary process determines the likelihood of these becoming part of the policy.

A final question is whether the fact that donors align their policy with the official partner country's policy implies that donors feel less responsible for the outcome of their support. Our research has shown that donors primarily feel responsibility toward their home constituency, i.e. the parliament and (to a lesser degree) the public opinion of the home country. Donors think that the prime responsibility for the impact of a policy on the local population lies with the partner country's government itself, as donors have merely provided support to this policy.[2]

2.2. NATIONAL OWNERSHIP

More recently, the concept of local ownership was extended and understood to mean national ownership. That is why organisations from civil society and more recently the population itself have been involved in developing and implementing the official transitional justice policy through consultations.

Initially, this debate searched for an answer to the question how the available transitional justice mechanisms could be localised, for example by adding a local flavour (such as the ritual cleansing of child soldiers) or including local stakeholders in the mechanisms (such as the involvement of the religious and traditional leaders in the TRC in Sierra Leone, at the request of civil society). This did not involve using local mechanisms or questioning international norms in light of divergent traditional norms. Even the Rwandan *gacaca* courts, which were created by the government as a hybrid mix of formal justice and traditional elements and were subject to quite some criticism by the human rights movement, do not question the need for criminal prosecution – i.e. they respect the international legal duty to prosecute. The debate in Northern Uganda lifts this discussion to another level by proposing tradition-based accountability and reconciliation mechanisms as full-fledged alternatives to criminal prosecution. This questioning came from the same local NGOs and traditional and local leaders that received support from donors and international NGOs to create local ownership of the peace process and the transitional justice policy. This local claim on the debate came unexpectedly and created a lot of resistance, especially among international legal experts. This is exactly where globalisation and localisation cross paths: global views on how to deal with past crimes, the need for criminal prosecution and respect for human rights clash with sometimes opposing or at least divergent views of local stakeholders, who were consulted to enhance local ownership.

Obviously, this is a simplification of reality: popular consultations in Northern Uganda have shown that their views and attitudes are much more nuanced than the religious and traditional leaders claimed. For example people differentiate between the responsibility of the government and of the LRA, and between the responsibility of the commanders and executors and, as a consequence, their opinions on the most appropriate response to these crimes vary. This means that one has to be careful with the supposed representation of the population by local leaders (religious, traditional, NGOs) and that consultations must involve a wide range of local stakeholders.

---

[2] Focus group discussion. Forum Cape Town, 22–25 March 2010.

Systematic and subsequent popular consultations during the conflict and the peace negotiations furthermore show that opinions evolve over time and that people are more in favour of mechanisms that address the accountability of those responsible if they feel safe, while they feel less inclined to opt for criminal prosecution if they fear that this could lead to new eruptions of violence. This is shown by our studies in Sierra Leone, but also by consecutive surveys in Northern Uganda (Pham and Vinck, 2010; UNOHCHR, 2007; Pham et al., 2007; Pham et al., 2005). This means that developing a solid transitional justice policy takes time, and that people have to be given the chance to return to more or less normal living conditions. Only then will it become clear what the needs for sustainable coexistence are, so that consultations and especially the use of transitional justice mechanisms should only start later. Although the end of an armed conflict often creates a window of opportunity in which tough decisions on how to deal with the past can be taken more easily, the local population often needs more time to develop an opinion, which means that the implementation of transitional justice at that level will take more time as well. That is why donors who intervene in transitional justice should extend the timeline of their peacebuilding programmes beyond the first post-conflict years and should at the same time, with support from civil society, ensure the momentum for transitional justice (on a state level but also at their own level) does not get lost.

It is unfortunate that in many consultations, civil society actors and the population are still asked for their opinion on specific mechanisms, instead of asking them what kind of response they feel is appropriate, considering the type of crime, the perpetrator and the circumstances, and which values are important for them in such cases. Apparently, the 'tool box' approach to transitional justice is still dominant in such consultations. For example, a survey in Northern Uganda (Pham and Vinck, 2010) included the question: 'What do you prefer: amnesty, amnesty with a truth commission, prosecutions on a national or international level, or traditional mechanisms?' The same survey, however, started by asking people what 'justice' meant for them, and collected the following responses: 'Most defined it in terms of holding offenders accountable (29%), holding trials (25%), being fair (18%), and reconciling (9%).' These are interesting answers that urge the authors to a completely unwarranted conclusion: 'In other words, most attached procedural and institutional concepts to the idea of justice.' These kind of surveys ask people limited, superficial questions which do not take the underlying values of their global vision on justice and social harmony into account. There is a strong need for more thorough, qualitative research (as opposed to having an expert flown in for a limited time or holding surveys with standard questions). In many countries, legal anthropology research is available dating from before the armed conflict, but it is only rarely taken into consideration. Such research could be a useful source of information, even though it needs updating to take into account the evolving opinions of the population during and after the conflict.

Obviously, the situation at the local level is not isolated from national and international levels. All these levels are interrelated and the local population is aware of developments at other levels. Hence, local tradition-based initiatives can be encouraged or discouraged by respectively good or bad examples at national or international levels, and the other way around. These may include criminal prosecutions (but also the selectivity or lack thereof), offering apologies or gestures of reconciliation by political leaders. Hence, the need to develop an integrated approach and to avoid reducing the responsibility for dealing with past crimes to a local problem, for example by emphasising the need for tradition-based mechanisms on the one hand while, on the other hand, the national responsibility for causing or perpetuating the conflict is ignored (Beyond Juba, 2009; Allen, 2006).

Civil society sometimes lacks power to enforce its proposals – such as for traditional mechanisms as an alternative to international criminal prosecution – and relies on the government to do this, while the latter possibly has other – more political – priorities, as the Uganda case study shows. In such event, the support of donors and other international actors will prove crucial for empowering civil society organisations to influence policy with diplomatic interventions. Where civil society organisations are weak and lack international support – for example because their proposals violate international norms or because donor countries themselves have other, often political, priorities – they will find it difficult to get their views accepted.

The government may have a political interest in influencing the results of consultations, for example through preliminary sensitisation campaigns. If one really wants to uncover the population's opinions, careful planning and supervision of the consultations are indispensable. Such precautionary measures will, however, not be enough to neutralise the lack of freedom of speech in some countries, and the corresponding tendency of the population to follow the government discourse.

On the other hand, the population's opinion will not be the sole determining factor in the debate, especially when it comes to international crimes, on which the international community is also a stakeholder: partly because of its interest to end conflict and to create sustainable peace, partly because the nature of the international crimes themselves – i.e. violations of international common law norms (including treaty stipulations) which are meant to protect values that are important for the entire international community (Cassese, 2003) – forces the international community to take action, following international agreements. That is why transitional justice needs a holistic approach in which all these views receive equal attention.

What should be taken into account is the fact that consultations and participation create the expectation that their outcomes will be considered, even if these run counter to the opinions of the international community. That is why consultations cannot be seen as just the latest standard or default condition in peacebuilding programmes: what is the point of consulting the population if decisions are made without taking their views into account? One could doubt whether such an approach can actually lead to local ownership.

Finally, consulting the population requires an open mind to understand and accept complex views that cannot be aligned with ready-made concepts about, for example, accountability and reconciliation. One of the requests that arose from the study is to reconsider the equivalence between accountability and criminal prosecution. Donors, however, are not always fully aware of the complexity of local views.

The recommendations that follow from the above analysis are expounded in Chapter 16.

3. FRAGMENTED APPROACH TO TRADITION

As donors have no specific policy regarding the use of tradition-based mechanisms in transitional justice, but attach importance mainly to local ownership, they are not really invested in the debate on the real or (re)invented nature of such mechanisms. Rather, the fact that an activity is labelled as 'traditional' is for donors a sign that this activity is familiar to the population and will therefore create legitimacy and ownership. This potential was often confirmed by the research. This was the case in Rwanda, regarding the use of *gacaca* (UNOHCHR, 1996), in Sierra Leone with the proposals of the TRC to use traditional methods (Manifesto '99, 2002, financed by UNOHCHR), and extensively in the debate in Northern Uganda. During our research, donors repeatedly pointed out that they work with what they find 'on the ground', meaning that they also collaborate with traditional leaders if these leaders are locally perceived as unavoidable gatekeepers to the community. However, they do this without questioning or at least critically assessing these traditional leaders' unavoidable position.

It was already mentioned above that the traditional leaders in Sierra Leone were involved in the TRC activities, as provided by the Commission mandate. This was a response to a request from the civil society and the Paramount chiefs themselves, who were consulted with support from UNOHCHR. Donors had already – after preliminary consultations – supported a project for the reinstatement of the Paramount chiefs, at the request of the government (which clearly had political motives in mind, given the role of the chiefs in Parliament and during elections).[3] At that time, the role the chiefs had played in causing the conflict did not appear to be an important issue, and they still seemed to enjoy a certain legitimacy, perhaps because the abuse of power was simply part of a widespread pattern of corruption, patronage and nepotism and was not considered exceptional. But the

3 Statement on the formal recognition of *Paramount chiefs*, by president Kabbah at Kenema, Bo, Makeni and Port Loko, 26–30 January 2003.

matter did gradually come to the forefront during the TRC hearings and finally urged the Commission to state in its report that it was 'surprised by the number of complaints about violations committed by many of the Chiefs during the conflict, for which they neither as a group nor individually expressed remorse or offered any explanation to their communities. In reality, while the Commission had to rely on the chiefs as leaders of their communities and had to work closely with them … the Commission has not felt entirely comfortable having to rely on traditional structures to help foster reconciliation' (TRC report, 2004, Vol. 3B). The TRC even identified the abuse of power by the traditional chiefs as one of the causes of the conflict, since these abuses alienated quite some young people from their communities, causing them to leave the communities and become part of the mass of dissatisfied and easily mobilised young people (TRC report, 2004, Vol. 3B). The TRC's recommendation that subsequent governments put the chiefs' role and manipulation on the national agenda for further debate, considering the high potential for future conflict, has been ignored. More thorough preliminary research could have revealed the dubious role the traditional chiefs played and might have led to a more critical approach to the proposal to include them, as well as to a more thorough examination of the issue by the TRC itself.

Donors, however, rarely see more than the outside of what is presented and have a superficial approach to tradition. This turns tradition into a kind of exotic spice to add some local flavour to a standard mechanism from the transitional justice 'toolbox', just to present it as authentically 'local'. Even if it is indeed a local mechanism, donors sometimes pay too little attention to the context in which the use of traditional mechanisms is proposed, or to the cosmovision a tradition is part of. This happens mostly in cases where mechanisms are used 'only' for reconciliation or reintegration. However, people's cosmovision or world views constitute a larger whole that will evolve over time and under outside influences. One cannot split it up to use what comes in handy at a given moment, while disregarding the overall picture.

This situation can best be illustrated by expanding on what was already mentioned above (section 2.3.1.) with regard to Sierra Leone. After the war, donors supported reintegration programmes for ex-combatants, many of whom were kidnapped as children. These reintegration ceremonies were inspired by tradition and involved, among others, ritual cleansing. What the donors did not consider at that time was that although these ceremonies allowed the involved ex-combatants to return home, they would not be accepted as full members of the community because they had not been initiated into one of the secret societies. Initiation into such a society (including genital mutilation for girls) provides the participants with the required social status in their community, gives them a voice in decision-making processes, grants them respect and allows them to marry a person of equal status. These days it is possible to refuse initiation, but this will oblige that person to leave the community, or to stay without enjoying any status and the right to marry an initiated person. Non-initiated males will be excluded from important decisions regarding the community, which are taken by the secret societies. Some young people who returned have yielded to social pressure and have undergone the initiation, including genital mutilation or other harmful practices such as scarification. Participants in the *Fambul Tok* project who opted for this after the end of the project saw the initiation as the final step of their reintegration process. Others refused (many girls had been raped and had children when they returned, making initiation pointless), but experience many difficulties in being fully accepted (Schotsmans, 2011).

International actors must therefore ask themselves whether the application of the 'do no harm' principle is limited to the activity they support, or reaches beyond and includes the indirect, contextual consequences, the inevitability of which would have been revealed by thorough preliminary research.

In addition, the risk of political manipulation of tradition leaders, of the tradition-based mechanisms or the use of the label 'traditional' is not always thoroughly assessed. The example of localising the conflict in Northern Uganda was already mentioned above, while in Sierra Leone the traditional leaders are known as '*agip*': '*any government in power*', meaning servants of those in power, and their restoration and subsequent participation in official mechanisms is therefore in the interest of the government. In Rwanda, the use of the label 'traditional' has taken a new turn with the promotion of the solidarity camps *ingando* and *itorero* – a new type of initiation and reintegration ritual for ex-combatants, former prisoners, university students and other professional groups – and other NURC activities, especially with a view of achieving national unity. The fact that reconciliation is imposed as a top-down policy by the authorities and the romanticised presentation of the country's pre-colonial history cause concern (Purdeková, 2008; Mgbako, 2005).

In the same vein, the impact of donor support on local power relations is insufficiently examined. Support for tradition-based mechanisms entails the risk of strengthening the same traditional structures that were sometimes identified as causes of the conflict, while change is just what is needed to prevent recurrence (Pouligny, 2006). The same goes for the risks related to the conservative and discriminatory nature of traditional mechanisms. A careful analysis and assessment thereof should lead to providing the necessary checks and balances, both at the top (i.e. the government and donors) and at the bottom (i.e. the beneficiaries). The integration of women and young people both in the preliminary decision-making process and in the implementation of decisions, as well as the involvement of local NGOs, can contribute to this goal. Furthermore, the way in which perpetrators and victims of sexual violence are treated should receive a lot more attention, since traditional mechanisms overly emphasise compensation for the family and cleansing of the victim, while the views of the women themselves are not sufficiently considered (Porter, 2012). These practices obviously reflect gender (in)equality in the society as a whole, which will be subject of other donor interventions. The recommendations of the above analysis will be expounded in Chapter 16.

4. HYBRIDISATION

Since the patriarchal nature of traditional mechanisms often entails a risk of unequal treatment of men, women and youths on the one hand and a violation of the rights of the defence on the other, donors often face a dilemma: to support local mechanisms, thereby running the risk of human rights violations, or to only support formal justice without contributing to justice and reconciliation at the local level. In practice, in supporting such mechanisms they have always disclaimed responsibility for possible human rights violations, while simultaneously supporting activities to promote human rights. The actual integration of traditional elements and human rights into hybrid mechanisms was mostly left to local partners.

This brings us to the dilemma donors face with regard to the tensions between divergent normative orders.

As said, international actors do not oppose the use of traditional elements in the framework of transitional justice if these elements are used only for reconciliation or reintegration purposes, insofar as human rights are respected (such as the prohibition of corporal punishment or the discrimination of women). Objections do arise, however, in cases where tradition-based mechanisms are proposed as alternatives to criminal accountability, as happened in Northern Uganda, since this violates the international paradigm and the duty to prosecute. Of all generally accepted objectives of transitional justice (accountability, truth finding, reparations, reconciliation and preventing recurrence), the objective of accountability is the one on which global and local views clash the most.

The study of legal pluralism – an angle of research only sparingly used in transitional justice (see for example: Nagy, 2009) – offers us some interesting ideas on how to handle this challenge. Some of these are already applied in transitional justice.

The study of legal pluralism points out that a single social field can present several normative orders, which neither ignore nor eliminate each other (see section 3.1.4.2). Every society comprises a number of social fields and each of these fields is semi-autonomous: meaning that each field is partly able to regulate its activities independently, but still has to take the norms of other, overlapping fields into account. Every social action always takes place in the context of plural, overlapping semi-autonomous fields (Moore, 1973).

Legal pluralism originally studied the interaction between formal and informal legal systems, but the field of research was gradually expanded to include the interaction between multiple formal legal systems. For our research, these are exactly the three relevant normative orders: the international, the state and the non-state (although again one can distinguish several orders within each of the three fields).

Scholars of legal pluralism have tried to distinguish models, i.e. possible ways to manage the overlaps. Some of these models can be grouped under the label of state-central legal pluralism (also known as 'weak' legal pluralism, Griffiths, 1986). This departs from a normative state perspective and entails that non-state sources of law can be accepted as long as they can be brought to state control in the framework of continual evolution toward an order in which the state is the sole source of law. For example, the official *gacaca* courts in Rwanda replaced the post-genocide *gacaca* and the so-called Christian *gacaca*. On the other hand, scholars distinguish 'strong' legal pluralism, in which the co-existence of equivalent legal orders is accepted as an empirical reality, regardless of their recognition by the state. Obviously, this means that legal pluralism is everywhere and unavoidable. This leads to complex conflict patterns, which legal centralists often negatively describe as competition, but which can be more positively interpreted as an opportunity for a very dynamic process of interaction and negotiation between several social fields. This dynamic process will eventually establish which norms will in fact be applied to a certain place and time (Griffiths, 1986). The outcome of the process will be determined by, among other things, the power structures in which it takes place. This can lead to an adjustment to the dominant legal order – such as an adjustment to the international human rights debate – but also to manipulation, resistance or other unexpected results (Merry, 2003; Merry, 1988).

In relation to our research on transitional justice, we found that this dialectical process is rarely granted enough time, while already-existing techniques of state-central legal pluralism are privileged.

First, the overlap can simply be ignored: this is the case when one assumes that tradition-based mechanisms are solely involved in reconciliation and reintegration and are ill-suited to establish criminal accountability. In this case, donors will have no difficulties in supporting the government's criminal prosecution on the one hand and supporting – usually indirectly – tradition-based mechanisms on the other, or leaving the latter to other parties. But, as said, these are often not distinct concepts on the ground, as they are all part of one, overall view on justice, meaning that the absence of accountability will impede reconciliation. Ignoring the problem, therefore, will not solve it.

Overlaps can also be managed by establishing priority or jurisdiction rules, in other words by establishing which mechanism applies to which case. Examples are the primacy of the ICTR and the complementarity of the ICC; the *ratione materiae* jurisdiction in Rwanda, where the assessment of the most serious crimes (first category) was – initially – left to the formal courts, while the other crimes (second and third categories) were tried by the *gacaca* courts; and *ratione personae* jurisdiction in Rwanda and Uganda, according to which military personnel can only be tried by military courts and not by tradition-based mechanisms. In the event that such choices are not made, rules will have to be established for the mutual recognition of decisions. Uganda's Agreement on Accountability and Reconciliation, for example, stipulates that the principle of *non bis in idem* applies between traditional and formal justice, meaning that the same individual will only have to answer to one of these (art. 3.10). Whether this provision will actually be turned into practice is not clear. In these examples, each mechanism is respected and the tasks are simply divided.

These rules, however, do not suffice to solve the problems that donors are faced with, as they wish to support only those mechanisms that respect international norms and human rights. The problem's essence is not that overlapping norms exist, but that normative orders clash.

Since tradition is not a static but a flexible phenomenon, always evolving, and as human rights education has become an automatic component of peacebuilding, modern norms are gradually being integrated in most tradition-based mechanisms: for example, women and youths are to a certain extent involved in activities, such as the *gacaca* courts and in the *Fambul Tok* project, although certain aspects of the dominant position of men cannot be questioned (such as the chief's function or the role of men in traditional rituals). The use of physical violence to reveal the truth or as a punishment is also gradually being eliminated, although some aspects of certain rituals can still be quite radical (such as the temporary house arrest and drinking animal blood during *mato oput* in Northern Uganda). The involved parties furthermore often receive training on modern mediation techniques, trauma and sexual violence, although this does not automatically lead to a shift in the mentality and the approach to sexual violence.

However, to the extent that tradition-based mechanisms are also used to establish accountability, they need to respect international fair trial standards, such as the impartiality and independence of the judge, and the rights of defence (arts. 14–15 International Covenant on Civil and Political Rights). It is in this respect that international and traditional norms clash most. Concerns about the lack of respect for these standards are entirely justified, considering the abuse of power by some traditional leaders in the past, and the fact that some mechanisms can lead to severe punishment. This puts donors in an uncomfortable position when asked to support such mechanisms. Generally, donors assume they can solve the dilemma by adding a clause that requires respect for human rights to peace treaties (e.g. 3.3. of the Agreement on Accountability and Reconciliation in Uganda) or funding agreements. Such clauses are now a standard practice and seem to become a kind of disclaimer allowing donors to cover their liability for human rights violations. In practice, simply adding a clause will not suffice to solve the conflict.

All the solutions mentioned above in fact try to solve the overlap between different normative orders by understanding globalisation as a hierarchy, in which the normative order of the international level has precedence over the order at the national level, which in turn has precedence over the order at the non-state level.

Just as components of traditional mechanisms for conflict resolution cannot be singled out to add some local flavour to existing transitional justice mechanisms, norms inherent to the international criminal law paradigm cannot be isolated and transplanted to tradition-based accountability and reconciliation mechanisms, which are based on a completely different view on conflict resolution (partiality, community participation, restoration of social harmony). This means that such tensions cannot be resolved by transplanting norms of a higher, dominant hierarchal order to a 'lower' normative order.

Instead of seeing this clash of views and paradigms as a conflict that should be resolved, one can also consider the confrontation of normative orders as an opportunity for an encounter, for a dynamic interaction to create a new, hybrid space, as proposed by 'strong' legal pluralism. The hybridisation of normative orders can concern different aspects: it can involve a mix of mechanisms (such as the mixed Sierra Leone tribunal), which Clark dubs external hybridisation. It can also take the shape of a mix of norms or even paradigms, i.e. internal hybridisation (Clark, 2010). The Rwandan *gacaca* courts are a clear mixture of both mechanisms and norms: they bring together both retributive and restorative aspects, both procedural rules of formal courts and those of traditional community participation, both a legal framework and room for local variation within the framework (Clark, 2010; Ingelaere, 2008; Waldorf, 2006). The more aspects of different semi-autonomous social fields are combined in a new normative order, such as the *gacaca* courts, the stronger the debate and the criticism will be, depending on the perspective of every critic and his or her social field(s). As we know, the *gacaca* courts were criticised by international legal experts because they do not respect international norms concerning criminal justice, while Rwandan respondents who participated in them criticised *gacaca* because of the lack of attention for the values of acknowledging accountability, apologies and reparation payments. *Gacaca*, however, does not question the equation of accountability and criminal prosecution but even reinforces it. In other countries, such as Northern Uganda, part of the non-state level (supported by part of the international level) does question this equation, arguing that the international normative order is in conflict with the traditional one. This view is, just as in the case of *gacaca*, criticised by international legal experts, but has also received international support. It is interesting to see that this support is not only provided by sociologists and legal anthropologists (Quinn, 2009; Baines, 2007), who, as expected, hold on to 'strong' legal pluralism (without naming it as such), but also by advocates of 'weak' pluralism, or state centralists (who, again, do not use such terms). The latter argue that tradition-based mechanisms (in Uganda) comply with the stipulations of art. 17 of the Rome Statute in order to be considered as prosecution 'by a State which has jurisdiction over it', which should make any prosecution of the same person for the same act by the ICC inadmissible. They furthermore argue that the use of tradition-based mechanisms should be a sufficient reason for the ICC to refrain from prosecution in 'the interest of justice.' (art. 53.1.C) (Keller, 2007).

This barricade war between legal centralists, legal pluralists and legal anthropologists creates only more confusion in the minds of the donors and does not help them in making policy choices. On the one hand, as members of the international community, they have an interest in seeing international crimes prosecuted; on the other hand, they support peace negotiations during which the transitional justice policy is usually developed and they need to identify locally anchored solutions.

Given the fact that both formal and tradition-based mechanisms are included in the Agreement on Accountability and Reconciliation in Uganda, it is no wonder that the actual implementation of the agreement turns out to be a lengthy process. To accept the interaction between these semi-autonomous normative orders on paper is one thing. To create from this an actually functioning hybrid order that is perceived as legitimate on an international, national and local level, and that operates in a coherent way, is a steeper challenge. In other words: the dynamic, dialectical process that should finally result in the hybridisation of international criminal law paradigms and local accountability paradigms is still ongoing and may require more time than expected. The fact that donors at the moment primarily support preparatory actions, such as consultations, studies, work groups, etc., is not at all a wrong decision, provided that these efforts can be sustained as long as needed and that the lengthy process is not an expression of the government's lack of political will.

The further course and outcome of this dialectical process will provide many lessons for other post-conflict situations in which similar normative conflicts arise. But considering that the process is unique to every context and in every post-conflict country, the resulting hybrid solutions are not eligible for transplantation to other post-conflict situations, since these will in turn comprise quite different semi-autonomous social fields. Nor can we create new standard models of tradition-based mechanisms. For the same reason, no general conclusions can be drawn regarding the position of such hybrid mechanisms with regard to other transitional justice mechanisms with which they might be combined, or with regard to timing and sequencing. It is possible that current processes of hybridisation of the international normative order regarding criminal prosecution and of the non-state, local normative orders regarding accountability for mass crimes will lead to the creation of a new, inclusive transitional justice paradigm (Brems and Viaene, 2010), but at the moment it is unclear what such a paradigm will look like. In any event, such a new paradigm will also have to develop principles to guide the hybridisation processes, such as respecting each other's values and interests and searching for common, underlying values (Berman, 2007). Finally, new, hybrid standards will have to be designed to assess the newly created hybrid mechanisms. The recommendations from the above analysis will be expounded in Chapter 16.

BIBLIOGRAPHY

Allen, T. (2006) *Trial Justice. The International Criminal Court and the Lord's Resistance Army*. London/New York: Zed Books.

Baines, E.K. (2007) The haunting of Alice: local approaches to justice and reconciliation in Northern Uganda, *The International Journal of Transitional Justice*, 1, 91–114.

Berman, P.S. (2007) Global Legal Pluralism, *Southern California Law Review*, 80, 1155–1237.

Beyond Juba (2009) A transitional justice project of the Faculty of Law, Makerere University, The Refugee Law Project and the Human Rights & Peace Centre, *Tradition in Transition*, Working Paper No. 1.

Boersch-Supan, J. (2009) The communities: the crossroads between reintegration and reconciliation. What can be learned from the Sierra Leonean experience?, Crise Working Paper No. 63.

Brems, E. and Viaene, L. (2010) Transitional Justice and Cultural Contexts: Learning from the Universality Debate, *Netherlands Quarterly of Human Rights*, 28(2), 199–224.

Cassese, A. (2003) *International Criminal Law*. Oxford: Oxford University Press.

Clark, P. (2010) *The Gacaca Courts, Post-Genocide Justice and Reconciliation in Rwanda. Justice without Lawyers*. Cambridge: Cambridge University Press.

Conciliation Resources (2010) *Choosing to return. Challenges faced by the Lord's Resistance Army's middle-ranking commander*. London, October 2010.

Daly, E. and Sarkin, J. (2007) *Reconciliation in divided societies. Finding common ground*. Philadelphia: University of Pennsylvania Press.

Griffiths, J. (1986) What is Legal Pluralism?, *Journal of Legal Pluralism*, 24, 1–56.

Huyse, L. and Salter, M. (eds.) (2008) *Traditional Justice after Violent Conflict. Learning from African experiences*. Stockholm, Sweden: IDEA.

Ingelaere, B. (2008) The *gacaca* courts in Rwanda. In Huyse, L. and Salter, M. (eds.) *Traditional Justice after Violent Conflict. Learning from African Experiences*, 25–59. Stockholm, Sweden: IDEA.

Keller, L.M. (2007) The False Dichotomy of Peace versus Justice and the International Criminal Court, *The Hague Justice Journal*, 3(1), 12–47.

Manifesto '99 (2002) *Traditional methods of conflict management/resolution of possible complementary value to the proposed Sierra Leone Truth and Reconciliation Commission*.

Merry, S. (1988) Legal Pluralism, *Law & Society Review*, 22(5), 869–896.

Merry, S. (2003), From law and colonialism to law and globalization, *Law & Social Inquiry*, 28(2), 569–590.

Mgbako, C. (2005) Ingando Solidarity Camps: Reconciliation and Political Indoctrination in Post-Genocide Rwanda, *Harvard Human Rights Journal*, 18, 201–224.

Moore, S. (1973) Law and Social Change: The Semi-Autonomous Social Field as an Appropriate Subject of Study, *Law & Society Review*, 7, 719–746.

Nagy, R. (2009) Traditional justice and legal pluralism in transitional context: the case of Rwanda's gacaca courts. In Quinn, J.R., *Reconciliation(s). Transitional justice in post-conflict societies*, 86–115. Montréal: McGill-Queen's University Press.

Pham, P.N., Vinck, P., Stover, E., Moss, A. and Wierda, M. (2007) *When the War Ends. A Population-Based Survey on Attitudes about Peace, Justice and Social Reconstruction in Northern Uganda*. Human Rights Center, University of California, Berkeley; Payson Center for International Development, Tulane University; International Center for Transitional Justice, New York.

Pham, P.N., Vinck, P., Wierda, M., Stover, E. and Di Giovanni, A. (2005) *Forgotten Voices: A Population-Based Survey of Attitudes about Peace and Justice in Northern Uganda*. International Center for Transitional Justice and the Human Rights Center, University of California, Berkeley.

Pham, P.N. and Vinck, P. (2010), *Transitioning to Peace. A population-based survey on attitudes about social reconstruction and Justice in Northern Uganda*. The Human Rights Center, University of California, Berkeley.

Porter, H.E. (2012) Justice and rape on the periphery: the supremacy of social harmony in the space between local solutions and established judicial systems in northern Uganda, *Journal of East African Studies*, 6(1), 81–97

Pouligny, B. (2003) UN peace operations, INGO's, NGO's, and promoting the rule of law: exploring the intersection of international and local norms in different post-war contexts, *Journal of Human Rights*, 2(3), 359–377.

Purdeková, A. (2008) Repatriation and Reconciliation in Divided Societies: The Case of Rwanda's 'Ingando'. Refugees Studies Centre Working Paper, University of Oxford, No. 43.

Quinn, J.R. (2009) What of reconciliation ? Traditional mechanisms of acknowledgment in Uganda. In Quinn, J.R. (ed.) *Reconciliation(s). Transitional justice in post-conflict societies*, 174–206. Montréal: McGill-Queen's University Press.

Schotsmans, M. (2011) No return home. The (non)reintegration of youth ex-combatants in Sierra Leone as a challenge to the contextualisation of DDR and transitional justice. In Derluyn, I., Parmentier, S. and Vandehole, W. (eds.) *Re-member. Rehabilitation and Reintegration of War-Affected Children*. Antwerp: Intersentia.

Truth and Reconciliation Commission (2004) *Witness to truth*, Report of the Sierra Leone Truth and Reconciliation Commission, Sierra Leone.

UNOHCHR (1996) *Gacaca. Le droit coutumier au Rwanda*. Rapport final de la première phase d'enquête sur le terrain, Kigali, 31/01/1996. Rapport de la deuxième phase d'enquêtes sur le terrain, Kigali, 30/06/1996.

UNOHCHR (2007) *Making peace our own. Victims' perceptions of accountability, reconciliation and transitional justice in Northern Uganda*.

Waldorf, L. (2006) Mass justice for mass atrocity: rethinking local justice as transitional justice, *Temple Law Review*, 79(1), 1–87.

PART III

INTERNATIONAL ACTORS AND TRADITIONAL JUSTICE IN JUSTICE SECTOR AID

CHAPTER 8
AT THE CROSSROADS OF THEORY AND PRACTICE

Giselle CORRADI

1. INTRODUCTION

Justice sector aid is a relatively new area of activity for international actors in Sub-Saharan Africa. Although the resources allocated to the justice sector are limited when compared to other sectors, international actors play an increasingly important role in this field. In this context, they are confronted with the fact that legal pluralism is prominent in the life of most Africans. In some countries as much as 80–90% of all disputes are resolved through so-called traditional justice mechanisms.[1] Though widely accessible, these institutions present a number of challenges, most notably in the area of human rights. For example, they tend to discriminate on the basis of gender and apply corporal punishments (Wojkowska, 2006). At the same time, these legal orders may also contain norms that protect human rights or that may allow their protection (Gomez Isa, 2011; Hellum, 2007). However, the legitimacy of some human rights is often contested in this region as these norms contradict certain aspects of African cultural and religious traditions (An-Na'Im, 2003). In other words, justice sector aid in Africa faces the task of contributing to building justice institutions that provide legitimate and effective remedies in legally plural contexts where state justice is not dominant and human rights remain contested.

At the crossroads of theory and practice, Part III of this book explores the connections between the policies and interventions of development actors that engage with local legal orders in the context of justice sector aid to Sub-Saharan Africa and important insights generated by socio-legal scholars on how to go about these challenges. The overall aim of this endeavour is to provide a critical analysis of the main strategies currently supported by development actors, and hopefully, contribute to the translation of socio-legal theory into guidance for further practice. Due to the relevance of the topic, particular attention is paid

[1] Wojkowska, 2006.

to a sub-field within justice sector aid, namely human rights assistance. In this context, Part III pays systematic attention to the relationship between local legal orders, legal pluralism and human rights, as well as the strategies pursued by international actors in this specific domain.

Part III of this book focuses on international assistance to the justice sector provided at national and local levels, targeting state and civil society actors. In order to analyse these interventions, four general types of interventions have been identified.[2] First, interventions may deal with law drafting and law reform. Examples of this type of intervention include drafting legislation, the removal of clauses that exempt customary laws from complying with the national constitution and the ascertainment or self-statement of customary laws, amongst others. Second, interventions may aim at supporting or reforming institutional arrangements. For instance, reforming the institutional framework for legal pluralism, (re)defining jurisdictional boundaries and referral procedures between state and local legal orders, and reforming appointment procedures within local justice forums. Third, interventions may attempt to build capacity amongst state and local justice providers by means of training state court judges, training local justice providers on national legislation and human rights dialogue with local justice providers, amongst others. Finally, interventions may focus on empowering justice users, such as initiatives for the dissemination of national legislation and the provision of mobile courts, legal aid and paralegal services. As the tables below clarify, each of these types of interventions may be conducted at the level of the state – the formal justice system – or at the level of local legal orders.

---

[2] Different international actors have produced various classifications of interventions in the justice sector. Although the terminology differs, there is a lot of overlap between the various typologies. For extensive lists of possible interventions, see Skaar et al. (2004) and Samuels (2006). The typology of interventions proposed in this introduction results from the analysis of data collected during field visits and an extensive review of grey literature.

Table 1.1. Examples of interventions dealing with legal pluralism at state level (formal justice institutions)

Law reform	Institutional support and reform	Building capacity of justice providers	Empowering justice users
- Removal of exemptions clauses for customary law - Introduction of compliance or repugnancy clauses for customary law - Development of 'conflict rules' for traditional and formal justice - Research related activities - etc.	- Recognition of traditional courts - Incorporation of traditional courts in state justice system - Regulation of jurisdiction of traditional courts - De/refining procedures for referrals and appeals between formal and traditional justice - etc.	- Training of formal justice providers on matters related to customary law, traditional justice and legal pluralism - Sensitisation of formal justice providers on linkages between formal and traditional justice such as referral procedures - etc.	- Provision of legal aid and paralegal assistance - Civic education programmes - Human rights awareness raising - Sensitisation on human rights of vulnerable groups - etc.

Table 1.2. Examples of interventions dealing with legal pluralism at the level of local legal orders

Law reform	Institutional support and reform	Building capacity of justice providers	Empowering justice users
- Self statement, ascertainment or codification of customary law - Appointment of experts to determine content of customary law - Participatory standard setting processes for customary law - Community debates on the content of customary law (including identification of structural, procedural, and substantial rules) - etc.	- Infrastructural and organisational support for traditional courts - Improvement of record keeping in traditional courts - De/refining procedures for appointment and removal of traditional justice providers - Procedures for monitoring and inspection of traditional courts - De/refining procedures for appeals, referrals and enforcement in traditional courts - etc.	- Training of traditional justice providers on national laws and human rights standards - Sensitisation of traditional justice providers on linkages between formal and traditional justice such as referral procedures - Training on record keeping and documentation of case outcomes - Training in techniques of dispute resolution - Provision of legal materials and advice services - etc.	- Provision of legal aid and paralegal assistance - Civic education programmes - Human rights awareness raising - Sensitisation on human rights of vulnerable groups - etc.

Chapters 11 to 14 rely on this typology for the presentation of a 'mapping' of interventions in the four case study countries.

2. CONCEPTUAL FRAMEWORK

Part III of this book relies more on the concepts of legal pluralism and 'local' (rather than 'traditional') legal orders. This is the case in view of the fact that these terms emphasise a users' perspective, i.e. the locally available justice options, which are often many. As already explained, in most cases this excludes formal justice institutions sponsored by the state. However, throughout Part III of this book, local legal orders are also identified in terms of 'customary', 'traditional' 'informal' and 'non-state', depending on the terminology that is most frequently employed in the different case study countries that were examined. Actually, there is no single word that captures all the dimensions implicated in the justice options that are locally available. For example, a legal NGO may not be a 'customary' legal actor but may nevertheless base much of its work on local custom. Similarly, official customary courts may belong to the justice structures of the state so that they cannot be called 'non-state' in *sensu stricto*, while in their operation they may combine local custom and state norms. For their part, local state actors, such as the police and the lower courts, may officially or unofficially endorse local normative orders. In other words, local legal orders often cross the boundaries of 'modern' vs. 'customary', 'formal' vs. 'informal', or 'state' vs. 'non-state' dichotomies. Bearing this in mind, these labels have been nevertheless employed since they are a useful way of distinguishing aid that is targeted towards these as compared to state sponsored formal justice institutions. The term 'legal orders' covers the norms, the actors and the mechanisms involved in local justice processes.

'International actors' refers to multilateral and bilateral assistance agencies, development banks, United Nations agencies, international non-governmental organisations, international consultancy firms and international foundations in their roles as donors, implementers, technical advisors and stakeholders in policy dialogue. The word 'donor' comprises all international providers of any kind of aid, such as loans and grants. However, it is necessary to bear in mind that justice sector aid entails a chain involving multiple links between international and domestic development actors (ICHRP, 2000). For example, it may include a primary donor, such as a bilateral agency, a donor country implementing agency, such as an international non-governmental organisation, a beneficiary country partner, such as a local non-governmental organisation, a primary beneficiary, such as local justice providers, and the ultimate beneficiaries, the justice users. In addition, despite justice sector aid often being delivered in the form of projects, i.e. grants and loans that are explicitly programmed to a series of inputs and outputs linked to some larger objective, there is a trend towards moving away from 'projectised' activities towards sector support modalities in which the recipient is typically a government through a ministry or an *ad hoc* body that manages and executes a programme (Bergling 2006). Therefore, the role of international actors is necessarily examined in relation to that of domestic actors, such as the government and local civil society organisations. In this sense, this part of the book refers to 'development actors', 'legal development actors' and 'development practitioners' meaning all the actors involved in the chain of justice sector aid. When necessary, a distinction is made between different kinds of international development actors. For example, the main focus of multilateral and bilateral development agencies and development banks is state building and strengthening the capacities of the state, whereas that of international non-governmental organisations entails closer collaboration with domestic civil society organisations and citizens in general. This may result in different or parallel 'chains' that may be constrained by different factors and pursue different strategies of action.

3. SITUATING THE STUDY WITHIN BROADER DEBATES

The topic of Part III of this book forms part of broader ongoing debates on law and development dealing with how justice sector aid can contribute to building equitable justice institutions that benefit the poor and disadvantaged (Golub, 2003; Sage and Woolcock, 2005; Van Rooij, 2009; Sage et al., 2010). In addition, some authors have examined this issue in the context of post-conflict peacebuilding efforts (Widner, 2001; Sannerholm, 2007; Amisi et al., 2007; Sending, 2009; Donais, 2009; Isser, 2011). In both cases, these discussions point out that so far most aid to the justice sector has been top-down and concerned with building formal state justice institutions, which mainly benefit and are dominated by wealthy, educated, urban elites, while neglecting the perspectives and experiences of the wider population (Golub, 2003; Sage and Woolcock, 2005; Sage et al., 2010; Isser, 2011). They also highlight that classical 'rule of law' approaches to justice sector reform focus on 'institution building' from a technical point of view, are based on an idealised western model of justice and ignore the role of local contexts and power relations. Therefore these initiatives have not delivered the expected outcomes (Golub, 2003; Sage and Woolcock, 2005; Sannerholm, 2007; Donais, 2009; Sending, 2009; Sage et al., 2010; Isser, 2011). As a result, these discussions underscore the importance of complementing these efforts with context sensitive 'bottom-up' approaches that promote local ownership, access to justice and the legal empowerment of the poor, including engagement with the local legal orders that most people actually resort to (Sage and Woolcock, 2005; Amisi et al., 2007; Sannerholm, 2007; Van Rooij, 2009; Sage et al., 2010; Isser, 2011).

In recent years, a growing body of literature started to examine the connection between justice sector aid and local legal orders (Le Roy and Kuyu, 1997; Penal

Reform International, 2000; Nyamu-Musembi, 2003; Thorne, 2005; Chirayath et al., 2005; Kimati, 2005; Odinkalu, 2005; Wojkowska, 2006; Weilenmann, 2007; ICHRP, 2009; Toomey, 2010; Mapaure, 2010; HAKI, 2011; Isser, 2011; Albrecht et al., 2011; Kyed, 2011; Ubink, 2011a, 2011b; Harper, 2011a, 2011b; UN Women, UNICEF and UNDP, 2012). Though the regional focus of these studies is not always Africa in particular, the sheer relevance of legal pluralism in this part of the world means that in practice many of them draw on examples from this region. As introduced very briefly in Chapter 1, in the first place, this literature emphasises why it is necessary for development actors to include local legal orders within justice sector aid in Sub-Saharan Africa. It is argued that development actors should pay attention to local legal orders since most Africans will continue to rely heavily on them (Le Roy and Kuyu, 1997; Penal Reform International, 2000; Chirayath et al., 2005). This is the case due to several reasons, such as that formal justice institutions may remain inaccessible despite reforms (Chirayath et al., 2005), that trying to wipe out local legal orders will not work since they are the expression of underlying visions of the cosmos (Le Roy and Kuyu, 1997), and that African customary institutions are closely linked to the social organisation of agrarian multiplex societies (Penal Reform International, 2000; Weilenmann, 2007). Secondly, it is pointed out that in many cases local legal orders have more authority and legitimacy than formal justice institutions so that excluding them from justice sector aid is exclusionary in itself (Chirayath et al., 2005). Third, it is highlighted that local legal orders often present problems in terms of accountability and human rights which justice sector aid cannot leave unaddressed (Nyamu-Musembi, 2003; Chirayath et al., 2005). Finally, it has been recently argued that supporting formal state justice institutions while ignoring local legal orders weakens the provision of justice as a whole, as poorly connected justice institutions generate confusion and jurisdictional gaps (HAKI, 2011).

In addition, most of these studies contain normative analyses of how development actors should engage with local legal orders. In this regard, there seems to be a consensus on a number of central issues. First, development actors need to understand the specific social, historical, political and cultural background of local legal orders (Nyamu-Musembi, 2003; ICHRP, 2009; Toomey, 2010; Clarcke, 2011; Obarrio, 2011; Isser, 2011; UN Women, UNICEF and UNDP, 2012). This includes a critical examination of the dialectic dynamics that constituted customary and modern justice institutions during the colonial and post-colonial periods as well as appreciating the internal logic, the social bases and the world view that underpin local legal orders (Le Roy et al., 1997; Obarrio, 2011; Isser, 2011). Second, development actors need to follow a user's perspective (Nyamu-Musembi, 2003; Isser, 2011; UN Women, UNICEF and UNDP, 2012). Methodologically, this requires meaningful local participation (ICHRP, 2009) and in-depth knowledge of local empirical realities, i.e. who the local justice providers are, which justice mechanisms are available, how provision is experienced by different groups of local justice users and what these groups see as legitimate forms of justice and security (Albrecht et al., 2011). This should lead to the formulation of practical solutions to the problems affecting local populations rather than investing in building ideal justice institutions (Isser, 2011). Third, development actors need to acknowledge the political dimension of their interventions and support processes that improve downwards accountability (Nyamu-Musembi, 2003; Odinkalu, 2005; ICHRP, 2009; Albrecht et al., 2011; Clarcke, 2011; Ubink et al., 2011). On the one hand, there is a concern that interventions may leave intact despotic community level power relations or even reinforce them by formally sanctioning them (Nyamu-Musembi, 2003; Odinkalu, 2005; Clarcke, 2011; Ubink et al., 2011). On the other hand, it is pointed out that the choice of supporting certain providers and agendas over others is in itself political and that national leaders often try to benefit politically from the inclusion of customary leaders into justice sector aid (Albrecht et al., 2011; Isser, 2011; Kyed, 2011). In this context, what international actors should do is facilitate processes of negotiation where a plurality of actors is considered and included in the dialogue (Albrecht et al., 2011; Isser, 2011; Kyed, 2011). This is related to a fourth key issue, namely that development actors should rethink the model of state that underpins justice sector aid and consider a political order that includes a plurality of institutions in a non-exclusive manner (Le Roy and Kuyu, 1997; Nyamu-Musembi, 2003; Weilenmann, 2007; Albrecht et al., 2011; Kyed, 2011). In other words, it is not an 'either/or' equation since in practice, both local and state justice institutions interact and play a role in the provision of justice (Isser, 2011). Therefore, interventions should support a variety of justice providers and enhance the negotiation capacities of all relevant stakeholders (Weilenmann, 2007), while blending the strengths and mitigating the weaknesses of both local and state legal orders (Clarcke et al., 2011). According to some authors, this entails a dual approach with top-down and bottom-up elements (HAKI, 2011) where international actors facilitate a constructive dialectic between locally driven initiatives and nationally determined policies (Albrecht et al., 2011). Finally, most authors coincide that addressing these issues demands a sustained, gradual and long-term commitment, which poses a challenge to international development actors, who are usually under pressure to show results in a relatively short term (Toomey, 2010; Wojkowska et al., 2010; Albrecht et al., 2011; Isser, 2011).

At the level of human rights, many of these studies stress that development actors need to be aware of the social purpose of local practices that contravene human rights (Isser, 2011; Harper, 2011a). In other words, development actors need to understand why these practices make sense locally and address the socio-cultural complexities that surround them (Isser, 2011). This relates to the fact that there may be fundamental differences in the *raison d'être* between local and state legal orders (Harper, 2011). Local legal orders are generally concerned with restoring intra-community harmony by repairing relationships and creating a framework for reintegration whereas state legal orders aim at protecting individual rights and cause deterrence through retributive punishments. Consequently, measuring the performance of the former by applying the logic of the latter is unhelpful and misleading (Harper, 2011).[3] Moreover, many human rights violations may have a social and economic explanation so that development actors need to devise solutions that go beyond modifying legal rules and practices to encompass broader processes of social change (Harper, 2011; Chopra et al., 2011).

In addition, a number of studies have analysed the relationship between legal plurality, local legal orders and human rights specifically. The International Council on Human Rights Policy has developed a framework for advocacy and policy in relation to human rights and plural legal orders (ICHRP, 2009). This framework highlights the need to critically assess any policy or demand for the preservation, reform or introduction of plural legal orders along six dimensions: the basis of the policy or demand, the motivation of those who advocate it, its internal coherence, the extent to which the policy advances human rights nationally, the wider national context and the impact of the policy on intra- and inter-group rights. It also proposes another six dimensions for assessing the operation of plural legal orders, including the process for developing the content and structure of plural legal orders, the resources of local and state legal orders, their substantive content and procedural functioning, safeguarding the existence of rights and whether the broader context is conducive to rights protection. The framework also highlights the need to move beyond 'balancing' human rights and culture, towards the adoption of intersectional approaches to identity, seeing culture, custom and religion as changing and internally contested and a situated analysis that regards rights-holders as simultaneously individuals and members of multiple collectives (ICHRP, 2009: 147). Furthermore, a study conducted by the Danish Institute for Human Rights identifies the main areas where local legal orders are at odds with human rights and discusses how development actors should address each of them (UN Women, UNICEF and UNDP, 2012). Based on case studies from different developing regions in the world, the study suggests that problematic issues need to be balanced against the performance of state justice in those same areas. While the study recognises that states have the duty to ensure human rights protection even by local legal orders, it recommends that international actors acknowledge the role of local legal orders in providing access to justice and adopt a pragmatic gradualist approach to meeting international requirements while providing support to that end.

As international actors begin to programme in relation to local legal orders, a recent generation of studies begins to produce knowledge on the practices of these actors from an empirical viewpoint (Mapaure, 2010; Albrecht et al., 2011; Chopra et al., 2011; Harper, 2011c; Harper et al., 2011; Leonardi et al., 2011; Rawls, 2011; Ubink, 2011a, 2011b, 2011c; Ubink et al., 2011). Some of these studies suggest that

[3] For example, this would happen if local legal orders were expected to comply with due process guarantees in a strict way, as this presupposes a context of adjudication, whereas local justice forums tend to mediate.

despite rhetoric acknowledgements, development actors have so far been hesitant to support local legal orders and take them seriously (Isser, 2011; Albrecht et al., 2011; Clarcke, 2011; Ubink et al., 2011; Kyed, 2011). For example, current initiatives to involve local justice providers within justice sector aid may reflect more an attempt to reclaim state sovereignty through the incorporation of non-state actors as allies than the intention to strengthen local legal actors in their own right (Albrecht et al., 2011; Clarcke, 2011; Kyed, 2011).[4] In relation to human rights, a number of authors explain that most interventions have so far addressed important challenges in a superficial way (Mapaure, 2010; Chopra et al., 2011; Harper, 2011c). First, based on the assumption that local legal orders are at odds with human rights due to a lack of knowledge, development actors have tried to educate local justice providers on human rights in a top-down way, which has often generated resistance (Mapaure, 2010; Chopra et al., 2011). Second, interventions have attempted to adapt local legal orders by requiring the participation of women, prohibiting harmful practices and ascertaining or modifying customary laws without grounding these initiatives on internal demands or generating changes in a participatory way (Chopra et al., 2011; Harper, 2011c; Leonardi et al., 2011). Finally, development actors have introduced linkages between local and state legal orders and have sought to expand local access to dispute resolution forums without always paying due attention to local power dynamics and the experiences of justice users (Chopra et al., 2011; Clarcke, 2011; Harper, 2011c). Nevertheless, a number of initiatives seem to be yielding positive results. For example, supporting local communities to 'self-state' customary laws that protect human rights in a specific domain and around which there is a widespread local consensus (Ubink, 2011c), and engaging in meaningful dialogue with local leaders about customary practices that contravene human rights (Chopra, 2007; Rawls, 2011). Based on an evaluation of seven interventions aimed at empowering local justice users Harper et al. conclude that:

> 'with the capacity to challenge power imbalances, access the law and legal services, exercise choice regarding alternative recourse options and obtain remedies that do not contravene minimum rights standards, people living in poverty can improve the justice outcomes available to them and become agents of change for their own betterment' (Harper et al., 2011: 173).

Part III of this book contributes to this growing body of knowledge from an empirical and normative point of view, and pays particular attention to the issues raised within the discussions on human rights. At the empirical level, it investigates how international development actors engage with legal pluralism

[4] This is less the case of international non-governmental organisations, which tend to focus on improving local access to justice as compared to bilateral or multilateral actors whose focus is state building (Albrecht et al., 2011).

and local legal orders within justice sector aid in Sub-Saharan Africa. What kind of policies and interventions do they support in this area? What strategies do they follow for advancing human rights at the level of local legal orders? At the normative level, it explores how socio-legal theories are of relevance to the practice of international development actors in this area and how they can be translated into guidance for practitioners. Why are these theories relevant for justice sector aid in Sub-Saharan Africa and how can they be applied?

4. MULTI-SITED QUALITATIVE RESEARCH METHODS

As explained in Chapter 1, the process of data collection and analysis took place in different phases. A first exploratory phase consisted in a systematic review of grey literature produced by international development actors, which was available online. During this phase, the focus laid on identifying which actors had produced documents discussing their views on local legal orders, legal pluralism and human rights in relation to justice sector aid. Subsequently, a revision of programme documents for the African region allowed the 'mapping' of countries in which these actors were supporting interventions in this area. On the basis of this mapping, four case studies were selected for fieldwork: Malawi, Mozambique, Sierra Leone and Zambia. This choice was motivated by the fact that different international agencies were active in each of these countries thereby allowing the collection of data from a broader spectrum of practices.[5] Prior to the field research, a broad range of information was gathered on the history of these countries, in particular how the colonial and post-colonial history affected the legal landscape, the characteristics of local legal orders and legal pluralism, and the relationship between local justice processes and human rights. The purpose of the fieldwork was to gather detailed information about the types of strategy that development actors support in relation to these issues and their rationales for doing so.

An interview guide was developed in advance on the basis of a review of socio-legal and grey literature and identified the topics that would be covered in the four case studies. At the same time, the semi-structured interview method allowed enough flexibility to incorporate new topics that emerged in the course of the field research. Interviews with representatives from multilateral and bilateral development organisations, government officers, international non-governmental organisations, and domestic non-governmental and civil society organisations

[5] At the time the empirical research was conducted, the main development actors providing support to local legal orders in Malawi were the British bilateral cooperation (DFID) and UNDP; in Sierra Leone the British bilateral cooperation (DFID), the United Nations Development Programme (UNDP) and the World Bank, in Mozambique the Danish bilateral cooperation (DANIDA), the European Union (EU) and UNDP, and in Zambia the Danish bilateral cooperation (DANIDA) and the European Union (EU).

led to a good overview of the different initiatives supported by development actors at different levels and their discourses on the reasons why they considered these approaches appropriate. Local justice providers that had been involved in interventions, such as traditional leaders and paralegals, were also interviewed on their perspectives on these initiatives and representatives from civil society organisations and local experts were consulted in respect of their ideas about the research topic. All interviews were conducted in English or Portuguese and most of them were recorded, except for a few in which the interviewee did not agree to it.

During the phase of analysis, all recordings were carefully listened to and interview notes taken on the field were expanded. Subsequently, a number of interviews were fully or partially transcribed by the researcher. Not all interviews were transcribed due to the fact that in many cases interviews yielded mainly factual information about the kinds of activities supported by development actors, which did not require a word-by-word analysis. Those interviews or parts of interviews where more complex issues were discussed, such as development actors' discourses on their rationales for engaging or not with local legal orders, the limitations of interventions and their perceived effects, were transcribed. Both the transcribed interviews, the expanded interview notes and the field notes taken on the basis of observations were coded inductively. The categories emerging from this process were analysed in the light of insights generated by the review of socio-legal literature and discussions held with peer researchers and colleagues.

In addition to the fieldwork, an international forum was organised in Cape Town from 23 to 25 March 2010, which brought together representatives of stakeholders identified during the field research, including officers from donor organisations, the government and international and local non-governmental organisations. The forum served as a platform to discuss preliminary findings and explore further questions with these actors. Invited representatives from the selected countries were asked to present their views and reflect on their experiences with regard to development actors' engagement with local legal orders. A series of focus group discussions were organised during the forum, which aimed at collectively exploring a range of relevant topics. The first focus group dealt with the normative framework for legal pluralism and reform proposals to state recognition and regulation of local legal orders. The second one explored development actors' current approaches to local legal orders and human rights. And the third one addressed how processes of social change unfold at grassroots level and what this implies for human rights interventions. All discussions were held in English. They were recorded, transcribed and analysed by inductive coding. Finally, a more refined version of the preliminary results was presented at an international seminar organised for this purpose in Brussels on 14 February 2011. The seminar was attended by a mixed public of academics and practitioners. The presentation of the research results was preceded by a keynote address and was followed by a discussion with a panel of experts.[6] The systematic involvement of different stakeholders throughout the whole process of the research proved to be a highly stimulating and enriching exercise, not only in terms of validation but also for acquiring more insights into development actors' ways of thinking about the provision of aid, human rights and local legal orders.

One of the limitations of this methodology is that it did not allow for an evaluation of the impact of interventions. The latter would have required the selection of one intervention in particular whereas this study aims at understanding a broader range of strategies deployed by development actors at different levels. In addition, time and budget constraints did not allow for long term fieldwork, which would have led to the generation of ethnographic insights into the processes through which interventions interplay with local realities or into how the political economy of justice sector aid and the internal logic of development organisations influences the policies and interventions that are supported. Again, this would have required the selection of one specific intervention or development agency in particular to be analysed for a longer period of time. That said, these limitations did not preclude the collection of relevant data on the basis of which to provide interesting results on the research questions and suggest complementary research agendas.

5. STRUCTURE OF PART III

Part III of this book contains eight chapters. Next to this introductory chapter, Chapters 9 and 10 present an analysis of the relationship between local legal orders, legal pluralism, human rights and justice sector aid in Sub-Saharan Africa in general. Chapter 9 deals with the context in which development actors operate and the background of their interventions. It first describes the main common threads running through the plural legal landscapes of Sub-Saharan Africa, as well as some of the salient characteristics of local legal orders in this region and how the latter relate to human rights. After providing important insights into the challenges involved in supporting local justice processes in this region, the chapter discusses the background of justice sector aid and human rights assistance in Sub-Saharan Africa and how international development actors purport to position themselves towards local legal orders. Building further on the contextual issues presented in Chapter 9, Chapter 10 explores how socio-legal theory on legal pluralism and human rights relates to the practice of justice sector and human rights aid in relation to local justice processes. The chapter discusses

[6] The keynote speaker was Prof. Anne Griffiths, University of Edinburgh, and the participants in the panel were Dr Tanja Chopra, independent consultant for international organisations such as the World Bank and UN Women, Mr Fergus Kerrigan, Danish Institute for Human Rights, Ms Kersty McCourt, Open Society Justice Initiative and Dr Albrecht Stockmayer, of the German International Cooperation.

a number of critical insights generated by socio-legal scholars on two significant challenges that development actors encounter in Sub-Saharan Africa: a context of legal pluralism where state justice is not dominant, and that of cultural and contextual diversity, where human rights are often not known, not accepted or considered irrelevant. The chapter explores how these theories and concepts may inform different kinds of intervention.

Chapters 11, 12, 13 and 14 present the four case studies on Malawi, Mozambique, Sierra Leone and Zambia respectively. These chapters follow the same structure. First, they outline a series of key contextual features, such as the historical background of each country and how the latter gave shape to current configurations of legal pluralism, the justice landscape, the institutional framework for legal pluralism and the status of human rights within local justice processes. Second, they present the empirical data on the kind of policies and interventions that international actors support in this area. And third, they provide an analysis of international actors' practices.

Chapter 15 closes Part III with a comparative analysis of the four case studies. The chapter identifies salient trends regarding the type of interventions that international actors are supporting in the region and examines how the latter relate to the theoretical insights presented in Chapters 9 and 10.

BIBLIOGRAPHY

Albrecht, P., Kyed, H.M., Isser, D. and Harper, E. (eds.) (2011) *Perspectives on Involving Non-State and Customary Actors in Justice and Security Reform*. Rome: International Law and Development Organisation.

Amisi, B. and Duffy, G. (2007) New Rules for the Rule of Law? External Actors and Rule of Law Development in Post-Conflict African Societies [online] http://citation.allacademic.com/meta/p_mla_apa_research_citation/1/8/0/7/3/pages180731/p180731-1.php (11/07/2012).

An-Na'Im, A. (ed.) (2003) *Human Rights Under African Constitutions, Realizing the Promise for Ourselves*. Philadelphia: University of Pennsylvania Press.

Bergling, P. (2006) *Rule of Law on the International Agenda: International Support to Legal and Judicial Reform in International Administration, Transition and Development Cooperation*. Antwerp: Intersentia.

Chirayath, L., Sage, C. and Woolock, M. (2005) Customary Law and Policy Reform: Engaging with the Plurality of Justice Systems [online] http://siteresources.worldbank.org/INTWDR2006/Resources/477383-1118673432908/Customary_Law_and_Policy_Reform.pdf (10/07/2012).

Chopra, T. (2007) Promoting Women's Rights by Indigenous Means: An Innovative Project in Kenya. *Justice for the Poor,* 1(2), 1–4.

Chopra, T. and Isser, D. (2011) 'Women's Access to Justice, Legal Pluralism and Fragile States'. In Albrecht, P., Kyed, H.M., Isser, D. and Harper, E. (eds.) *Perspectives on*

Involving Non-State and Customary Actors in Justice and Security Reform. Rome: International Law and Development Organisation.

Clark, S. and Stephens, M. (2011) 'Reducing Injustice? A Grounded Approach to Strengthening Hybrid Justice Systems: Lessons from Indonesia'. In Ubink, J. (ed.) *Customary Justice: Perspectives on Legal Empowerment*. Rome: International Legal Development Organisation.

Clarcke, R. (2011) Customary Legal Empowerment: Towards a More Critical Approach. In Ubink, J. (ed.) *Customary Justice: Perspectives on Legal Empowerment*. Rome: International Legal Development Organisation.

DANIDA International Development Cooperation (2010) *How To Note. Informal Justice Systems* [online] http://www.danidadevforum.um.dk/NR/rdonlyres/FE725502-ACF5-42C2-B677-C0D411AE2660/0/InformalJusticeSystemsfinalprint.pdf (30/03/2012).

DFID Department for International Development (2000) Justice and Poverty Reduction [online] http://www.gsdrc.org/docs/open/SSAJ35.pdf (18/06/2012).

DFID Department for International Development (2004) *Non-State Justice and Security Systems* [online] http://www.gsdrc.org/docs/open/SSAJ101.pdf (30/03/2012).

Donais, T. (2009) Empowerment or Imposition? Dilemmas of Local Ownership in Post-Conflict Peacebuilding Processes, *Peace & Change*, 34(1), 3–26.

Golub, S. (2003) Beyond Rule of Law Orthodoxy, The Legal Empowerment Alternative. Rule of Law Series Carnegie Endowment for International Peace, 41, 1–46.

HAKI Legal Empowerment Network (2011) Engaging Customary Justice Systems, White Paper [online] http://www.hakinetwork.org/resource-center/ (11/07/2012).

Harper, E. (2011a) *Customary Justice: From Program Design to Impact Evaluation*. Rome: International Law and Development Organisation.

Harper, E. (ed.) (2011b) *Working With Customary Justice Systems: Post-Conflict and Fragile States*. Rome: International Law and Development Organisation.

Harper, E. (2011c) Engaging with Customary Justice Systems. In Ubink, J. (ed.) *Customary Justice: Perspectives on Legal Empowerment*. Rome: International Legal Development Organisation.

Harper, E., Wojkowska, E. and Cunningham, J. (2011) Conclusion: Enhancing Legal Empowerment through Engagement with Customary Justice Systems. In Harper, E. (ed.) *Working with Customary Justice Systems: Post-Conflict and Fragile States*. Rome: International Law and Development Organisation.

ICHRP – International Council on Human Rights Policy (2000) *Local Perspectives: Foreign Aid to the Justice Sector*. Versoix: International Council on Human Rights Policy.

ICHRP – International Council on Human Rights Policy (2009) *When Legal Worlds Overlap: Human Rights, State and Non-State Law*. Versoix: International Council on Human Rights Policy.

Isser, D. (ed.) (2011) *Customary Justice and the Rule of Law in War-Torn Societies*. Washington DC: United States Institute of Peace Press.

KIMATI, L.W. (2005) Non-State Institutions as a Basis of State Reconstruction: The Case of Justice Systems in Africa. Paper presented for CODESRIA's 11th General Assembly, Maputo, 6–10 December 2005.

LEONARDI, C., ISSER, D., MORO, L. and SANTSCHI, M. (2011) The Politics of Customary Law Ascertainment in South Sudan, *Journal of Legal Pluralism*, 63, 111–142.

LE ROY, E. and KUYU, C. (1997) La Politique Française de Coopération Judiciaire: Bilan et Perspectives. Observatoire de la Coopération Française, Rapport 1997, 36–65. Paris: Karthala.

MAPAURE, C. (2010) Accused and Cherished: Traditional and Informal Systems as Seen by International Organisations. In Hinz, M.O. and Mapaure, C. (eds.) *In Search of Justice and Peace. Traditional and Informal Justice Systems in Africa.* Windhoek: Namibia Scientific Society.

NYAMU-MUSEMBI, C. (2003) Review of Experience in Engaging with 'Non-State' Justice Systems in East-Africa [online] http://www.gsdrc.org/docs/open/DS37.pdf (10/07/2012).

OBARRIO J. (2011) Traditional Justice as Rule of Law in Africa: An Anthropological Perspective. In Sriram, C.L., Martin-Ortega, O. and Herman, J. (eds.) *Peace Building and Rule of Law in Africa.* New York: Routledge.

ODINKALU, C.A. (2006) Poor Justice or Justice for the Poor? A Policy Framework for Reform of Customary and Informal Justice Systems in Africa. In Sage, C. and Woolcock, M. (eds.) *The World Bank Legal Review, Law, Equity and Development Vol. 2,* 141–165. Washington DC: Martinus Nijhoff.

PENAL REFORM INTERNATIONAL (2000) *Access to Justice in Sub-Saharan Africa. The Role of Traditional and Informal Justice Systems.* London: Astron Printers.

PIRON, L.H. (2005) Donor assistance to justice sector reform in Africa: living up to the new agenda? In Open Society Justice Initiative (ed.) *Human Rights and Justice Sector Reform in Africa: Contemporary Issues and Responses*, Governance and Social Development Resource Centre.

RAWLS, A. (2011) Policy Proposals for Justice Reform in Liberia: Opportunities under the Current Legal Framework to Expand Access to Justice. In Ubink, J. (ed.) *Customary Justice: Perspectives on Legal Empowerment.* Rome: International Legal Development Organisation.

SAGE, C. and WOOLCOCK, M. (2005) *Breaking Legal Inequality Traps: New Approaches to Building Justice Systems for the Poor in Developing Countries.* Paper presented at the conference 'New Frontiers of Social Policy', Arusha, 12–15 December 2005.

SAGE C., MENZIES, N. and WOOLOCK, M. (2010) Taking the Rules of the Game Seriously: Mainstreaming Justice in Development. The World Bank's Justice for the Poor Program. In Golub, S. (ed.) *Legal Empowerment: Practitioners' Perspectives.* Rome: International Development Law Organisation.

SAMUELS, K. (2006) *Law Reform in Post-Conflict Countries. Operational Initiatives and Lessons Learnt.* World Bank Working Paper Series No. 37. Washington DC: The World Bank.

Sannerholm, R. (2007) Legal, Judicial and Administrative Reforms in Post-Conflict Societies: Beyond the Rule of Law Template, *Journal of Conflict and Security Law*, 12(1), 65–94.

Sending, O.J. (2009) Why Peacebuilders Fail to Secure Ownership and be Sensitive to Context. NUPI Working Paper No. 755. Norwegian Institute of International Affairs.

Skaar, E., Samset, I. and Gloppen, S. (2004) *Aid to Judicial Reform: Norwegian and International Experiences*. CMI Report R 2004: 12. Bergen: Chr. Michelsen Institute.

Thorne, K. (2005) Rule of Law through Imperfect Bodies? The Informal Justice Systems of Burundi and Somalia [online] www.hdcentre.org (10/07/2012)

Toomey, L. (2010) A Delicate Balance: Building Complementary Customary and Sate Legal Systems, *The Law and Development Review*, 3(1), 156–208.

Ubink, J. (ed.) (2011a) *Customary Justice: Perspectives on Legal Empowerment*. Rome: International Law and Development Organisation.

Ubink, J. (2011b) *Research and Policy Note: Customary Justice Sector Reform*. Rome: International Law and Development Organisation.

Ubink, J. (2011c) Stating the Customary: An Innovative Approach to the Locally Legitimate Recording of Customary Law in Namibia. In Ubink, J. (ed.) *Customary Justice: Perspectives on Legal Empowerment*. Rome: International Legal Development Organisation.

Ubink, J. and Van Rooij, B. (2011) Towards Customary Legal Empowerment: An Introduction. In Ubink, J. (ed.) *Customary Justice: Perspectives on Legal Empowerment*. Rome: International Legal Development Organisation.

UNDP – United Nations Development Programme (2004) Access to Justice. Practice Note [online] http://www.undp.org/content/undp/en/home/librarypage/democratic-governance/access_to_justiceandruleoflaw/access-to-justice-practice-note/ (18/06/2012).

UNDP – United Nations Development Programme (2006) UNDP and Transitional Justice. An Overview. New York: United Nations Development Programme [online] http://www.unrol.org/doc.aspx?d=2296.

UN Women, UNICEF and UNDP (2012) Informal Justice Systems. Charting a Course for Human Rights Based Engagement [online] http://www.undp.org/content/dam/undp/library/Democratic%20Governance/Access%20to%20Justice%20and%20Rule%20of%20Law/Informal-Justice-Systems-Charting-a-Course-for-Human-Rights-Based-Engagement.pdf (15/10/2012).

United Nations (2004) The Rule of Law and Transitional Justice in Conflict and Post-Conflict Societies. Report of the Secretary-General. 23 August 2004. S/2004/616

Van Rooij, B. (2009) Bringing Justice to the Poor: Bottom-Up Legal Development Cooperation [online] http://papers.ssrn.com/sol3/papers.cfm?abstract_id=1368185 (10/07/2012)

Weilenmann, M. (2007) Legal Pluralism: A New Challenge for Development Agencies. In Penal Reform International and Bluhm Legal Clinic of the Northwestern University School of Law (eds.) *Access to Justice in Africa and Beyond: Making the Rule of Law a Reality* [online] http://www.penalreform.org/files/rep-2007-access-africa-and-beyond-en.pdf (06/07/2012).

WIDNER, J. (2001) Courts and Democracy in Post-conflict Transitions: A Social Scientist's Perspective on the African Case, *The American Journal of International Law*, 95(1), 64–75.

WOJKOWSKA, E. (2006) *Doing Justice: How Informal Justice Systems Can Contribute.* United Nations Development Programme. Oslo Governance Centre [online] http://www.democraciaejustica.org/cienciapolitica3/sites/default/files/doingjustice ewawojkowska130307.pdf (30/03/2012).

WOJKOWSKA, E. and CUNNINGHAM, J. (2010) Justice Reform's New Frontier: Engaging with Customary Systems to Legally Empower the Poor. In Golub, S. (ed.) *Legal Empowerment: Practitioners' Perspectives.* Rome: International Law and Development Organisation.

WORLD BANK (2006) World Development Report, Equity and Development [online] http://siteresources.worldbank.org/INTWDR2006/Resources/477383-1127230817 535/082136412X.pdf (10/07/2012).

CHAPTER 9

JUSTICE SECTOR AID IN LEGALLY PLURAL AFRICA

Giselle CORRADI

1. INTRODUCTION

In order to understand the context in which development actors operate and the nature of their interventions regarding local legal orders in Sub-Saharan Africa, it is necessary to sketch out two issues. On the one hand, a number of common threads running across the justice landscapes of the continent, including a brief overview of how historical developments affected current configurations of legal pluralism, some of the features that are usually associated with an 'African approach' to justice, and how local legal orders relate to human rights.[1] And on the other, the background of justice sector aid and human rights assistance in this region as well as the kind of policies and interventions that international development actors support in the area of legal pluralism and human rights. This chapter outlines these issues and provides the background to the discussion in Chapter 10.

2. THE PLURAL JUSTICE LANDSCAPES OF SUB-SAHARAN AFRICA

2.1. LEGAL PLURALISM IN HISTORICAL PERSPECTIVE

As documented by different authors, the colonial encounter modified African endogenous legal orders in important ways, so that it is not possible to see current customary law institutions as a 'surviving' pre-colonial form of social control (Snyder, 1981; Mann and Roberts, 1991; Daannaa, 1994; Mamdani, 1996;

[1] Obviously, this entails an oversimplification of what are otherwise complex, diverse, and at times contradictory realities. The purpose of this section is to illustrate some of the key issues that need consideration in relation to legal pluralism and human rights in this region.

Chanock, 1998; John-Nambo, 2002). Moreover, pre-colonial Africa was far from a static, unified and egalitarian universe in which an immutable customary order maintained a stable peace (Chanock, 1998).[2] A variety of forms of social organisation, ranging from acephalous societies to kingdoms and conquest states, gave rise to different legal orders. Appointed chiefs, kin-based hereditary chiefs, spiritual leaders, Islamic leaders and a number of authorities within age and gender groups shared jurisdiction over persons and were kept in check by elders, lineage based councils or the clan organisation (Mamdani, 1996; John-Nambo, 2002). Neither in small-scale communities nor in larger groupings there existed a single 'tribal' identity, as most Africans belonged to overlapping networks of association and exchange that placed them under the authority of a chief for a certain matter and under that of a professional association for another (Ranger, 1983). Pre-colonial customs were flexible and adaptive to competition and shifting power imbalances, rather than reflecting a homogeneous, static and consensual order (Ranger, 1983; Chanock, 1998).

As from the final decades of the nineteenth century, colonial domination transformed certain aspects of these justice institutions.[3] In particular, existing checks and balances on authority and the fluid nature of custom were undermined (Mamdani, 1996; Ranger, 1983). This resulted from the introduction of 'indirect rule', a bifurcated system of governance, whereby the colonial powers governed directly in the colonies where they settled and indirectly through co-opted chiefs in territories under colonial domination but which were not occupied.[4] Indirect rule went hand in hand with legal dualism. In the colonies, European legal orders were transplanted and applied to resolve disputes involving non-natives, whereas in the hinterlands selectively reconstituted or imposed chiefs were granted the right to rule over the people allocated to their tribes by passing rules (bylaws), executing them and settling disputes according to local customs (Mann and Roberts, 1991; Mamdani, 1996). This mainly covered personal relations, such as marriage, succession, and access to productive resources, while colonial administrators reserved the jurisdiction over serious criminal offenses for themselves (Mamdani, 1996). Next to the 'native courts' presided over by chiefs, an intermediate level of courts, staffed by white officials who were charged with the general administration of the native population, listened to appeals and tried to resolve the cases presented to them according to their understanding of local customs, except in cases where the latter were considered 'repugnant' to public order (Mamdani, 1996).

2 In Central Africa for example, the late pre-colonial period in the last decades of the nineteenth century saw the rise of conquest states and an increase in the slave trade, constituting a time of violence and rapid change (Chanock, 1998).

3 Christian missionaries also played a role in this by promulgating rules of behaviour based on the bible (Nader, 2001).

4 Indirect rule was originally introduced in the territories under British domination, but other colonial powers, such as the French and the Portuguese, also resorted to this form of governance later on (Mann and Roberts, 1991).

In this process, colonial administrators understood African customs as unchanging rules that had always governed local societies and that needed to be pinned down in the form of official customary laws (Ranger, 1983). In addition, chiefs became part of an authoritarian framework for local governance. Their authority was unbound from local checks and balances and they were the sole local authority recognised (Mamdani, 1996).[5] Their power was enhanced and backed by the colonial administration in order to extract forced labour, forced crops, forced sales and forced taxes, leading to abuses and popular discontent (Mamdani, 1996). All of this happened in a period in which the introduction of cash crops and migrant labour caused important transformations in relations of production resulting in far reaching consequences in generational and gender relations that shifted existing power bases and hierarchies (Chanock, 1998). In this context, the reification of customs as fixed 'customary laws' was manipulated by vested interests as a means of asserting and increasing control. As explained by Ranger:

> 'Elders tended to appeal to "tradition" in order to defend their dominance of the rural means of production against challenge by the young. Men tended to appeal to "tradition" in order to ensure that the increasing role, which women played in production in the rural areas, did not result in any diminution of male control over women as economic assets. Paramount chiefs and ruling aristocracies in polities that included numbers of ethnic and social groupings appealed to "tradition" in order to maintain or extend their control over their subjects. Indigenous populations appealed to "tradition" in order to ensure that the migrants who settled amongst them did not achieve political and economic rights' (Ranger 1983: 254).

Upon independence, the colonial masters transferred control over these power structures to local elites without popular participation (An Na'Im, 2003). All African states kept the law institutions imported from Europe as their official justice system, but due to their accessibility, customary law institutions were often retained as a temporary solution, until modern courts could be spread out (Mamdani, 1996). During the phase of decolonisation, between the late 1960s and the mid-1970s, three kinds of policy were adopted regarding legal pluralism. First, the continuation of a bifurcated system of common law and customary law, with parallel sets of courts and laws, such as in Sierra Leone (Mamdani, 1996). Second, the unification of the system of courts with different levels of retention of customary law, which varied between (i) the adoption of a dual structure of courts with a single review process, such as in Chad and the Central African Republic,

[5] Though according to Englebert (2002), in some cases, colonial authorities granted traditional authorities more autonomy so that collaboration with the colonial powers did not always result in a loss of legitimacy.

(ii) the abolition of customary courts but the retention of customary law to be applied by a unified system of courts, such as in Tanzania, Niger and Mali, and (iii) the integration of civil or common law and customary law in one body of law to be applied by one system of courts, such as in Senegal and Ghana (Mamdani, 1996). The third and less common policy entailed the abolition of both customary courts and customary laws and the top-down introduction of one single modern justice system for the whole country, as it was the case in Mozambique (Mamdani, 1996).

These policies resulted in official customary courts and laws operating next to unofficial ones. Though in many cases civil or common law was open to all in theory, in practice, it remained out of reach to most who continued to access justice through locally available forums, even if the latter were not recognised by law. According to Mamdani (1996), this means that reforms tended towards deracialisation rather than democratisation of justice processes. In some cases, such as Malawi, the official customary courts became in effect a state court system abused as a political tool throughout the one party era of Banda (Manda, 2012). In several countries, these frameworks were subsequently reviewed as a result of changing political circumstances, and in particular with the end of the Cold War and the wave of democratisation that took place throughout the continent, though this did not necessarily mean a turn towards more democratic processes of local governance (Englebert, 2002; Buur and Kyed, 2007). Independently from changes in the framework for legal pluralism, the prevalence of official and unofficial customary justice processes remained a common thread throughout Sub-Saharan Africa, as well as most states' lack of capacity to provide justice services to the majority of the population through the law institutions inherited from the former colonial powers (Penal Reform International, 2000).[6] As a matter of fact, official state justice remained chronically under-resourced and understaffed in most of the region until today, with decaying infrastructures and outdated legal frameworks (Piron, 2005). This has been exacerbated in those regions that went through violent conflict (Isser, 2011). This is particularly relevant from the viewpoint of human rights, as it means that the justice institutions of the state, which are supposed to be the primary agents in the protection and promotion of human rights, are not only far from the population in terms of physical distance and capacity, but also in terms of ownership. An Na'Im goes even further to explain that African societies tolerate the existence of the post-colonial state with profound mistrust and prefer to have little interaction with its institutions and processes (2003: 14).

---

6 In some cases, this includes Islamic courts and laws, which are often intertwined with 'local custom'.

2.2. LOCAL NORMATIVE ORDERS AND DISPUTE PROCESSING FORUMS

Despite considerable variation in the normative orders and justice mechanisms that can be found throughout Sub-Saharan Africa, a number of common features are often associated with 'an African approach' to justice. Different scholars emphasise that local justice processes in Sub-Saharan Africa are generally geared towards the negotiation or mediation of an agreement rather than being concerned with deciding who is right and wrong according to a priori defined impersonal rules that are applied in a derivative way, as it is normally the case within formal state justice (Allot, 1968; Holleman, 1974; Alliot, 1983, 1985; Le Roy, 1995, 2004). In these processes, rules, customary, religious or statutory, may be resorted to as 'resources' and even combined in the negotiation of a decision by a local forum, but they tend not to determine the outcome of a dispute (Oomen, 2005; Comaroff et al., 1981). Moreover, customs cannot be considered to diverge from statutory rules in terms of content only, for it is their nature that makes them different: they are oral and derive from the social practices that are locally observed constituting models of conduct and behaviour rather than rules in a strict sense (Bennett, 2004). Therefore, they are highly flexible and adaptive to new circumstances (Bennett, 2004). At the same time, these customs are very local, resulting in a rich variety of normative repertoires (Eberhard, 2001; Menski, 2006: 424–425).

In rural areas in particular, where social relations are based on past and future economic and social interdependence amongst community members, disputes are not handled in isolation from their overall context but tend to focus on the roots of the conflict beyond the particular incident that brought the parties to the forum (Penal Reform International, 2000). Conflicts can potentially create disorder affecting the community as a whole and are therefore not seen as involving the two parties only (Lubkemann et al., 2011). Consequently, dispute processing does not necessarily result in a consensual agreement between the parties, but rather in an outcome that is acceptable and backed by the community (Nader, 2001; Lubkemann et al., 2011). Next to the fact that the problem is viewed from the perspective of corporate rather than individual interests, which implies a high degree of public participation, the emphasis lies on reconciliation and the restoration of social order. This means that like cases are not necessarily treated alike (Penal Reform International, 2000). For example, the claims that individuals can make and the solutions that are sought depend on the status of the parties and of those who have a stake in the case at hand (Lubkemann et al., 2011). Power dynamics are therefore at the core of the disputing process (Oomen, 2005). Decisions often include restorative penalties, the enforcement of which relies on social pressure and sometimes physical violence (Lubkemann et al., 2011). No professional legal representation is provided and arbitrators are appointed from the community according to their status (Penal Reform International, 2000).

Some authors emphasise the link between this approach to justice, with its emphasis on mediation and models of behaviour, and the cosmologies that are at play in African societies (Alliot, 1983, 1985; John-Nambo, 2002; Le Roy, 1995, 2004; Okafor, 2006). The *Laboratoire d'Anthropologie Juridique de Paris* has developed this perspective in detail by showing how different founding myths are intimately related to our perceptions of reality and social practice, including our understanding of justice institutions, even in secular contexts (Alliot, 1983, 1985; Le Roy, 1995, 2004). In Africa, founding myths often rest on the idea that the world emerged from chaos (ibid). As such, it is the multiple, the unstable and the unorganised which constitute the foundation of the world (ibid). Therefore, the unity of society is not perceived as the result of obedience to a uniform and superior order embodied in impersonal rules and adjudication by a higher authority, as it is the case in the Judaeo-Christian tradition, but as the affirmation of complementarities and mutual interdependence (ibid). Since this order is always fragile,

> 'the ideal is not to let conflicts lead to an open confrontation. And if the latter cannot be avoided, a solution is sought, not so much by relying on previously fixed rules, but in conformity to what is perceived case by case as being in the interest of the group' (Alliot, 1985: 87 in Eberhard, 2001: 16).

The aim is thus to solve conflicts inside the group where they emerged, emphasising the responsibility of the group for its own future (Le Roy, 1995; Eberhard, 2001; John-Nambo, 2002).[7] In addition, justice processes in Africa often have a supernatural dimension (John-Nambo, 2002; Okafor, 2006) and the emergence of a conflict is often seen as a 'social disease' with different forces at play, where the behaviour of the living can have serious repercussions in the invisible world and vice-versa (John-Nambo, 2002; Okafor, 2006).

This is not to say that all these characteristics are 'essential' to local disputing processes in Africa. Different world views, life strategies and approaches to justice co-exist for a while in this region. Such interactions have often resulted in hybrid legal configurations (Santos, 2006). Moreover, the prevalence of violent conflicts in many parts of Africa poses several challenges to the operation of these institutions, such as breakdown of internal accountability mechanisms, mass displacement and population movements, returning refugees and changes in lifestyle (Isser, 2011). In addition, the prominence of these features may vary depending on the setting (e.g. rural vs. urban) and the type of forum (e.g. official vs. unofficial ones), amongst others. For example, in urban contexts, where social cohesion may be less intense than in rural ones, social pressure may not be as

---

7 According to John-Nambo (2002), this explains why it is not possible to ascertain or codify custom, as this would take away the responsibility to solve a conflict from the group where it emerged.

efficient in ensuring compliance with the decision of a local forum.[8] The kind of justice forums people resort to in urban as compared to rural contexts may differ too and official low courts may rely more often on official customary law than unofficial traditional authorities.[9] In other words, there exists considerable diversity in the justice processes that people encounter on their pathways to justice. This diversity can be found at various levels. On the one hand, multiple legal actors participate in disputing processes, e.g. courts created by the state to apply customary law, traditional authorities that administer justice officially or unofficially, religious leaders, gender group leaders, spirit mediums, legal NGOs, community policing councils, the police and in a minority of cases, formal state courts. These instances may compete or collaborate with each other so that local justice processes can be conceptualised as multi-layered and polycentric (Oomen, 2005). On the other hand, the modalities of dispute processing may also vary depending on the actors involved, ranging from adjudication or arbitration according to state or customary law by some forums to mediation by others.

This plurality in normative orders and forms of dispute processing has a number of consequences for the advancement of human rights. First of all, the polycentric nature of local justice processes entails that there are many sites where struggles with human rights implications may take place, ranging from official and easily identifiable forums, such as a chief's court, to more 'hidden' spaces, such as gender and age groups. Therefore, it is paramount to understand the relevance of all locally available justice actors and the extent to which their practices respect human rights. Secondly, the tendency towards mediating disputes rather than adjudicating them according to specific rules means that if the outcome of a dispute is at odds with human rights the problem may not reside exclusively at the level of the content of local norms since, as explained above, the role of norms is relative. In addition, customary norms are flexible and may adapt to changing circumstances, so in principle they cannot be regarded as being inherently at odds with human rights.[10] This is not to deny that norms play a role in the decision of an outcome and if local normative orders are in line with human rights, the chances that they can inspire a decision that respects human rights may be higher. However, it is necessary to look at other factors that may play a greater role. Nader (2001) has noted that mediation and negotiation require conditions of relative equal power in order to produce fair outcomes. If decisions are embedded socially within the community, power disparities between individual disputants may be mitigated by corporate interests but this may not always be the case, especially in urban contexts. Finally, if outcomes and their enforcement are strongly linked to some publicly backed understanding of social order, and this understanding leads to violations of human rights, changing the practices of justice providers so

[8] Chapter 6 shows this trend in the area of family law.

[9] This is the case for example in Sierra Leone. See Chapter 4.

[10] This might be less the case with religious norms, though their interpretation also provides quite a margin for adaptability.

that they respect and protect human rights also requires bringing about broader social changes so that such decisions are not totally out of tune with local notions of what is legitimate to enforce.

2.3. LOCAL LEGAL ORDERS AND HUMAN RIGHTS

When assessing the relationship between local legal orders and human rights, two distinct but interconnected issues need to be considered. On the one hand, the extent to which local practices and normative orders are in line with human rights. And on the other, the extent to which local dispute processing forums operate according to human rights norms, are responsive to human rights claims and take decisions that are in line with human rights. Both are interconnected since, as explained above, local dispute processing forums are generally embedded in local understandings of social order. This adds another dimension to such assessments, namely, the extent to which human rights are locally known and accepted.

In terms of how local practices and normative orders relate to human rights, it is well documented that several customs and certain interpretations of Islamic law in the area of family relations and access to resources infringe the rights of women and children (Howard, 1982; Armstrong et al., 1995; Butegwa, 2002; Nyamu-Musembi, 2002; Uchechukwu, 2002; Banda, 2005; Ssenyonjo, 2007; UN Women, UNICEF and UNDP, 2012). Most of these laws and customs derive from pre-colonial forms of social organisation, which despite being hierarchical, with entitlements depending on status, gender and age, did not necessarily imply patriarchal oppression (Ilumoka, 1994).[11] However, communal forms of support provided by the extended family and the clan have tended to erode due to new forms of social, political and economic structures (Ilumoka, 1994). In a context where there is a growing tendency toward urbanisation and nuclearisation of the family, the survival of customs that perpetuate gender inequality, but not of others, which emphasise men's responsibilities and reciprocal duties in the family, poses great challenges to women's wellbeing and, by implication, to those who depend on them (Armstrong et al., 1995).

Several customs in the area of family relations do not confer the same rights to men and women in marriage, divorce, succession and custody of children (Howard, 1982; Armstrong et al., 1995; Uchechukwu, 2002; Banda, 2005; Ssenyonjo, 2007; UN Women, UNICEF and UNDP, 2012). Bridewealth, i.e. the transfer of cattle or livestock and/or money by a prospective bridegroom or his family to the family of the woman whom he intends to marry, is a widespread

[11] Colonial administrators reinforced and 'froze' such practices by constructing a version of official customary law in which women were considered minors under the guardianship of a male (Armstrong et al., 1995).

practice throughout most patrilineal African societies and is generally considered one of the legal conditions for a valid customary marriage (Armstrong et al., 1995; Banda, 2005; UN Women, UNICEF and UNDP, 2012). Traditionally, bridewealth is given to the father of the bride, but there are cases in which single mothers receive it for their daughters, showing the flexible nature of customs (Banda 2005: 108). The practice binds together the two families and compensates for the transference of the woman's productive and reproductive capacities from her lineage to that of the husband.[12] In other words, it allows the husband and his family to acquire control over both the wife and her offspring (Armstrong et al., 1995). Many African women value this practice as it supposedly shows a man's commitment and acts as a guarantee that he will not abandon the marital home or he would lose his investment (Banda, 2005). However, bridewealth makes it difficult for women to choose with whom they want to marry since their custodians may easily give preference to the best offer. It also easily traps women in undesirable or violent marriages because the repayment of bridewealth is generally a requisite for granting a divorce (UN Women, UNICEF and UNDP, 2012). In addition, men often interpret that the payment of bridewealth gives them almost total power over their wives and children as they have 'paid' for them (Armstrong et al., 1995). In a context where the reproductive role of women is to produce children for her husband's lineage, it is easy for men to regard their wives as their 'sexual property' and demand sexual services against the will of the wife (Banda, 2005). This not only exposes women to sexual and psychological violence, but it also infringes their sexual and reproductive rights (Howard, 1982). The practice also contributes to child betrothal as girls are given in marriage in order to receive cattle or other property from the prospective husband, who may be a polygamist much older than the girl (Armstrong et al., 1995).

Local customs also tend to grant different rights to men and women in marriage.[13] For instance, the custom of polygyny violates the principle of gender equality because men can take more than one wife, while the same does not apply to women. Men can also resort to more substantive grounds for requesting a divorce. For example, women's 'barrenness', adultery or disobedience is often considered a legitimate reason when invoked by men but not when invoked by women (Howard, 1982; Banda, 2005). If a woman cannot bear children or dies prematurely without having borne a child, the wife's family may have to provide a 'substitute wife' in sororate marriage in order to avoid having to pay back the bridewealth; violating the rights of girls and women to free choice in marriage (Armstrong et al., 1995; Banda, 2005). In addition, it is most common that marital property and commonly acquired freehold land is registered on the name of men

12 In matrilineal societies, women continue to live within their own lineage and therefore bridewealth is not applicable.

13 This is also the case in Islamic law, which is often interpreted in conservative ways that deny women's rights, such as in many parts of Sudan, Kenya and Nigeria (Halim, 1994; Banda, 2005).

exclusively, because it is considered that marital property belongs to the husband, while men increasingly dispose of it as they see fit without the consent of their wives (Butegwa, 2002).

In patrilineal rural societies, the wife resides with the family of her husband and is allocated fields for cultivation and/or livestock in his ancestral lands. Therefore, upon divorce she is expected to return to her natal family, losing access to this land, animals and most of her possessions (Armstrong et al., 1995). Despite the fact that many current unions include marital property such as freehold land, houses and cars, which are acquired with the income generated by women, many men continue to expect that women will leave all this property behind (Armstrong et al., 1995). The assumption is that upon return to their homes, women will be cared for by their families, which is often not the case. In patrilineal societies, it was also customary that upon divorce the children would remain within the family of the man, who considered them an asset (Armstrong et al., 1995). However, this is no longer a clear-cut practice because children need to go to school and thus begin to represent a burden rather than a working force (Armstrong et al., 1995). Customarily, maintenance is linked to affiliation and custody, so many men refuse to pay maintenance for a child who is not living within his family (Armstrong et al., 1995; Banda, 2005). In some parts of Africa, the increasing number of single mothers is giving rise to significant changes in customary land allocation practices, so that women are now allocated residential sites, though this is often done in the name of a relative male (Claassens and Mnisi, 2009).

Similarly, local customs generally exclude women from inheritance rights. For example, it tends to forbid widows from inheriting her husband's property and it often concedes them no right to bury a husband (Armstrong et al., 1995; Uchechukwu, 2002; Banda, 2005). Widows are often in a difficult position, having to choose between returning to their natal group under harsh conditions, accepting a male relative of the husband in a levirate marriage, or residing with married children (Uchechukwu, 2002). Furthermore, a widow often faces expulsion by the husband's family, who grabs both the personal and jointly acquired property and leaves her (and often her children) totally destitute, while blaming her for killing the husband by means of witchcraft (Uchechukwu, 2002). In addition, in some parts of Africa widows are subjected to burial and mourning rituals, such as 'cleansing ceremonies' entailing sexual intercourse, confinement and restricted freedom of movement, which run against their dignity, right to health and sometimes life (Uchechukwu, 2002). Refusal to go through these rituals may have severe consequences, such as disinheriting the children (Armstrong et al., 1995). This is not the case of widowers, who can resume normal lives after the burial of the wife (Uchechukwu, 2002). In some parts of Africa, orphan children also find themselves in a vulnerable position as their custodians may want to take care of them in order to have access to their inheritance, while sending them to work rather than to school (Save the Children, 2007). Moreover, under customary laws, women frequently have fewer inheritance rights within their own family as compared to their male counterparts and succession to positions of authority also tends to exclude them (Armstrong et al., 1995). Family land usually goes to male children or the eldest son, who is expected to administer it in the benefit of all members of the family, though the latter is not certain, with many men disposing of inherited land and property for their own personal benefit (Butegwa, 2002).

Another problematic issue is that local customs allow or even encourage wife-beating and physical violence against children for disciplinary purposes, with only 'abusive' forms of aggression being condemned (Howard, 1982; Armstrong et al., 1995). Such violence is often exercised by those in a position of authority, such as a father or a husband in respect of a daughter or wife or the custodians of children (Armstrong et al., 1995). Also, a number of harmful traditional practices, such as female genital cutting, ritual scarification and puberty rites as well as female and child religious bondage are sustained by local customs in some parts of Africa despite their detrimental effects on the physical, psychological and emotional integrity of women and children (Howard, 1982; Banda, 2005).

Many of these practices are based on an ideology of male superiority that perpetuates the subordination of women. Men are given more value as they are supposed to take care of the wellbeing of the family, while female socialisation devalues their own interests in favour of those of men (Armstrong et al., 1995). Such discrimination begins early. For instance, girls are more likely to assume more tasks in the household or be sent to work, while boys remain at school due to the expectation that later on they will provide for the family (Armstrong et al., 1995). This means that women have heavier responsibilities in the household, inferior employment and income, inferior access to land and positions of authority and lower levels of health and education, which is not only problematic because it seriously curtails the human rights of women and those depending on them, but it also leads to the feminisation of poverty, constituting a great obstacle to sustainable development (Morrison et al., 2007).

At the same time, local normative orders may contain norms that provide a strong protection of socio-economic and cultural rights, and in particular subsistence rights, such as the right to food and water. For example, in Mhondoro, Zimbabwe, local norms protect livelihood rights, such as the right to drinking water, in ways that resonate with human rights and without any form of discrimination (Hellum, 2007).

In view of how local justice forums relate to human rights, it is necessary to consider substantive, procedural and structural aspects of their operation (UN Women, UNICEF and UNDP, 2012). Though it is impossible to present a picture of how all local justice providers in all of Sub-Saharan Africa operate, a number of issues have been identified as widespread amongst different local justice providers and in particular customary justice forums. In substantive terms, decisions are often inconsistent with human rights, either because they breach the rights of women and children by endorsing the discriminatory practices that were described above, or because they sanction cruel and inhuman forms of punishment (UN Women, UNICEF and UNDP, 2012). For example, amongst the Shona of Zimbabwe, the family of a murder victim can be compensated in 'blood' by receiving a woman, often a young girl, in marriage from the family of the perpetrator so that she will bear a child to replace the person who has been murdered (Banda, 2005: 121). In more traditional areas of Nigeria, the police have been reluctant to intervene to protect women victims of violence if the level of the alleged abuse did not exceed the customary norms of those areas (Ssenyonjo, 2007: 52). In Somalia, a woman who is raped is often forced to marry her attacker in order to protect her honour, ensure the payment of the bridewealth, and establish a bond between the clan of the man and the woman in order to prevent future violence (Wojkowska, 2006). Many local justice forums also hold individuals accountable on the basis of witchcraft (UN Women, UNICEF and UNDP, 2012). In some regions, such as central Mozambique, the supposed perpetrator is subjected to insults and severe physical violence from spirit mediums and their assistants (Jacobs, 2010). That said, there are also instances in which local forums and customs provide better protection of certain rights, such as access to land (Nyamu-Musembi, 2002). For example, in Kenya local clan authorities are more likely to recognise customary land tenure rights of women as compared to formal state courts, where formal titles are the only legal basis to protect these rights (Nyamu-Musembi, 2002), and in South Africa, women living on family land resist being evicted by male relatives by relying on their customary 'birthright' to belong, while formal laws offer them no protection (Claassens and Mnisi, 2009).

At the level of procedure, the operation of these forums is generally known to the parties. The right to be present at the hearing and present evidence and witnesses are normally respected (Penal Reform International, 2000). Moreover, these forums tend to operate in the local language, are available within walking distance and resolve many cases on the spot or within days (Wojkowska, 2006). However, amongst the problems associated with local justice forums are the non-observance of the principle of the presumption of innocence and that some of the methods that are used for extracting a confession are physically harmful, which jeopardises the right to a fair trial (Penal Reform International, 2000). For example, in Liberia trial by ordeal is a common practice in order to identify a guilty party, make a party confess the truth and 'get rid of the witch' (Isser et al., 2009). Some forms of this practice entail the ingestion of poison, the application of hot metal to the skin and the immersion of one's hand in a pot of boiling oil, while it is supposed that the supernatural power of the ritual will protect the innocent from harm (Isser et al., 2009). Many local justice procedures also tend to discriminate against women. For instance, in Sudan, Islamic religious courts give less worth to female witnesses (UN Women, UNICEF and UNDP, 2012) and in much of Sub-Saharan Africa, where customary law treats women as minors, women cannot stand in court but need to be represented by their male custodians (Howard, 1982). It is also problematic that women do not have the same possibilities to access local forums as men (Banda, 2005). For example, women may not dare present claims for fear of being rejected by their families or bringing shame to the family's honour (Banda, 2005). However, this may vary from local to local forum. In Malawi, for example, women prefer to bring their cases to village mediators rather than to the courts of the chiefs since the former offer them more confidentiality as compared with the public proceedings of the latter (UN Women, UNICEF and UNDP, 2012). Finally, local justice forums tend not to respect the right of children to meaningful participation in cases affecting their interests (UN Women, UNICEF and UNDP, 2012)

At the structural level, the lack of formal procedural and substantive rules in combination with the erosion of local accountability mechanisms often leads to abuses of power, arbitrariness and unpredictability of decisions and politicisation of local justice processes (Wojkowska, 2006). In addition, in most of Africa customary courts remain male-dominated so that men are in a privileged position to define what is custom (UN Women, UNICEF and UNDP, 2012). The same applies to religious forums and the interpretation of religious norms (UN Women, UNICEF and UNDP, 2012). Though more equal gender representation in local justice forums is not a guarantee that female justice providers will enjoy the same level of authority as their male counterparts or that female litigants will see their position improved, it is nevertheless desirable that they participate in the internal dynamics of shaping custom (Nyamu-Musembi, 2002).

Finally, there are a number of human rights concerns that arise out of the co-existence of various legal orders (ICHRP, 2009). For instance, the risk that the *non bis in idem* principle is violated where different legal orders compete with each other, barriers in access to justice that may arise out of powerful litigants exerting pressure to have a case heard in a forum that will favour them and lack of clarity over jurisdiction and the applicable law (ICHRP, 2009).

All these challenges take place in a context where, despite human rights being generally endorsed by formal legal orders, they are often not known at grassroots level or partially rejected. On the one hand, there is the problem of local knowledge of human rights, which tends to be low amongst justice seekers and many local justice providers (UN Women, UNICEF and UNDP, 2012). Nyamu-Musembi (2002: 138) explains that familiarity with rights plays a role in shaping interactions at a local level as well as the choices that people make in specific situations. She gives the example of Kenya, where women are disadvantaged by not being familiar with local institutions that were created to protect their rights in land (Nyamu-Musembi, 2002). In a similar vein, Banda (2005: 129, 174) describes how most rural women with unregistered customary law unions in Uganda do not consider themselves entitled to anything and therefore rarely advance claims on property, while many women in Sierra Leone believe that a husband has the right to beat his wife and that it is the duty of the wife to have intercourse with her husband whenever he demands it. On the other hand, even when human rights are locally known, this does not mean that they are all equally embraced. For instance, in much of Liberia and Namibia the term human rights has negative connotations (Isser et al., 2009; Mapaure, 2010). In Liberia, children's rights and the rights of criminals are generally considered as a threat to social order and waywardness among the youth (Isser et al., 2009), while in Namibia human rights are called 'monsters' (Mapaure, 2010). According to Ibhawoh (2000) and An Na'Im (2003) this is partly related to the fact that the development of human rights regimes in Africa has not often been grounded on cultural traditions while there is an urgent need to pursue this goal. Eventually, most of the human rights problems raised in this section, and certainly those related to gender, need to be seen in the context of evolving power relations. As the next chapter shows, it is also against this backdrop that challenges to the cultural legitimacy of human rights in Africa need to be evaluated and addressed.

3. JUSTICE SECTOR AND HUMAN RIGHTS AID IN SUB-SAHARAN AFRICA: THE EMERGENT ENGAGEMENT WITH LOCAL LEGAL ORDERS

Justice sector aid and human rights assistance are relatively new areas of intervention for international development actors in Sub-Saharan Africa (Piron, 2005). Nonetheless, this field has already experienced a number of important shifts affecting the way in which local legal orders have been approached (Bennett et al., 2013). Some of these shifts relate to general trends in international development aid while others relate specifically to the nature of international aid to the justice sector (Bennett et al., 2013).

In Sub-Saharan Africa, justice sector assistance started to gain momentum by the early nineties, with the wave of democratisation that followed the end of the Cold War. The fall of authoritarian regimes, the introduction of multiparty democracy and the adoption of international human rights instruments in much of the region coincided with the emergence of 'governance' as a new concept in aid policy. In this context, effective state institutions were regarded as essential for establishing a stable and predictable environment that would facilitate international investment. This led international development actors in the region to provide aid for strengthening state institutions, and in particular the capacity of the justice sector (Piron, 2005). Initially, these interventions followed what is generally called the 'rule of law orthodoxy', i.e. a top-down, state centred institutional approach (Golub, 2003). During this initial phase, international development actors provided support for courthouse construction and repair, purchase of furniture, computers, and other equipment and materials, drafting new laws and regulations, training judges, lawyers and other legal personnel, establishing management and administration systems for judiciaries, building up bar associations and international exchanges for judges, courts administrators and lawyers (Golub, 2003; Piron, 2005). During this same period, some bilateral agencies also started to provide support to civil society organisations to advance human rights as a late response to Apartheid in South Africa and the increased political repression in Rwanda in the years that preceded the genocide (Piron, 2005). The idea that human rights would not be realised automatically as a result of economic development but had to be pursued as independent goals started to take root during this period as well (Trubek, 2003). At the same time, justice sector assistance to the region began to increase due to the prevalence of violent conflicts and the need for post-conflict justice sector reform (Piron, 2005). During this period international development actors showed little interest in local legal orders, which were rather considered an obstacle to development and human rights that would disappear by itself with the reinforcement of state justice (Corradi and Schotsmans, 2012).

About a decade later, the field of development assistance went through an important paradigm shift. On the one hand, the adoption of the Millennium Declaration and the Millennium Development Goals made poverty reduction the official objective of international cooperation. On the other hand, important changes took place in relation to how official aid was to be provided in order to improve its effectiveness. The Paris Declaration (2005) and the Accra Agenda for Action (2008) set out the principles of this new consensus that commits donors to harmonising their efforts, aligning their support to the strategies and policies of partner countries and managing aid for results and mutual accountability, while partner countries are expected to exercise leadership and coordinate support, thus enhancing ownership of development aid. These two developments had different repercussions on justice sector aid and human rights assistance in Africa, and in particular on how local legal orders were approached in relation to human rights. The poverty reduction paradigm led to a reflection on how justice sector aid contributed to alleviate poverty and as a result some donors felt compelled to adapt their approach to assisting this sector and be more responsive to local realities (Piron, 2006). For example, the World Bank went to emphasise that criminal law and justice programmes were necessary for improving the lives of the poor, who were disproportionately affected by high levels of crime and insecurity (World Bank, 2003). This resulted in an increased concern with enhancing access to justice and promoting human rights at local level by means of support to civil society organisations to provide legal aid services and legal education campaigns.[14] In Africa, different international development actors also realised that state justice was not available to the majority of the population who rather resorted to a variety of local forms of justice. Bearing in mind that building justice institutions is a complex and lengthy task, particularly in post-conflict situations, international agencies started to consider how local legal orders could contribute to improving access to justice.[15]

[14] See for example DFID, 2000 and UNDP, 2003.

[15] See for example, DFID, 2004; UNDP, 2005 and DANIDA, 2010.

In many cases these actors came to the conclusion that it was necessary to reinforce the relationship between local justice processes and human rights. For example, the World Bank launched a specific research and development programme called 'Justice for the Poor' that focuses on grassroots governance and justice institutions in Kenya and Sierra Leone. The main objectives of this programme are to understand how justice works at the local level, and to inform and support pro-poor programme design and implementation in the domain of justice reform.[16] Amongst the rationales found within this programme for engagement with local justice frameworks are the following two arguments: on the one hand, the fact that these frameworks form a fundamental aspect of a community's identity and belief system, and on the other, the need to act on discriminatory practices they may perpetuate.[17] In a similar vein, UNDP expresses the view that local justice can 'fill in the gap' or 'compensate' for the state's inability or unwillingness to provide justice (UNDP, 2005: 101). As regards possible areas of tension between local justice and human rights, UNDP suggest that interventions should promote the positive features of these justice frameworks and reform the negative ones (UNDP, 2005). In South Sudan for instance, this organisation provides support for training traditional leaders on human rights so that they incorporate these standards into traditional dispute resolution mechanisms.[18] The German Federal Ministry for Economic Cooperation and Development also states that in cases where local norms contradict international human rights, it is necessary to develop strategies to alter those values and facilitate the implementation of statutory or customary law in compliance with human rights and the national constitution (GMECD, 2002). In line with this, the German International Cooperation agency has supported a number of projects in Ghana and Ethiopia that discussed how local customs related to women's rights (Weilenmann, 2007). DFID also identifies a range of activities that donors can support in order to address non-state justice institutions' non compliance with human rights, such as facilitating the development of state policy and legislation requiring non-state justice to comply with constitutional provisions, funding trainings for traditional authorities, establishing alternative forums to which cases can be appealed and modifying non-state norms so that they become more responsive to the needs of disadvantaged groups (DFID, 2004). Finally, the Ministry of Foreign Affairs of Denmark also recognises the role of informal justice in promoting access to justice and recommends engagement with these frameworks as an integrated part of support to justice sector reform. In this context, the Ministry deems of particular importance to assess the likelihood that these interventions lead to gradual adherence to human rights in areas such

16 http://web.worldbank.org/WBSITE/EXTERNAL/TOPICS/EXTLAWJUSTICE/EXTJUSFORPOOR/0,,menuPK:3282947~pagePK:149018~piPK:149093~theSitePK:3282787,00.html.

17 Ibid.

18 http://www.ss.undp.org/content/south_sudan/en/home/operations/projects/democratic_governance/access_to_justice.html.

as accountability, non-discrimination, equality in procedures and outcomes, impartiality of decisions and respect for the physical integrity of justice users (DANIDA, 2010).

Conversely, the evolutions in the area of aid effectiveness brought about new aid modalities that reinforced state centred assistance, such as direct budget support and 'sector-wide approaches', where partner countries define a national poverty reduction strategy and sector policies that embody the government's priorities. In many cases, national policies in the justice sector focus on reinforcing formal state justice and tend to neglect local legal orders and their impact on human rights. As it will be shown in Part III of this book, these two contradictory trends seem to constrain the way in which justice sector aid addresses the promotion of human rights within local legal orders.

4. CONCLUSION

International actors providing justice sector and human rights aid in Sub-Saharan Africa are confronted with several considerable challenges. In the first place, they face a context of legal pluralism, where state justice is not dominant. At the same time, state justice has historically benefited from a privileged epistemological position. However, given the characteristics of the justice landscapes in Sub-Saharan Africa, it is problematic to assume that state courts and laws can provide justice services and advance human rights on their own, or that they are per se in a better position to do so as compared to other locally available legal orders. Secondly, local legal orders differ in many ways from the justice institutions that most international and domestic development actors are familiar with. Customary justice institutions, which are prominent in the region, are neither backward vestiges from the past nor idyllic and harmonious. Colonial and post-colonial dynamics shaped them in important ways. On the one hand, these dynamics often led to a gap between the official customary law institutions recognised by the state and the unofficial local legal orders that are the living reality at grassroots level. On the other hand, they tended to erode customary checks and balances and undermine the downward accountability of traditional authorities. In addition, local legal orders are multi-layered and polycentric, including a wide array of actors and dispute processing mechanisms. While various local customs and legal practices contravene human rights in important ways, these legal orders also contain elements that protect human rights or that may allow their protection. Moreover, they are dynamic and adaptive to new circumstances and demands. However, human rights are not always known or accepted by local populations.

International development actors start to grapple with these realities in a context that presents contradictory dynamics. The shift towards poverty reduction means that they are more prone to engage with local realities, including local legal orders, and support the implementation of human rights at this level, whereas new aid modalities centre development assistance around state institutions. As it will be shown by Chapters 11 to 15, these two contradictory trends seem to have an effect on how international and domestic development actors address legal pluralism and the promotion of human rights within local legal orders. But before turning to the empirical findings, the next chapter discusses how important insights generated by the socio-legal scholarship on legal pluralism and human rights relate to the practice of development actors in the justice sector.

BIBLIOGRAPHY

Alliot, M. (1983) Anthropologie et Juristique. Sur les Conditions de l'Elaboration d'une Science du Droit, *Bulletin de Liaison du LAJP,* 6, 83–117.

Alliot, M. (1985) La Coutume dans les Droits Originellement Africains, *Bulletin de Liaison du LAJP,* 7–8, 79–100.

Allot, A. (1968) African Law. In Derret, J.D. *An Introduction to Legal Systems,* 131–156. London: Sweet & Maxwell.

An Na'Im, A. (ed.) (2003) *Human Rights Under African Constitutions, Realizing the Promise for Ourselves.* Philadelphia: University of Pennsylvania Press.

Armstrong, A., Chuulu, M., Himonga, C., Letuka, P., Mokobi, K., Ncube, W., Nhlapo, T., Rwezaura, B. and Vilakazi, P. (1995) Towards a Cultural Understanding of the Interplay between Children's and Women's Rights: An Eastern and Southern African Perspective, *The International Journal of Children's Rights,* 3, 333–368.

Banda, F. (2005) *Women, Law and Human Rights: An African Perspective.* Oxford/ Portland, OR: Hart Publishing.

Bennett, T. (2004) *Customary Law in South Africa.* Cape Town: Juta.

Bennett, T., Brems, E., Corradi, G., Nijzink, L. and Schotsmans, M. (2013) *Internationale Actoren en Traditioneel Recht in Sub-Sahara Afrika. Beleid en Interventions op het Vlak van Transitional Justice en Ontwikkelingshulp aan de Justitiesector.* Ghent: Academia Press.

Bergling, P. (2006) *Rule of Law on the International Agenda: International Support to Legal and Judicial Reform in International Administration, Transition and Development Cooperation.* Antwerp: Intersentia.

Butegwa, F. (2002) Mediating Culture and Human Rights in Favour of Land Rights for Women in Africa: A Framework for Community Level Action. In An-Na'im, A. (ed.) *Cultural Transformation and Human Rights in Africa.* London: Zed Books.

Buur, L. and Kyed, H.M. (2007) Introduction: Traditional Authority and Democratization in Africa. In Buur, L. and Kyed, H.M. (eds.) *State Recognition and Democratization in Sub-Saharan Africa.* New York: Palgrave MacMillan.

Chanock, M. (1998) *Law, Custom and Social Order. The Colonial Experience in Malawi and Zambia.* Portsmouth: Heinemann.

Claassens, A. and Mnisi, S. (2009) Rural Women Redefining Land Rights in the Context of Living Customary Law, *South African Journal of Human Rights*, 25, 491–516.

Comaroff, J. and Roberts, S. (1981) *Rule and Processes. The Cultural Logic of Dispute in an African Context*. Chicago: University of Chicago Press.

Corradi, G. and Schotsmans, M. (2012) Introduction. In Bennett, T., Brems, E., Corradi, G., Nijzink, L. and Schotsmans, M. (eds.) *African Perspectives on Tradition and Justice*. Antwerp: Intersentia.

Daannaa, H.S. (1994) The Acephalous Society and the Indirect Rule System in Africa. British Colonial Administrative Policy in Retrospect, *Journal of Legal Pluralism*, 34, 61–85.

DANIDA International Development Cooperation (2010) How To Note. Informal Justice Systems [online] http://www.danidadevforum.um.dk/NR/rdonlyres/FE725502-ACF5-42C2-B677-C0D411AE2660/0/InformalJusticeSystemsfinalprint.pdf (30/03/2012).

DIFD – UK Department for International Development (2000) Justice and Poverty Reduction [online] http://www.gsdrc.org/docs/open/SSAJ35.pdf (05/07/2012).

DFID – UK Department for International Development (2004) Non-State Justice and Security Systems [online] http://www.gsdrc.org/docs/open/SSAJ101.pdf (30/03/2012).

Englebert, P. (2002) Patterns and Theories of Traditional Resurgence in Tropical Africa, *Mondes en Développement*, 30, 118–151.

German Federal Ministry for Economic Cooperation and Development (2002) Paper 405, Division of Development Education and Information.

Golub, S. (2003) *Beyond Rule of Law Orthodoxy, The Legal Empowerment Alternative*. Rule of Law Series Carnegie Endowment for International Peace 41, 1–46.

Halim, A.M.A. (1994) Challenges to the Application of International Women's Rights in the Sudan. In Cook, R. (ed.) *Human Rights of Women. National and International Perspectives*. Philadelphia: University of Pennsylvania Press.

Holleman, J.F. (1974) *Issues in African Law*. The Hague/Paris: Mouton.

Howard, R. (1982) Human Rights and Personal Law: Women in Sub-Saharan Africa, *Journal of Africanist Opinion*, 12(1/2):, 45–52.

Ibhawoh, B. (2000) Between Culture and Constitution: Evaluating the Cultural Legitimacy of Human Rights in the African State, *Human Rights Quarterly*, 22(3), 838–860.

Idowu, W. (2006) African Jurisprudence and the Reconciliation Theory of Law, *Cambrian Law Review*, 37, 1–16.

Ilumoka, A. (1994) African Women's Economic, Social, and Cultural Rights – Toward a Relevant Theory and Practice. In Cook, R. (ed.) *Human Rights of Women. National and International Perspectives*. Philadelphia: University of Pennsylvania Press.

ICHRP – International Council on Human Rights Policy (2009) *When Legal Worlds Overlap: Human Rights, State and Non-State Law*. Versoix: International Council on Human Rights Policy.

Isser, D., Lubkemann, S. and N'Tow, S. (2009) *Looking for Justice. Liberian Experiences with and Perceptions of Local Justice Options.* Washington, DC: United States Institute of Peace Press.

Jacobs, C. (2010) *Plurality of Religion, Plurality of Justice. Exploring the Role of Religion in Disputing Processes in Gorongosa, Central Mozambique.* PhD Thesis, Wageningen University, the Netherlands.

John-Nambo, J. (2002) Quelques heritages de la justice colonial en Afrique noire, *Droit et Société*, 51/52, 325–344.

Le Roy, É. (1995) L'Accés à l'Universalisme par le Dialogue Interculturel, *Revue Générale de Droit*, 26, 5–26.

Le Roy, É. (2004) *Les Africains et l'Instituition de la Justice. Entre Mimetismes et Métissages.* Paris: Dalloz.

Lubkemann, S., Kyed, H.M. and Garvey, J. (2011) Dilemmas of Articulation in Mozambique: Customary Justice in Transition. In Isser, D. (ed.) *Customary Justice and the Rule of Law in War-Torn Societies.* Washington, DC: United States Institute of Peace Press.

Mamdani, M. (1996) *Citizen and Subject. Contemporary Africa and the Legacy of Late Colonialism.* Princeton: Princeton University Press.

Manda, K.T. (2012) Courts and the Application of Customary Law in Malawi: Towards the Reintroduction of Local Courts. In Bennett, T., Brems, E., Corradi, G., Nijzink, L. and Schotsmans, M. (eds.) *African Perspectives on Tradition and Justice.* Antwerp: Intersentia.

Mann, K. and Roberts, R. (1991) Law in Colonial Africa. In Mann, K. and Roberts, R. (eds.) *Law in Colonial Africa.* Portsmouth: Heinemann.

Mapaure, C. (2010) Accused and Cherished: Traditional and Informal Systems as Seen by International Organisations. In Hinz, M.O. and Mapaure, C. (eds.) *In Search of Justice and Peace. Traditional and Informal Justice Systems in Africa.* Windhoek: Namibia Scientific Society.

Menski, W. (2006) *Comparative Law in a Global Context. The Legal Systems of Asia and Africa.* New York: Cambridge University Press.

Morrison, A. and Dhushyanth, R. (2007) *Gender Equality, Poverty and Economic Growth.* Policy Research Working Paper No. 4349, Washington: The World Bank.

Nader, L. (2001) The Underside of Conflict Management in Africa and Elsewhere, *IDS Bulletin*, 32(1), 19–27.

Nyamu-Musembi, C. (2002) Are Local Norms and Practices Fences or Pathways? The Example of Women's Property Rights. In An-Na'im, A. (ed.) *Cultural Transformation and Human Rights in Africa.* London: Zed Books.

Okafor, F. (2006) From Praxis to Theory: a Discourse on the Philosophy of African Law, *Cambrian Law Review*, 37, 37–48.

Oomen, B. (2005) *Chiefs in South Africa. Law, Power and Culture in the Post-Apartheid Era.* New York: Palgrave.

Penal Reform International (2000) *Access to Justice in Sub-Saharan Africa, the role of traditional and informal justice systems.* London: Penal Reform International.

Piron, L.-H. (2005) Donor assistance to justice sector reform in Africa: living up to the new agenda? In Open Society Justice Initiative (ed.) *Human Rights and Justice Sector Reform in Africa: Contemporary Issues and Responses*, Governance and Social Development Resource Centre.

Piron, L.-H. (2006) Time to Learn, Time to Act in Africa. In Carothers, T. (ed.) *Promoting the Rule of Law Abroad: In Search of Knowledge*. Washington, DC: Carnegie Endowment for International Peace.

Ranger, T. (1983) The Invention of Tradition in Colonial Africa. In Hobsbawm, E. and Ranger, T. (eds.) *The Invention of Tradition*. Cambridge: Cambridge University Press.

Santos, B. (2006) The Heterogeneous State and Legal Pluralism in Mozambique, *Law and Society Review*, 40(1), 39–76.

Save the Children (2007) *Denied Our Rights: Children, Women and Inheritance in Mozambique* [online] http://www.savethechildren.org.uk/en/docs/denied-our-rights.pdf (27/07/2010).

Snyder, F. (1981) Colonialism and Legal Form: The Creation of 'Customary Law' in Senegal, *Journal of Legal Pluralism*, 19, 49–90.

Ssenyonjo, M. (2007) Culture and the Human Rights of Women in Africa: Between Light and Shadow, *Journal of African Law*, 51(1), 39–67.

Thorne, K. (2005) Rule of Law through Imperfect Bodies? The Informal Justice Systems of Burundi and Somalia [online] www.hdcentre.org (04/07/2012).

Trubek, D. (2003) The 'Rule of Law' in Development Assistance: Past, Present, and Future [online] http://www.law.wisc.edu/facstaff/trubek/RuleofLaw.pdf (accessed 05/07/2012).

Uchechukwu, E. (2002) Post-Colonialism, Gender, Customary Injustice: Widows in African Societies, *Human Rights Quarterly*, 24(2), 424–486.

UNDP – United Nations Development Programme (2003) Poverty Reduction and Human Rights: A Practice Note [online] http://www.undp.org. (05/07/2012).

UNDP – United Nations Development Programme (2005) Programming for Justice: Access for All [online] http://regionalcentrebangkok.undp.or.th/practices/governance/a2j/tools/index1.html (30/03/2012).

UN Women, UNICEF and UNDP (2012) Informal Justice Systems. Charting a Course for Human Rights Based Engagement [online] http://www.undp.org/content/dam/undp/library/Democratic%20Governance/Access%20to%20Justice%20and%20Rule%20of%20Law/Informal-Justice-Systems-Charting-a-Course-for-Human-Rights-Based-Engagement.pdf (15/10/2012).

Weilenmann, M. (2007) Legal Pluralism: A New Challenge for Development Agencies. In Penal Reform International and Bluhm Legal Clinic of the Northwestern University School of Law (eds.) *Access to Justice in Africa and Beyond: Making the Rule of Law a Reality* [online] http://www.penalreform.org/files/rep-2007-access-africa-and-beyond-en.pdf (06/07/2012).

Wojkowska, E. (2006) *Doing Justice: How Informal Justice Systems Can Contribute.* United Nations Development Programme. Oslo Governance Centre [online]

http://www.democraciaejustica.org/cienciapolitica3/sites/default/files/doingjusticeewawojkowska130307.pdf (30/03/2012).
WORLD BANK (2003) *Legal and Judicial Reform: Strategic Directions*. Washington, DC: The World Bank.

CHAPTER 10

LINKING SOCIO-LEGAL THEORY AND JUSTICE SECTOR AID

Giselle CORRADI

1. INTRODUCTION

As explained in the previous chapter, international actors providing justice sector and human rights aid in Africa encounter specific challenges, such as a context of legal pluralism, where state justice is generally weak or distrusted, and of cultural diversity and contextual specificity, with human rights not necessarily being known or considered legitimate by all. This chapter analyses how important insights generated by the socio-legal scholarship on these two challenges relate to the practice of legal development actors and can feed into it. The first part of the chapter examines the main discussions in the field of legal pluralism and the second one in that of human rights' universality and cross-contextual application. At the same time, this chapter lays the foundations for the analysis presented in Chapter 15.

2. LEGAL PLURALISM AND JUSTICE SECTOR AID

While there are numerous definitions of legal pluralism, Woodman's characterisation of this phenomenon from a 'top-down' as well as from a 'bottom-up' perspective is particularly useful for the purposes of the present analysis. According to him:

> 'Legal pluralism in general may be defined as the state of affairs in which a category of social relations is within the fields of operation of two or more bodies of legal norms. Alternatively, if it is viewed not from above in the process of mapping the legal universe but rather from the perspective of the individual subject of law, legal pluralism may be said to exist whenever a person is subject to more than one body of law' (Woodman, 1996: 157).

The advantage of this double outlook is that it makes it possible to examine the relationship between legal plurality and human rights assistance from two complementary perspectives. From a structural point of view, it is possible to analyse how legal pluralism affects individual and collective actors' possibilities to claim their human rights and how interventions may impinge on these structures while they are affected by them. From an agency standpoint, it is possible to examine how interventions can build on local actors' individual and collective strategies in navigating plural legal orders, including the use of 'resources' that may become available or disappear as a result of interventions.

It is also necessary to make a distinction between two aspects of this phenomenon, i.e. 'normative pluralism' and 'pluralism in forums of dispute resolution' (Le Roy, 2004: 260). The former refers to pluralism as it is manifested at the level of norms, rules and values that inform daily life and that might be mobilised in conflictive situations, whereas the latter consist of the multiplicity of legal actors, institutions and processes that might be involved in different forms of dispute processing. The remainder of this section analyses how key insights generated within discussions on legal pluralism are relevant for development actors seeking to advance human rights within local legal orders in Sub-Saharan Africa.

2.1. LOOKING BEYOND STATE JUSTICE

The concept 'legal pluralism' departs from the observation that individual and social behaviour are regulated by more than one normative order (Vanderlinden, 1971, 1989; Moore, 1973; Galanter, 1981; Griffiths, 1986). This results from the fact that human activity takes place in a multitude of social fields (Moore, 1973) or social networks (Vanderlinden, 1989), each of which generates and coerces its own rules. As a result, individuals are subject to as many regulatory orders as social networks they participate in (Vanderlinden, 1989). The concept shows that, from an empirical point of view, it is inadequate to regard the state as the sole source of normative ordering. Such a position would amount to an 'ideology of legal centralism' since regardless of whether or not a state recognises different bodies of law as official (e.g. statutory, religious or customary), a multitude of regulatory orders coexist de facto in all societies (Griffiths, 1986). In addition, a distinction is made between 'weak' or 'state' legal pluralism and 'strong' or 'deep' legal pluralism (Griffiths, 1986; Woodman, 1996). The former follows a normative standpoint by considering the state as the source of legal plurality and it examines how different bodies of law, e.g. religious or customary, may be accommodated within the state institutional framework. The latter is concerned with an empirical reality, namely how different sources of normative authority coexist de facto in a given society, independently from whether a state gives them official recognition.

What is relevant to the present discussion is the acknowledgement that justice sector and human rights aid always operates in a context of legal pluralism, regardless of whether a state officially endorses more than one legal order. This means that different kinds of interventions might be set up in response to these different aspects of legal pluralism. While 'weak' or 'state' legal pluralism raises questions related to the coordination of different bodies of laws within the state institutional framework (e.g. how linking statutory and customary justice may enhance the protection of human rights), 'strong' or 'deep' legal pluralism confronts development practitioners with the issue of the relative capacity of the state to effectively influence and regulate the conduct of its citizens as compared to other sources of authority, such as chiefs and traditional leaders, who may actually exert more influence at local level. At the same time, it means that it is necessary to consider both aspects of this phenomenon for they complement each other. On the one hand, it is necessary to examine who is actually involved in local justice processes and how these actors stand towards human rights, and on the other, what the official status of these actors is and how the latter affects the protection of human rights.

2.2. CONSIDERING HOW LEGAL ORDERS INTERSECT EACH OTHER

This bring us to another central tenet of legal pluralism, namely the fact that normative orders, including state laws and institutions, do not operate in isolation but intersect and interpenetrate each other. In other words, they are semi-autonomous, i.e. each social field generates and coerces its own rules but these fields operate in a dialectic and mutually constitutive manner (Merry, 1988). As explained by Merry:

> 'state law penetrates and restructures other normative orders through symbols and through direct coercion and, at the same time, ... non-state normative orders resist and circumvent penetration or even capture and use the symbolic capital of state law' (Merry, 1988: 881).

The fact that normative orders exist in relation to each other has different implications. In the first place, it precludes any sharp divide between 'customary' and 'modern' legal orders. Secondly, it implies that these interactions affect the way people get access to justice and human rights (Forsyth, 2009: 36–37). By considering the interaction between state and local justice providers, interventions can attempt at promoting supportive rather than competitive relations between different legal actors. On the contrary, totally ignoring the relative position of state justice providers in a legally plural context could at best result in missing an opportunity to engage in meaningful interaction with local actors and at worst generate unexpected resistance or even the rejection of state justice institutions. This is relevant in the context of intervention that aim at improving local access to justice by building state courts at lower administrative levels or by supporting 'mobile courts'. Such interventions can enhance their legitimacy by sensitising state court judges about legal pluralism and local legal orders and by promoting dialogue between them and local legal actors.

At another level, this insight reveals that the social space between the legislator and the legal subject cannot be conceived of as a 'normative vacuum' for state laws necessarily 'travel' through a social medium that is full of non-state normative activity (Griffiths, 1986: 34). By implication, it is the interaction between state law and other forms of normative ordering that gives shape to the law as people experience it on the ground and which determines how conduct is regulated in practice (Moore, 1973; Griffiths, 1986). From this standpoint, it is possible to reconsider the role of legal reform in generating social changes. While state laws may enjoy significant symbolic power, they do not have the monopoly of social control. Therefore, it becomes necessary to assess how these laws are likely to interact with other normative orders and local practices.[1] The other side of this coin is to view the semi-autonomous nature of legal orders as the result of an inter-subjective process. Since the life of most individuals and social groups takes place at the intersection of legal orders, the latter are combined and mixed giving rise to a phenomenon called 'inter-legality' (Santos, 2002: 437). According to Santos (2002: 437), as different legal spaces interact, intersect each other and are superimposed in our lives, a mixture and interpenetration of elements from different legal orders arises both in our minds and in our actions. Consequently, social practice is a constant bridging between legal orders (Santos, 2002: 437).

Understanding the legal experiences of justice seekers from this perspective can provide a more solid basis for programming in certain areas, such as legal education and human rights awareness raising (Tsanga, 2007). Instead of assuming that access to justice and human rights is mainly constrained by a lack of knowledge so that the dissemination of state laws will 'enlighten' local actors, practitioners need to understand that these interventions rather provide a new layer of normativity that may compete with or enrich other locally existing normative repertoires. As pointed out by Tsanga (2007: 438), 'the lack of familiarity with the state system … does not mean that people are not familiar with any justice system at all.' Therefore, legal education should go beyond state laws and engage the wider context where national legislation is supposed to operate within (Tsanga, 2007).

[1] See Griffith (2003) for a critique to instrumentalist approaches to legislation and a sociological theory of how and under which circumstances legislation is likely to influence social behaviour.

2.3. ASSESSING THE LEGAL NATURE OF NORMATIVE ORDERS AND THE DISTINCTIVENESS OF STATE LAW

So far, the terms 'normative', 'regulatory' and 'legal' have been used interchangeably. However, a series of debates can be found in the academic literature about 'the question of the distinctiveness of state law' and 'the question of the distinction between non-state law and social order generally' (Woodman, 1998).[2] The first discussion revolves around the issue of whether a difference should be made between state law and other forms of normative ordering, whereas the second one focuses on how to determine when a normative order is also 'legal'.[3] Up until today, no ultimate answers have been provided to these questions. Nevertheless, there is an increasing recognition of the importance of analysing these topics in concrete contexts, while considering who is asking the question and for which purposes (Forsyth, 2009; Twinning, 2003; Von Benda-Beckman, 2002; Merry, 1988).

There are several reasons why these debates are relevant to justice sector and human rights aid in Sub-Saharan Africa. In the first place, there is the question of whether interventions should privilege state law and justice above other sources and processes of social ordering. While there is no evidence that the state offers a superior form of justice than other legal orders, it is not difficult to imagine why the development of state capacity to deliver justice services and respect and protect human rights is seen as crucial within justice sector aid. On the one hand, there is the empirical reality that state law has considerable coercive and symbolic power (Merry, 1988). On the other hand, it is the state that will eventually provide an overarching framework when conflicts between different legal orders arise. Moreover, in the current global architecture, states are the primary actors who are expected to organise and provide justice services, including the protection and promotion of human rights. However, from a legally plural point of view, even when 'state building' is the main objective of interventions, and by implication it is the capacity of the state to respect, protect and fulfil human rights that is privileged, such efforts need to take account of other relevant legal forces that are present in the social space for they will anyway influence the way the state is able to operate. As was shown in Chapter 2, this is particularly relevant in the Sub-Saharan region where state justice coexists to a great extent with other legal orders. Moreover, this issue confronts us with the question of who gets to define the forms of justice that are embraced by a state and how human rights are interpreted within them.

---

2 See also Tamanaha, 1993, 2000; Von Benda-Beckman, 2002.

3 Ultimately, these debates revolve around the question of what is law. The fact that there is so far no satisfactory answer to this question has led some scholars to dismiss the concept of legal pluralism (Tamanaha, 1993), whereas other doubt the usefulness of the question itself (Merry, 1988; Woodman, 1998; Santos, 2002).

As regards the second discussion, if interventions engage with legal plurality, those normative orders and actors that get the label of 'law' or 'legal' might have more chances of being considered for programming purposes than those that are merely viewed as informal or diffuse forms of social control. Differently put, these issues relate to the question of what normative orders and justice providers should justice sector aid consider for programming next to state justice, which ones not, and why. In this sense, it could be argued that no single form of ordering should be excluded a priori, since it is their actual role in relation to the provision of justice that should determine their inclusion or not. As a result, the question of whether a certain normative order constitutes or not a form of 'law' becomes irrelevant, and it could even be counterproductive if interventions fail to identify actors and processes that are crucial to advancing access to justice and human rights just because they do not present typically 'legal' characteristics.[4] As regards assistance to local legal orders, it is not necessarily those structures that are most visible, formally defined or even officially recognised that are the only or the most important ones at grassroots level. As the next point illustrates in more depth, it is necessary to depart from an analysis that is grounded on the experiences of those who navigate plural legal orders.

2.4. UNDERSTANDING LEGAL ORDERS AS RESOURCES

One crucial insight generated by the socio-legal scholarship is that law functions as a resource that can be mobilised for reproducing or contesting power relations and negotiating social realities (Starr et al., 1989; Lazarus-Black et al., 1994; Oomen, 2005). In addition, a distinction is made between two sides of a continuum where power struggles can manifest themselves, i.e. hegemony and ideology (Lazarus-Black et al., 1994: 6). The former refers to a form of power that naturalises 'the way things are', while it tends to sustain the interests of dominant groups. The latter refers to the oppositional practices that resist and question this order, making it unstable and dynamic. Legal orders, state or customary, can therefore both enable or constrain hegemonic and oppositional discourses and practices (Nyamu-Musembi, 2005; Lazarus-Black et al., 1994; Starr et al., 1989). In other words, even if local legal orders tend to operate in ways that are at odds with human rights, the contestation of such practices need not necessarily be found in state law but can come from within.

Moreover, in legally plural contexts, legal orders can be either selectively invoked or ignored both by users and by providers depending on how they are expected to serve the purposes of the actors concerned. On the one

[4] For example, interventions in the area of women's rights show that the family, the religious sphere, and other spaces that do not necessarily show typically 'legal' characteristics are of utmost importance in the regulation of gendered relations.

hand, individuals and collective actors can attempt to navigate these orders strategically in pursuing certain interests, a phenomenon that has been termed 'forum shopping' (Von Benda-Beckman, 1981). Furthermore, norms can be borrowed from different frameworks as resources in the negotiation of certain interpretations of the law (Oomen, 2005). This means that it is important to make human rights norms and forums that protect them available and known at local level so that they can be resorted to as a 'resource' in local negotiations.

On the other hand, the term 'shopping forums' has been coined to describe situations where forums compete for disputes, which they use to advance their own political ends (Von Benda Beckman, 1981). As highlighted by Kyed (2009), the distribution of power deriving from the administration of justice is a contentious and politically sensitive field at several levels: legal actors compete for authority and income deriving from the provision of justice, political party interests are pursued by supporting and forming alliances with strategic local actors, and tensions around the hierarchy of state and non-state authority can emerge. This is important at the level of interventions that modify the official status of a local legal order. Since all legal orders, state or customary, can both serve hegemonic and oppositional practices, it is necessary to examine empirically whose interests are served by modifying the official status of a certain legal order and how this is likely to affect access to justice and human rights (ICHRP, 2009: 84).

2.5. HOW 'THE LEGAL' IS DEFINED

By way of introducing the next section, an important question to consider is whether the ontological and epistemological categories of meaning that define 'legal orders' within justice sector aid are of cross-cultural application. From this perspective, 'law' might be just one of the many possible ways whereby societies put their reproduction into form (Eberhard, 2001: 174). Consequently, one of the central concerns of cross cultural approaches to law is avoiding that the own experience of 'the legal' is taken as the universal point of reference against which other traditions are measured and (mis)understood (Vachon, 1990; Eberhard, 2001). By breaking away from a conception of legal pluralism in terms of 'different versions of a same phenomenon', where this 'same phenomenon' is implicitly constructed by reference to the own experience, a pluralist conception of legal pluralism gives up the idea of unity and introduces the need for an intercultural and dialogical approach (Vachon, 1990; Eberhard, 2001). The analysis then moves towards the underlying paradigms of reality or '*mythos*' that shape our visions of the cosmos and therefore give rise to different social institutions for the regulation of behaviour. As explained by Alliot, it is especially the invisible realm that matters in this regard:

> '[Societies] construct their own mental universe, carrying fundamental models which produce meaning, which are revealed through the vision of the visible and the invisible of each of its members, through his/her vision of peoples, of his/her society, of the groups to which he/she belongs and with whom he/she is in relation, and his/her vision of him/herself. Each partial view refers to the others and sheds light on them. But the view a society has of the world and of itself explains more specifically the legal behaviour and the limits of the legal' (Alliot, 1983: 90 in Eberhard, 2001: 179).

While understanding law in a plural way requires the kind of openness towards diversity that takes seriously the role of cosmologies in mediating our experiences of the world, it is as crucial to avoid a cultural essentialist trap since various *mythoi* may coexist in a same social space and relate to different aspects of reality (Le Roy et al., 1997). Therefore a pluralist methodology moves beyond 'either (modern) / or (traditional)' dichotomies towards 'and / and' articulations and blends that acknowledge the hybrid practices of real-life people (Le Roy et al., 1997). In other words, attention for plurality in relation to the law entails both discarding monist conceptions of justice, e.g. 'Western-like' justice as the only option to development and the advancement of human rights, as well as discarding binary approaches, i.e. state vs. traditional justice. At the same time, it reveals the importance of considering how the diverse forms of normative ordering that are present in a society can be combined into hybrid configurations that respond to different needs at the local, regional, national and international levels (Le Roy et al., 1997).

The next section expands on this and related issues, this time with a focus on the challenges entailed when advancing human rights in diverse contexts and milieus.

3. ADVANCING HUMAN RIGHTS CROSS-CONTEXTUALLY

The promotion of human rights within local legal orders in Sub-Saharan Africa and beyond is not immune to the well-known universalism vs. relativism debates on human rights. Bluntly put, universalist arguments sustain that human rights are universal since they flow from the inherent dignity of every human person, whereas cultural relativists argue that human rights reflect only the particular cultural viewpoint of the West on morality. Against this backdrop it would seem that, depending on the position one follows, promoting human rights within local legal orders may either be a moral duty or an act of cultural imperialism. However, one of the ways out of this conundrum is to question the kind of ideas that lie behind key concepts, such universality and cultural diversity (Merry, 2006a; Cowan et al., 2001), and examine how they inform the policies and interventions of development actors.

3.1. RECONCEPTUALISING HUMAN RIGHTS' UNIVERSALITY

At the level of human rights, several authors have shown that instead of looking at their universality as an a priori given, it might be worth considering how this framework can become a universal construction a posteriori. This implies looking at human rights as flexible and evolving, so that they can make room to accommodate inputs from different cultural traditions (Messer, 2009; Donelly, 2007, 1984; Brems, 2001; Hellum, 1998; An-Na'Im, 1992). In other words, universality can be seen as a multidimensional process of inclusion, where on the one hand standards at a transnational level can evolve in order to incorporate contributions from different contexts, and on the other hand, at the national and local levels, human rights can be flexibly interpreted and implemented in order to respond to different needs and realities, while at the same time they can operate as pointers for social and cultural change (Brems, 2001). As several scholars argue, universality does not require uniformity (Messer, 2009; Donelly, 2007, 1984; Brems, 2001; Hellum, 1998; Wilson, 1997).

Moreover, human rights are more likely to be observed if they enjoy some degree of local ownership and legitimacy. For this purpose, intercultural dialogues have been advanced as one of the ways forward (De Sousa Santos, 2002: 271; Eberhard, 2002; An-Na'Im, 1992). An-Na'Im (1992: 21) identifies two levels where these dialogues should take place, i.e. 'internal reinterpretation' of local ideas and values within communities and 'cross-cultural dialogue' amongst cultural traditions on the meaning and scope of human rights. He sets the task as follows:

> 'The cultural legitimacy thesis accepts the existing international standards while seeking to enhance their cultural legitimacy within the major traditions of the world through internal dialogue and struggle to establish enlightened perceptions and interpretations of cultural values and norms. Having achieved an adequate level of legitimacy within each tradition, through this internal stage, human rights scholars and advocates should work for cross-cultural legitimacy, so that peoples of diverse cultural traditions can agree on the meaning, scope, and methods of implementing these rights. … I propose to broaden and deepen universal consensus on the formulation and interpretation of human rights through internal reinterpretation of, and cross-cultural dialogue about, the meaning and implication of basic human values and norms' (An-Na'Im, 1992: 21).

De Sousa Santos (2002: 271–272) adds that these dialogues need to lead to 'cosmopolitan human rights', i.e. the globalisation of moral and political struggles against social oppression and human suffering. He departs from the premise that each cultural tradition is incomplete, implying that all cultures are problematic vis-à-vis human rights. The objective of intercultural dialogues on human rights is thus to raise the consciousness of reciprocal incompleteness and weaknesses.

Therefore, it is necessary to base such dialogues on discursive tolerance and readiness to incorporate alternative and marginalised forms of knowledge (De Sousa Santos, 2002: 272). The call to move from 'globalised Western human rights' to 'cosmopolitan human rights' indicates that it is not enough to take other perspectives into account. What is at stake is the possibility to participate and share in the construction of global knowledge (De Feyter, 2007, 2011; Eberhard, 2001). This entails harnessing spaces within the global human rights architecture for bottom-up contributions and processes of right discovery that are based on lessons learned from attempts to put human rights into practice at local level (De Feyter, 2007, 2011; De Feyter et al., 2011). In addition, it is a matter of opening up spaces where hegemonic ideas can be questioned and where those participating in the intercultural encounter allow themselves to be changed by it (Eberhard, 2001).

The first question that is then relevant for legal development actors when engaging with local legal orders is what kinds of human rights ideas lie at the basis of their praxis and how they position themselves explicitly or implicitly around the issue of human rights universality? In other words, what kind of universality are they promoting? One of the areas where this question can be examined is that of programming for human rights training and awareness raising. Are these interventions conceptualised as an exercise in 'bringing' a priori defined human rights to communities? How much room do they make for bottom-up contributions and to what extent do they engage in intercultural dialogues? Are they aware of and adapted to the cosmologies and local realities where human rights are supposed to operate? To what extent do they consider the differences between implementing human rights within forums of dispute resolution that operate according to a logic of adjudication as compared to forums that rather resort to the logic of mediation, as it is often the case of local legal orders in Africa? If human rights are flexibly and cross-culturally understood, their 'localisation' does not necessarily involve a process of cultural homogenisation since depending on the context, different actors will understand and relate to this framework in a different way (De Feyter et al., 2011; De Feyter, 2011, 2007; Merry, 2006a; Wilson, 1997: 12). The next point builds further into these insights by examining the role of cultural diversity in these processes.

3.2. RECONCEPTUALISING CULTURE AND CUSTOMS

If different 'cultural traditions' should be able to contribute to inclusive definitions of human rights, it is also worth exploring how we think about culture. In this sense, various scholars have pointed to the dangers of conceptualising culture as homogeneous, reified, bounded, coherent and determining (Cowen, 2009; Benhabib, 2002; Cowen et al., 2001; Wilson, 1997). Such a view obscures the internal heterogeneity and contestation that takes place inside any cultural group. On the contrary, a critical approach to culture acknowledges its many voices, its dynamism and the power that inhabits meaning (Wilson, 1997; Wolf, 1980). In addition, culture does not only consist of beliefs, values and ideas, but also of practices and habits that predispose people to act in certain ways (Merry, 2003: 67; An-Na'Im, 2002). As shown in the previous chapter, the same line of reasoning can be applied to local customs, which cannot be captured by essentialist approaches. An essentialist view of culture and local customs, or the assumption that each individual belongs to only one culture and by implication one legal order, is thus highly problematic (Cowen et al., 2001; Cowen, 2009). Therefore, understanding these terms in a critical way implies that 'cultures' and 'local customs' are not by definition for or against human rights. Certain aspects of a cultural and legal tradition may be supportive of human rights, others may undermine them, while this is in a constant process of change (Merry, 2003).

In the first place, this implies that development actors should not look at culture and local legal orders as enemies of human rights (Merry, 2003). Actually, these frameworks may possess valuable 'tools' for protecting and advancing human rights (Merry, 2003). For example, they may provide ways of framing the protection of human dignity with a great potential for the realisation of subsistence rights (Gomez Isá, 2011; Hellum, 2007). Development actors may thus play an important role by supporting research that uncovers areas of synergy between international standards and local normative orders, which may feed into critical assessments of national policies and legislation and contribute to the development of human rights standards that respond to local realities (De Feyter, 2011; Hellum, 2007). Moreover, it means that development actors are confronted with the need to consider plurality and power dynamics both amongst different cultural traditions and within them. On the one hand, this is relevant at the level of how human rights are interpreted by state court judges and to what extent they are aware of the need for flexibility in this domain. On the other hand, this relates to the relationship between individual and collective rights. For example, collective rights to culture may be interpreted to include the right to access endogenous forms of justice, leading to legal reforms that grant official status to local justice institutions. While this could represent a progressive measure that aims at accommodating legal and cultural pluralism, it is also necessary to consider how participatory the process is by which these institutions are defined (Buur et al., 2007; ICHRP, 2009). This insight is also relevant for interventions that promote 'internal reinterpretations' and intra-group dialogues on customary norms and values, such as 'self-statement' or 'ascertainment' of customary law initiatives. Next to the discussion on whether this kind of intervention 'freezes' tradition, it is crucial to consider that there might be impediments to internal contestation due to power differentials amongst community members (An-Na'Im, 2002: 27). Therefore, cultural claims and definitions of customary laws need to be critically scrutinised in terms of who is asking the questions, who is providing the answers and whose interests they advance (UN Women, UNICEF and UNDP, 2012). Some authors argue that it is the task of external actors to support disadvantaged members to participate more equally in the process of defining and contesting culture (Benhabib, 2002). As regards local customs, this could be done by means of facilitating access to legal resources, such as the dissemination of laws that promote human rights and the provision of accessible legal services to enforce them. As illustrated in the previous section, rather than displacing local normativites, these initiatives could provide a new normative layer that may become a useful resource for negotiating the interpretation of customs and facilitate that 'the shadow of the law' influences the way local legal orders operate (Galanter, 1981; Wilson, 2006: 78; Oomen, 2005).

3.3. UNDERSTANDING AND SUPPORTING LOCAL DYNAMICS OF CHANGE

Next to a critical understanding of human rights' universality, culture and local customs, the promotion of human rights within local legal orders requires an analysis of how the economic, political and socio-cultural context interplays with them. In this sense, Chopra et al. (2011) argue that legal development actors need to move away from approaches that aim at 'amending' justice systems towards an understanding of the underlying socio-economic, cultural and political structures that lie at the root of human rights violations. According to them, development actors need to depart from the lived realities of justice seekers on their pathways to justice (Chopra et al., 2011). Two key issues emerge from this perspective. First, the need for an 'actor-oriented' approach to human rights (Nyamu-Musembi, 2005), and second, the acknowledgment that the advancement of human rights can be externally supported but, for it to be sustainable, it needs to be demanded 'from within' (Chopra et al., 2011; An-Na'Im, 1992, 2002; Nyamu-Musembi, 2002).

Actor-oriented approaches to human rights depart from the views of local actors. They examine how rights are mobilised in concrete situations by focusing on how people understand their rights, how they claim them and what they hope to achieve with them.[5] Nyamu-Musembi defines this approach as follows:

> 'Actor-oriented perspectives are based on the recognition that rights are shaped through actual struggles informed by people's own understandings of what they are justly entitled to. They imply an approach to needs, rights and priorities that is informed by the concrete experiences of the particular actors who are involved in, and who stand to gain directly from the struggles in question' (Nyamu-Musembi, 2005: 31).

[5] By implication, certain contexts may require an examination of whether people think in terms of 'rights' at all.

In other words, this perspective seeks to understand the strategies of action that people are able to mobilise in pursuing their goals, including their ability to draw on locally available legal resources (An-Na'Im, 2002; Swidler, 1986). In this sense, human rights can be a powerful framework on condition that local actors perceive them as an effective 'tool'. Coming back to legal pluralism and the idea that all individual and collective actors participate in various social fields that produce and enforce norms in a semi-autonomous way, it is important to bear in mind that some of these fields may support human rights ideas, some may resist them, and not all of them may exert the same influence in regulating the behaviour of these actors. In other words, individual agency is deeply shaped by social relations that may support or constrain human rights related strategies of action (Cowen, 2009).

When combined with structural analyses, actor-oriented perspectives reveal the need to assess through which channel(s) human rights ideas are supposed to be implemented locally and how these relate to the rest of the normative forces that operate in that same context (Hellum, 1995). For example, if development actors provide human rights support to the formal courts only, it is necessary to consider how effective these courts are in dealing with local stakes as compared to other justice providers. This is crucial since those who resort to formal justice will assess how this 'resource' works in practice. Depending on this, formal justice may or may not take root in a local context and become part of the 'legal consciousness' of justice seekers (Merry, 2006a). But ideally, interventions should take account of all relevant local normative forces, which include not only the most formalised justice institutions, but also other social fields that generate and enforce norms, such as the family, the church, the school and the local community. This is important since these spaces may not only reproduce norms that contravene human rights but they may also generate norms and practices that can be harnessed for protecting human rights. Therefore, various parallel and not necessarily only 'legal' interventions might be necessary in order to address the various fields of human interaction that affect the possibilities of local actors to access human rights. For example, human rights aid can follow a multi-layered strategy, where legal reforms that promote human rights nationally are complemented by human rights dialogue with local justice providers and the population at large and, depending on the operation of local legal orders, the provision of alternative justice options that protect human rights. As explained above, grassroots dialogue needs to go beyond local practices that contravene human rights. As a matter of fact, it is equally important to identify and reinforce those local practices that protect human rights and build on them when devising certain interventions, such as legal education, so that a link can be established between local normative orders and national legislation (Tsanga, 2007).

This is related to the importance of promoting progressive changes 'from within'. As different scholars argue, for human rights to fulfil their emancipatory potential, they need to be locally grounded (An-Na'Im, 1992, 2002; Merry,

2006a, 2006b; Hinz, 2010; Zwart, 2012). The process of appropriation and reinterpretation of international standards to fit local struggles has been termed the 'vernacularisation' of human rights (Merry, 2006a, 2006b). This implies a bi-directional process. On the one hand, international standards are framed in terms of local symbols and terminology, and on the other hand, local struggles and grievances start to be understood and fought in the language of human rights (Merry, 2006a, 2006b). This means that in order to make sense locally, human rights ideas need to be presented in terms that resonate with local cultural norms, values and practices. Here, a central concept is that of 'framing', which is the way an idea is packed and presented so that it generates shared beliefs, motivates collective action and defines appropriate strategies for action (Merry, 2006b: 41). This can be achieved by collaborating with the right local actors, who can act as intercultural 'translators' or 'brokers' (Merry, 2006b: 41). These actors are in a position to understand the logic of emancipation that international human rights seek to promote and at the same time their embedment in the local context allows them to think 'systemically' and estimate the kinds of reactions and consequences that these ideas may have locally. Therefore, they are in a more legitimate position to challenge local practices and ideas. These actors can range from religious and customary leaders and healers to local NGOs, community mediators and paralegals, who can be local partners in awareness raising campaigns, human rights dialogue and self-statement of customary law interventions, amongst others. However, the identification of local partners might not be an easy task as development actors need to be enough acquainted with each particular context and its dynamics (Chopra et al., 2011). Moreover, there might be no 'intercultural brokers' readily available, so that it becomes necessary to engage in a long-term process of mutual capacity and trust building.

Another way to implement human rights by relying on local socio-cultural arrangements is the 'receptor approach' (Zwart, 2012). This approach seeks to identify local values that can act as 'receptors' for human rights principles. This can be done by detecting and making visible social arrangements that protect human rights and, if these fall short of human rights, by adding elements to adapt these institutions without eliminating them (Zwart, 2012). Similarly, the 'soft approach' to human rights grounds human rights on indigenous foundations while emphasising the latter's flexibility to respond to new needs and demands (Hinz, 2010). In both cases, this requires a detailed analysis of how social institutions work and how their internal logic relates to human rights (Hinz, 2010; Zwart, 2012). Development actors can finance such research and provide support for local capacity building to conduct this kind of research, while facilitating that it feeds into subsequent interventions, such as human rights dialogue at grassroots level and trainings for state court judges, amongst others. The main point within these approaches is that implementing human rights across diverse socio-cultural contexts is more a matter of looking for home-grown solutions rather than of replacing local institutions by externally imposed ones. In this sense, it could be argued that human rights do not require the wholesale elimination of institutions that present challenges to human rights, but only of those elements that are harmful. Moreover, people tend to follow strategies of action that are more or less well known to them and they are unlikely to take new paths that imply serious ruptures with established ways of life (An-Na'Im, 2002; Swidler, 1986). Consequently, abolitionist approaches are not likely to bring about the desired results, not the least because they might be perceived as cultural imperialism (Nyamu-Musembi, 2000, 2002). Therefore, interventions need to focus on discussing the concrete negative consequences of certain local practices in order to forge a common ground with local actors to pursue solutions to problems that are locally identified as such.[6]

4. CONCLUSION

Departing from the premise that legal pluralism and the implementation of human rights across diverse socio-cultural contexts constitute two challenges that legal development actors are confronted with in Sub-Saharan Africa, this chapter has shown how socio-legal theory on these issues can provide valuable entry points for devising interventions. As a matter of fact, development practice constitutes a significant channel through which these theories can be applied in the real world and it is necessary to continue exploring how development practitioners can capitalise on this knowledge.

Indirectly, this chapter has also shown that as long as interventions pay thorough attention to the *how* question, promoting human rights within local legal orders does not need to represent in itself an exercise in cultural imperialism. Much to the contrary, this kind of undertaking could represent an excellent opportunity for understanding international standards in a critical way and contribute to more inclusive definitions of human rights. As has been discussed above, human rights as well as culture and local customs are flexible and dynamic so that they may be reconciled. The chapter has illustrated several ways in which legal development actors may contribute to this goal. This requires looking beyond state justice institutions, understanding the interaction amongst local legal actors and normative repertoires, looking at how behaviour is regulated from an empirical point of view, being sensitive to different paradigms of reality, conceptualising human rights, culture and custom in a critical way and supporting ongoing dynamics of change 'from within'.

The next four chapters present empirical data on how development actors have approached this topic so far in four case studies, i.e. Malawi, Mozambique,

6 See for example Chopra (2007) in respect of human rights dialogue on widow's inheritance rights in Kenya and Ubink (2011) on self-statement of customary laws protecting widow's inheritance rights in Namibia.

Sierra Leone and Zambia, while Chapter 15 reflects on what can be learned from these experiences.

BIBLIOGRAPHY

Alliot, M. (1983) Anthropologie et Juristique. Sur les Conditions de l'Elaboration d'une Science du Droit, *Bulletin de Liaison du LAJP*, 6, 83–117.

Alliot, M. (1985) La Coutume dans les Droits Originellement Africains, *Bulletin de Liaison du LAJP*, 7–8, 79–100.

An-Na'Im, A. (1992) Towards a cross-cultural approach to defining international standards of human rights: the meaning of cruel, inhuman, or degrading treatment or punishment. In An-Na'im, A. (ed.) *Human Rights in Cross-Cultural Perspectives: A Quest for Consensus*. Philadelphia: University of Pennsylvania Press.

Benhabib, S. (2002) *The Claims of Culture: Equality and Diversity in the Global Era*. Princeton: Princeton University Press.

Brems, E. (2001) *Human Rights: Universality and Diversity*. The Hague: Nijhoff.

Buur, L. and Kyed, H.M. (2007) Introduction: Traditional Authority and Democratization in Africa. In Buur, L. and Kyed, H.M. (eds.) *State Recognition and Democratization in Sub-Saharan Africa*. New York: Palgrave MacMillan.

Chopra, T. (2007) Promoting Women's Rights by Indigenous Means: An Innovative Project in Kenya, *Justice for the Poor*, 1(2), 1–4.

Chopra, T. and Isser, D. (2011) Women's Access to Justice, Legal Pluralism and Fragile States. In Albrecht, P., Kyed, H.M., Isser, D. and Harper, E. (eds.) *Perspectives on Involving Non-State and Customary Actors in Justice and Security Reform*. Rome: International Law and Development Organisation.

Cowan, J. (2009) Culture and Rights after *Culture and Rights*. In Goodale, M. (ed.) *Human Rights. An Anthropological Reader*. Sussex: Wiley-Blackwell.

Cowan, J., Dembour, M.B. and Wilson, R. (eds.) (2001) *Culture and Rights: Anthropological Perspectives*. Cambridge: Cambridge University Press

De Feyter, K. (2007) Localising Human Rights. In Benedek, W., De Feyter, K. and Marella, F. (eds.) *Economic Globalisation and Human Rights*. Cambridge: Cambridge University Press.

De Feyter, K. (2011) Sites of Resistance. In De Feyter, K., Parmentier, S., Timmerman, C. and Ulrich, G. (eds.) *The Local Relevance of Human Rights*. Cambridge: Cambridge University Press.

De Feyter, K. and Parmentier, S. (2011) Introduction: Reconsidering Human Rights from Below. In De Feyter, K., Parmentier, S., Timmerman, C. and Ulrich, G. (eds.) *The Local Relevance of Human Rights*. Cambridge: Cambridge University Press.

Donelly, J. (1984) Cultural Relativism and Universal Human Rights, *Human Rights Quarterly*, 6(4), 400–419.

Donelly, J. (2007) The Relative Universality of Human Rights. *Human Rights Quarterly*, 29(2), 281–306.

EBERHARD, C. (2001) Human Rights and Intercultural Dialogue, An Anthropological Perspective. Lecture for the Summer Course 'Cultural Identities and Human Rights' organized by the International Institute for the Sociology of Law in Oñati, 9–13 July 2001.

EBERHARD, C. (2002) *Droit de l'Homme et Dialogue Interculturel*. Paris: Editions Des Ecrivains.

FORSYTH, M. (2009) *A Bird that Flies with Two Wings: the Kastom and State Justice Systems in Vanuatu*. Canberra: Australian National University Press.

GALANTER, M. (1981) Justice in many rooms: courts, private ordering and indigenous law, *Journal of Legal Pluralism*, 19, 1–47.

GOMEZ ISA, F. (2011) Freedom from Want Revisited from a Local Perspective: Evolution and Challenges Ahead. In De Feyter, K., Parmentier, S., Timmerman, C. and Ulrich, G. (eds.) *The Local Relevance of Human Rights*. Cambridge: Cambridge University Press.

GRIFFITHS, J. (1986) What is Legal Pluralism?, *Journal of Legal Pluralism and Unofficial Law*, 24, 1–55.

GRIFFITHS, J. (2003) The Social Working of Legal Rules. *Journal of Legal Pluralism and Unofficial Law*, 48, 1–3.

HELLUM, A. (1995) Actor Perspectives on Gender and Legal Pluralism in Africa. In Petersen, H. (ed.) *Legal Polycentricity: Consequences of Pluralism in Law*. Boston: Dartmouth Publishing.

HELLUM, A. (1998) Women's Human Rights and African Customary Laws: Between Universalism and Relativism – Individualism and Communitarism, *The European Journal of Development Research*, 10(2), 88–104.

HELLUM, A. (2007) Human Rights Encountering Gendered Land and Water Uses. Family Gardens and the Right to Water in Mhondoro Communal Land. In Hellum, A., Stewart, J., Sardar Ali, S. and Tsanga, A. (eds.) *Human Rights, Plural Legalities and Gendered Realities. Paths are Made by Walking*. Harare: Southern and Eastern African Regional Centre for Women's Law.

HELLUM, A., STEWART, J., SARDAR ALI, S. and TSANGA, A. (eds.) (2007) *Human Rights, Plural Legalities and Gendered Realities. Paths are Made by Walking*. Harare: Southern and Eastern African Regional Centre for Women's Law.

HINZ, M. (2010) Justice for Justice and Justice for Peace: Legal Anthropological Observations on Traditional and Informal Justice Systems. In Hinz, M. and Mapaure, C. (eds.) *In Search of Justice and Peace. Traditional and Informal Justice Systems in Africa*. Windhoek: Namibia Scientific Society.

ICHRP – INTERNATIONAL COUNCIL ON HUMAN RIGHTS POLICY (2009) *When Legal Worlds Overlap: Human Rights, State and Non-State Law*. Versoix: International Council on Human Rights Policy.

KYED, H.M. (2009) The Politics of Legal Pluralism: State Policies on Legal Pluralism and their Local Dynamics in Mozambique, *Journal of Legal Pluralism and Unofficial Law*, 59, 87–121.

LAZARUS-BLACK, M. and HIRSCH, S. (eds.) (1994) *Contested States: Law, Hegemony, and Resistance*. New York: Routledge.

Le Roy, E. (2004) *Les Africains et l'Institution de la Justice. Entre Mimetisme et Metissages.* Paris: Dalloz.

Le Roy, E. and Kuyu, C. (1997) La Politique Française de Coopération Judiciaire: Bilan et Perspectives. Observatoire de la Coopération Française, Rapport 1997, 36–65. Paris: Karthala.

Merry, S.E. (1988) Legal Pluralism, *Law & Society Review*, 22(5), 869–96.

Merry, S.E. (2003) Human Rights Law and the Demonization of Culture (And Anthropology Along the Way), *Polar*, 26(1), 55–76.

Merry, S.E. (2006a) *Human Rights and Gender Violence: Translating International Law into Local Justice.* Chicago: University of Chicago Press.

Merry, S.E. (2006b) Transnational Human Rights and Local Activism: Mapping the Middle, *American Anthropologist*, 108(1), 38–51.

Messer, E. (2009) Anthropology, Human Rights and Social Transformation. In Goodale, M. (ed.) *Human Rights. An Anthropological Reader.* Sussex: Wiley-Blackwell.

Moore, S.F. (1973) Law and social change: the semi-autonomous social field as an appropriate subject of study, *Law & Society Review*, 7/4, 719–746

Moore, S.F. (1978) *Law as Process: An Anthropological Approach.* Oxford: Oxford University Press.

Nyamu, C. (2000) How Should Human Rights and Development Respond to Cultural Legitimization of Gender Hierarchy in Developing Countries?, *Harvard International Law Journal*, 41(2), 381–418.

Nyamu-Musembi, C. (2002) Are Local Norms and Practices Fences or Pathways? The Example of Women's Property Rights. In An-Na'im, A. (ed.) *Cultural Transformation and Human Rights in Africa.* London: Zed Books.

Nyamu-Musembi, C. (2005) Towards an Actor Oriented Perspective on Human Rights. In Kabeer, N. (ed.) *Inclusive Citizenship, Meanings and Expressions.* London/New York: Zed Books.

Oomen, B. (2005) *Chiefs in South Africa, Law, Power & Culture in the Post-Apartheid Era.* New York: Palgrave.

Santos, B. de Sousa (2002) *Towards a New Legal Common Sense.* Edinburgh: Butterworths Lexis Nexis.

Starr, J. and Collier, J. (eds.) (1989) *History and Power in the Study of Law, New Directions in Legal Anthropology.* Ithaca/London: Cornell University Press.

Swidler, A. (1986) Culture in action: symbols and strategies, *American Sociological Review*, 51(2), 273–286.

Tamanaha, B. (1993) The Folly of the 'Social Scientific' Concept of Legal Pluralism, *Journal of Law and Society*, 20(2), 263–323.

Tamanaha, B. (2000) A Non-Essentialist Version of Legal Pluralism, *Journal of Law and Society*, 27(2), 296–321.

Tsanga, A. (2007) Reconceptualising the Role of Legal Information Dissemination in the Context of Legal Pluralism in African Settings. In Hellum, A. et al. *Human Rights, Plural Legalities and Gendered Realities, Paths are Made by Walking.* Harare: Southern and Eastern African Regional Centre for Women's Law.

Twining, W. (2003) A Post-Westphalian Conception of Law, *Law & Society Review*, 37(1), 199–258.

Ubink, J. (2011) Stating the Customary: An Innovative Approach to the Locally Legitimate Recording of Customary Law in Namibia. In Ubink, J. (ed.) *Customary Justice: Perspectives on Legal Empowerment*. Rome: International Legal Development Organisation.

UN Women, UNICEF and UNDP (2012) Informal Justice Systems. Charting a Course for Human Rights Based Engagement [online] http://www.undp.org/content/dam/undp/library/Democratic%20Governance/Access%20to%20Justice%20and%20Rule%20of%20Law/Informal-Justice-Systems-Charting-a-Course-for-Human-Rights-Based-Engagement.pdf (15/10/12).

Vachon, R. (1990) L'Etude du Pluralisme Juridique, *Journal of Legal Pluralism*, 29, 163–173.

Vanderlinden, J. (1971) Le Pluralisme Juridique: Essai de Synthèse. In Gilissen, J. (ed.) *Le Pluralisme Juridique*. Brussels: Université Libre de Bruxelles.

Vanderlinden, J. (1989) Return to Legal Pluralism: Twenty Years Later, *Journal of Legal Pluralism and Unofficial Law*, 28, 149–157.

Von Benda-Beckmann, F. (2002) Who's Afraid of Legal Pluralism?, *Journal of Legal Pluralism*, 47, 37–83.

Von Benda-Beckmann, K. (1981) Forum shopping and shopping forums – Dispute settlement in a Minangkabau Village in West Sumatra, *Journal of Legal Pluralism*, 19, 117–159.

Wilson, R. (1997) Human Rights, Culture and Context: An Introduction. In Wilson, R. (ed.) *Human Rights, Culture and Context: Anthropological Perspectives*. London: Pluto Press.

Wilson, R. (2006) Afterword to 'Anthropology and Human Rights in a New Key': The Social Life of Human Rights, *American Anthropologist*, 108(1), 77–83.

Wolf, E. (1980) Facing Power, *American Anthropologist*, 92(3), 586–596.

Woodman, G. (1996) Legal Pluralism and the Search for Justice, *Journal of African Law*, 40(2), 152–167.

Woodman, G. (1998) Ideological Combat and Social Observation: Recent Debate about Legal Pluralism, *Journal of Legal Pluralism*, 42, 21–59.

Zwart, T. (2012) Using Local Culture to Further the Implementation of International Human Rights: The Receptor Approach, *Human Rights Quarterly*, 34(2), 546–569.

CHAPTER 11

TRADITIONAL LAW THROUGH A STATE LENS: A CASE STUDY ON MALAWI

Lia NIJZINK

1. INTRODUCTION

This chapter discusses how international development actors providing aid to the justice sector in Malawi position themselves regarding legal pluralism and the promotion of human rights within traditional law. The chapter begins with an overview of the main colonial and post-colonial developments in the field of law and justice. After describing the main features of the justice landscapes of Malawi and their main challenges in terms of human rights, the chapter depicts how international development actors engage with these realities and provides a mapping of their interventions. The conclusion argues that because most interventions in the justice sector were aimed at the formal legal system, the way in which the state approaches the justice sector and the role of traditional law in it plays a crucial role in development actors' position vis-à-vis legal pluralism and local legal orders.

2. HISTORICAL BACKGROUND

Malawi's traditional leaders have applied a system of traditional law since time immemorial. The customary law forums for settling disputes, also known as *Pabwalo*, date from long before 1891, when the British colonial rule over what was then known as Nyasaland began. The colonial period saw the establishment of the so-called Native Courts. In this system, formally introduced in 1933, traditional law was applied by the state, i.e. by the provincial commissioners assisted by traditional leaders, who acted as advisors or assessors. This system was an attempt by the colonial rulers to incorporate the unofficial system of traditional law into the formal legal system.

When Malawi gained independence in 1964, the Native Courts were replaced by the so-called Local Courts. The Local Courts Act determined their authority, which allowed them to pass judgement on all issues of private and criminal law, with the exception of homicides and other criminal offences for which the death penalty or life imprisonment could be imposed. Another exception were those cases related to marriages that did not fall under customary law. In certain cases, the personal authority of the Local Courts also included non-African citizens.

In 1969, the local courts were renamed and transformed into so-called traditional courts. The authority of these courts was extended to cases for which the death penalty could be imposed. This took place after the infamous Chilobwe murders case, for which the suspects were acquitted by the Supreme Court. A year later, in 1970, the Traditional Court of Appeal became the highest appellate body for customary law cases, instead of the Supreme Court. This meant that the traditional legal system became in fact an official legal system operating separate from and parallel to the recognised Western legal system. This situation persisted throughout the period of Banda's one-party regime in Malawi. During Banda's dictatorship, the traditional legal system was abused to suppress political opponents and to prosecute dissidents and people advocating political change. Although the traditional leaders did not take part in the traditional courts, they did play an important role in selecting their members. This is how both the traditional leaders and the traditional courts gained the reputation of being collaborators working with Banda.[1]

After a multiparty democracy was introduced in Malawi in 1994, the two parallel legal systems were integrated in the sense that the Traditional Supreme Court of Appeal and the regional Traditional Appeal Courts were abolished and the Traditional Courts were absorbed in the judicial power. The chairs of the traditional courts and other staff became part of the courts of first instance that functioned under auspices of the Supreme Court. In practice, this meant that customary law was applied by that part of the judicial system, which up until then had not dealt with customary law cases. This led to a number of issues, such as a lack of expertise concerning customary law within the justice system, a lack of expertise concerning criminal law among the former chairs and the former staff of the traditional courts, confusion with regards to authority, especially in cases concerning traditional marriages and landed property in areas that fell under traditional authorities, arrears in settling conflicts, and a decline in access to the legal system – especially in rural areas. Scharf et al. (2002) and Manda (2012) offer an extensive analysis of the integration process and the problems that this entailed. Because of these problems, the Malawi Law Commission began a revision of the Traditional Courts Act and presented a report in September 2007 that proposed far-reaching reforms (Malawi Law Commission, 2007). These reforms will be discussed below.

1 This description of the history of the Malawi traditional legal system is principally based on Cammack et al., 2009; Kanyongolo, 2006; and Malawi Law Commission, 2007.

3. THE JUSTICE LANDSCAPE

In Malawi, traditional law enjoys constitutional recognition. The Constitution stipulates that traditional law is applied by the formal legal system, but only when it does not contradict justice. The problem, however, is that the majority of the population has no access to the formal legal system. An estimated 80% of the population takes recourse to other forms of conflict settlement. Although the traditional courts were absorbed by the formal legal system in 1994, traditional leaders – chiefs and village chiefs – continued to settle disputes based on traditional law, and village tribunals that are not recognised by the state are still operational (Scharf et al., 2002). Furthermore, there are a number of actors in communities that are involved in non-tradition-based dispute settlement. There are units for victims support in police stations throughout the country. Also, there are volunteer village mediators and legal aid workers active in many rural communities (Stapleton, 2009).

4. THE INSTITUTIONAL FRAMEWORK FOR LEGAL PLURALISM

In its report of September 2007, the Malawi Law Commission suggested to reintroduce local courts into the legal system in order to allow ordinary Malawians access to a law that is affordable and that the people are used to (Malawi Law Commission, 2007). The most important motivation for this proposal was the objective to improve access to the law for all citizens. The Commission pointed out that access to the law is severely limited, especially for Malawians in rural areas, if all cases – including private law traditional cases – are handled by formal courts of first instance. Since their procedures and practices are based on Western law, there courts are ill equipped to treat customary law cases.

That is why the Commission decided to reintroduce local courts into the formal legal system. The Commission envisioned them applying traditional law and having the authority to handle private law in traditional cases and certain less serious criminal offences. Because several elements of traditional law contradict women and children's rights, certain cases were excluded from the authority of the proposed local courts, such as cases concerning inheritance, parental authority over children, witchcraft, landed property and the division of marital goods. The establishment of local courts of appeal on a district level was another part of the Commission's proposal. From the district level, the next step was supposed to be an appeal to the Supreme Court. In other words: there was no provision for a separate Traditional Court of Appeal. The Local Courts Act in which these reforms were included was approved by the Malawi Parliament in February 2011.

Figure 1. The institutional framework for legal pluralism in Malawi before February 2011

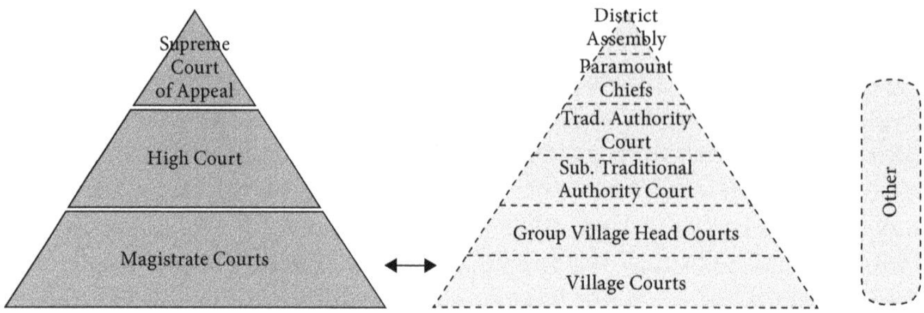

Figure 2. Reforms to the institutional framework for legal pluralism in Malawi as approved in February 2011

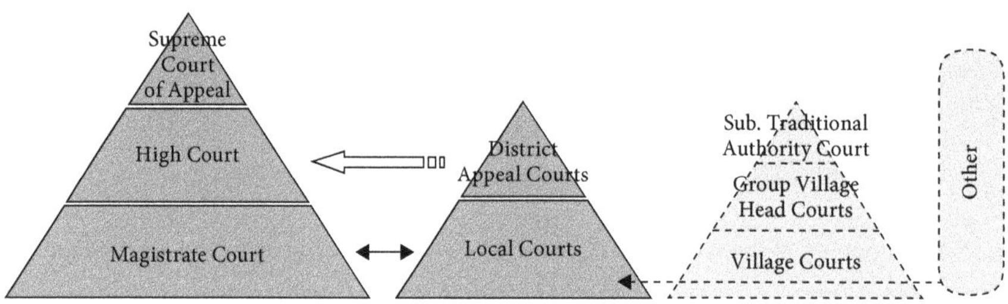

These figures are a graphical representation of the institutional framework for legal pluralism, as it existed in Malawi until recently, and the proposed reforms as approved by Parliament in February 2011. The dotted lines and light colour indicate traditional bodies and actors that are not officially recognised by the state and therefore are not part of state-recognised legal pluralism. However, both in the old and in the new situation, there is informal interaction between the formal and informal component of the legal system. As the second figure shows, it cannot be expected that the establishment of the new local courts for the application of traditional justice will cause the complete informal traditional law system to vanish. Actually, this is not the primary objective of the new system of local courts. The proposal for the establishment of local courts for the application of traditional law within the formal legal system is primarily based on the fact that the formal system was overburdened with less serious offences and traditional law cases for which it had neither the capacity nor the expertise. Moreover, in the new system there is a strong emphasis on separation of powers, especially between the judicial and executive powers. Therefore, in the new system the traditional leaders who join the local governing structures will be separated from the judiciary. They will not be part of the new local courts.

5. THE HUMAN RIGHTS LANDSCAPE

Although Malawi is still a strongly traditional society, the traditional leaders suffer from a poor reputation that originates in their role under Banda's single-party dictatorship. Moreover, the traditional leaders are heavily politicised in the current multiparty system. As a consequence, the role of traditional leaders as guardians of traditional law is weaker than one might expect, and the chiefs and village chiefs are not the most active participants in the current public debate on the tension between human rights and traditional norms and practices.[2] The most important areas where this tension is part of the public debate in Malawi are inheritance law and women's rights, arranged marriages/sexual relations with young girls, children's rights and the parental authority over children, as well as cases regarding witchcraft (Malawi Law Commission, 2009). The current debate shows that there is no strong lobby in Malawi that rejects human rights on basis of tradition. In other words: there is a reasonably fertile climate for addressing the tensions between traditional law and human rights and one can find several initiatives with this objective, as the description of interventions concerning traditional law below will show.

6. INTERNATIONAL ACTORS AND LOCAL LEGAL ORDERS

When the research was conducted, three development actors were active in the Malawi legal sector: the European Union, the British organisation for development cooperation DFID, and the United Nations via its United Nations Development Programme (UNDP). The majority of the activities and support that these actors provided to the sector was by far aimed at institutions and actors that are embedded in the formal legal system. Besides the programmes of the DFID, no particular attention was paid to traditional law and these development actors had not taken any specific policy position in the role of legal pluralism and local legal orders in the Malawi justice sector.

There was in fact a clear task division between these three organisations. The European Union executed the so-called Rule of Law programme. This programme was coordinated by the Malawi Ministry of Justice with the EU providing technical support through a unit that was specifically established in the Ministry for this purpose. The programme, which commenced in 2006, was exclusively aimed at the formal legal system and was not specifically concerned with traditional justice. Several organisations from the civil society were supported in the framework of the programme, such as the Malawi Human

2 Personal interviews with traditional leaders and other stakeholders, Lilongwe (Malawi), August–September 2009.

Rights Commission and the Initiative for Civic Education (NICE). In certain cases, the work these organisations did was indirectly related to traditional law and the role of traditional leaders in communities (see below). Nevertheless, the EU, as far as we could ascertain in our fieldwork, had not taken a specific policy position in this matter.

The UNDP had taken the initiative to introduce the so-called Sector-Wide Approach (SWAP, cf. Stone et al., 2005) into the Malawi justice system. This would basically lead to more and better coordination between the diverse donors and to a more significant role for the Malawi government in the implementation and evaluation of the donor programmes aimed at strengthening the justice sector (Malawi Ministry of Justice, 2009). A study tour to Uganda organised by the UNDP took place. Since Uganda was already working with a SWAP in the justice sector, the involved Malawi organisations were able to get a better idea of what a SWAP entails. It does seem, however, that such an approach would be somewhat premature in the Malawi context. Anyway, there are a large number of questions regarding the coordinating role and the capacity of the Ministry of Justice, and which organisations fall within or outside of the justice sector, and about the role of civil society organisations in a SWAP. Furthermore, there are questions surrounding the independence of the judiciary and the organisations such as the Malawi Human Rights Commission that are relevant should a SWAP be implemented. Our fieldwork showed that implementing a sector-wide approach would probably make developmental aid to the Malawi justice sector even more state-oriented than it already is. Unless the Malawi government makes haste with implementing the new local courts, it seems that a possible justice SWAP would leave too little room for traditional law or traditional law institutions. Nevertheless, the UNDP turned out to have no clear policy position concerning the role of traditional law in a sector-wide approach.[3]

The British organisation for development cooperation DFID had been active in the Malawi justice sector since 2000 through her MaSSAJ programme – Malawi Safety, Security and Access to Justice. This programme was designed as an ambitious long-term programme aimed at policy development for the entire justice sector, including unofficial traditional forums for dispute settlement (DFID, 2003). The programme was therefore aimed specifically at the traditional authorities not recognised by the state, to improve the access to and quality of traditional law and to align it with international human rights standards. The interventions regarding traditional law in the MaSSAJ programme proved not to be trouble-free and the DFID decided to focus its attention on so-called *primary justice*: an initiative for more collaboration between traditional and non-traditional organisations, including state institutions, to promote effective conflict settlement – whether or not by traditional norms and practices – in

[3] Personal interviews with representatives of international actors in development cooperation and other stakeholders, Lilongwe (Malawi), August–September 2009.

communities. One of the DFID's most recent interventions in this context was an educational programme organised by the judiciary for a group of layman judges without any specific legal training who were active in the formal legal system within courts of first instance.

DFID furthermore supported the Catholic Commission for Justice and Peace, an organisation from the civil society that is specifically involved in traditional law and which organises education programmes for members of the unofficial village tribunals. The Commission was active in 28 districts in Malawi and provided training for both the chiefs and the village chiefs in the communities on human rights, gender issues and matters that pertain to 'good governance'. The trainings were also aimed at clarifying and easing the authority of and the task division between the unofficial traditional legal system and the formal legal system. To improve the relationship between the unofficial traditional legal system and the formal legal system and to increase the trust in the much-applied traditional system, the Commission introduced a register to document cases in the village tribunals. The Commission also offered a successful programme to increase the number of female members in village tribunals.

Besides these interventions, which bear directly on traditional law, there were a number of interventions that were more indirectly related to traditional law. The above-mentioned organisation National Initiative for Civic Education (NICE) that received support from the European Union and stemmed from the civic society, aimed to support groups with a social-economic disadvantage. NICE worked with rural communities in a number of development projects and was specifically focused on mobilising communities to promote democracy and good governance. NICE organised awareness campaigns for human and women's rights, and its work here indirectly touched upon the role of traditional leaders. The work of the Paralegal Advisory Service Institute (PASI) was aimed at legal awareness but also at alternative forms of dispute settlement. PASI trained so-called village mediators that act as legal aids in rural communities and handle both private law cases and criminal cases. In a sense, the village mediators furnish an alternative for the village tribunal and thereby touch indirectly upon the role of traditional forums for dispute settlement (Stapleton, 2009). Certain elements of the work of the Malawi Human Rights Commission also indirectly bear on traditional law. For example, the Commission investigated existing traditional practices and made an inventory of norms and practices that violate human rights. During our fieldwork, it did not become clear what had been done with the results of this study. The following table maps these interventions according to the typology developed in Chapter 8:

Type of interventions	At state level	At local level
Law reform interventions		Research-related activities (Malawi Human Rights Commission – EU); stimulating the community debate on procedural and substantial traditional law norms (Catholic Commission for Justice and Peace – DFID)
Institutional support and reform interventions	Proposal for the reintroduction of local courts (Malawi Law Commission – no involvement of development actors)	Introducing a register for case documentation, revision of appointment procedures for members of village tribunals, reinforcing the relations with the formal legal system (Catholic Commission for Justice and Peace – DFID)
Strengthening the legal community (justice providers)		Human rights training, national legislation and several techniques for dispute settlement (Catholic Commission for Justice and Peace – DFID)
Empowering justice users	Human rights education and awareness programmes (NICE – EU and Catholic Commission for Justice and Peace – DFID); Programmes aimed at legal assistance and alternative dispute settlement (PASI – several development actors)	

The above table offers an overview of interventions regarding traditional justice as executed in Malawi at the time the research was conducted. The reform proposal for the introduction of local courts into the formal legal system has also been included in this table. It is interesting to see that the development actors who were active in the legal sector in Malawi were not involved in this proposal and had hardly engaged themselves with it. During our fieldwork they turned out to have practically no knowledge of the proposal's details, and also that they had not taken a position vis-à-vis the proposals of the Malawi Law Commission.

7. CONCLUSION

The description of the situation in Malawi that was given above allows us to draw the following conclusions regarding the question how international actors that are active in the field of justice sector aid in Malawi handle legal pluralism and traditional law.

First of all, it is clear that some development actors in Malawi had no intention to concern themselves with legal pluralism and traditional law and they had therefore not developed a (policy) position in this field. They were exclusively engaged in the formal legal system and seem to take their lead from the Malawi government for their position on traditional justice. The institutional framework for legal pluralism as it existed in Malawi up until recently apparently offered little reason to pay attention to traditional law in justice sector aid. Development actors were also hardly aware of existing proposals to adjust this legal framework.

This had led to a certain dichotomy in justice sector aid in Malawi. Interventions were either exclusively aimed at formal law or at unofficial traditional law. There were no interventions concerned with the customary law elements in the formal law. For example, development actors in Malawi had not concerned themselves with the lack of expertise regarding traditional norms and practices within the judiciary. Nor had they been active in relation to the institutional framework for legal pluralism or the proposals for the reintroduction of local courts in the judicial power. Development actors, therefore, seemed to have little awareness of legal pluralism approaches to law. In general, justice sector aid in Malawi seemed to pay too little attention to the existence of several legal orders that are interconnected and influence each other. Moreover, attention for traditional law was only paid by programmes concerned with unofficial forums for traditional law, but not by the more substantial support for formal law. The instalment of the new local courts may change this, if development actors were to support the establishment for these new courts for the practice of traditional law.

Secondly, it is clear that in cases where interventions by development actors were specifically related to traditional law, these were implemented by organisations of the civil society. These organisations seemed generally sensitive to the characteristics of traditional law and to also opt for an intercultural approach to promote human rights. The extent of these programmes, however, was limited and does not seem to result in more influence of the law users on policy issues within the justice sector.

This Malawi case study shows that, because most interventions in the justice sector were aimed at the formal legal system, it is crucial how the state approaches the justice sector and the role of traditional law. In Malawi, the state does not consider the development of the unofficial traditional justice sector to be a priority. Attention is paid to creating official local courts that apply traditional law and the role these local courts could have in easing the burden on the current formal legal system. This might create renewed interest in legal pluralism and traditional law, but this interest is still limited to a certain institutional interpretation and a certain concept of traditional law that are principally not concerned with the views, experiences and expectations of justice seekers. The implementation of the new system could in principle lead to a proper task division between the customary law and other parts of the formal legal system and thereby alleviate the tensions between traditional law and human rights. Considering the experiences in Zambia, however, there is reasonable doubt as to whether this will happen in practice (see Chapter 9).

Development actors in Malawi had not concerned themselves with these proposals but now that these have been accepted by Parliament this situation could change. This might lead justice sector aid in Malawi to become even more focused on the formal legal system. It is, however, much too early to determine whether this development will translate into improved access to and quality of the law in Malawi.

BIBLIOGRAPHY

Cammack, D., Kanyongolo, E. and O'Neil, T. (2009) Town Chiefs in Malawi, APPP Working Paper No. 3, Overseas Development Institute.

DFID – Department For Development Cooperation (2003) Malawi Safety, Security and Access to Justice Programme, Output to Purpose Review, September/October.

Kanyongolo, F.E. (2006) Malawi: Justice Sector and the Rule of Law, Open Society Initiative for Southern Africa [online] http://www.refworld.org/pdfid/46728e072.pdf (12/09/2014).

Malawi Law Commission (2007) Report on the Review of the Traditional Courts Act.

Malawi Ministry of Justice (2009) Creating a Coordinated Justice Sector for Malawi, Draft Concept Note.

Manda, K. (2012) Courts and the application of customary law in Malawi: Towards the reintroduction of local courts. In Bennett, T. et al. (eds.) *African Perspectives on Tradition and Justice*. Antwerp: Intersentia.

Scharf, W., Banda, C., Roentsch, R., Kaunda, D. and Shapiro, R. (2002) *Access to Justice for the Poor of Malawi? An Appraisal of Access to Justice Provided to the Poor of Malawi by the Lower Subordinate Courts and the Customary Justice Forums*. Report prepared for the UK Department of International Development [online] www.gsdrc.org/go/display/document/legacyid/1293 (27/05/2011).

Stapleton, A. (2009) *Empowering the Poor to Access Criminal Justice – A Grass-roots Perspective*. Rome: IDLO [online] http://www.afrimap.org/english/images/documents/LEWP_Stapleton.pdf (12/09/2014).

Stone, C., Miller, J., Thornton, M. and Trone, J. (2005) Supporting Security, Justice, and Development: Lessons for a New Era. Vera Institute of Justice [online] http://www.gsdrc.org/docs/open/CON24.pdf (12/09/2014).

CHAPTER 12

POLYCENTRIC LEGAL LANDSCAPES: A CASE STUDY ON MOZAMBIQUE

Giselle Corradi

1. INTRODUCTION

This chapter discusses how international development actors providing aid to the justice sector in Mozambique position themselves regarding legal pluralism and the promotion of human rights within local justice processes. The chapter begins with an overview of the main colonial and post-colonial developments that led to the highly polycentric configurations of justice provision that can be found throughout the country. After describing the main features of the justice landscapes of Mozambique and their main challenges in terms of human rights, the chapter depicts how international development actors engage with these realities and provides a mapping of their interventions. The concluding discussion analyses the latter in the light of the socio-legal insights presented in Chapter 10 and argues that despite some efforts to incorporate informal justice within justice sector aid, most initiatives reflect a state centric perspective.

2. COLONIAL AND POST-COLONIAL BACKGROUND OF LEGAL PLURALISM

Portuguese colonial presence in Mozambique stretches from 1500 to 1975. However, until the 20th century, Portuguese influence was limited to trading settlements along the coast and rivers. It was only between 1929 and 1941 that the territory came under direct control of the Portuguese colonial government.[1] This went hand in hand with the introduction of a dualistic system of local government called '*Indigenato*', which divided the population into *civilised* (Europeans and

[1] For an extensive account of Mozambique's history see Malyn Newitt, *A History of Mozambique* (London: Hurst & Co., 1995).

assimilados) and *natives*.[2] In line with this bifurcated system, the territory of Mozambique was organised into territorial units that were supervised by colonial officials, whereas sub-divisions of these structures fell under the administration of co-opted traditional authorities, who were also charged with the administration of local justice.[3] In 1961, under pressure from ILO to stop forced labour, the *Indigenato* regime was revoked and all natives of the Portuguese colonies were granted Portuguese citizenship. That same year, the movement for independence began to organise in Mozambique with the formation of an anti-colonial political group called 'Front for the Liberation of Mozambique' (FRELIMO). Under the ideology of socialist revolution, FRELIMO carried out an armed campaign against Portugal from 1964 to 1974 (the Colonial War).[4] Eventually, it negotiated independence with the government of Portugal in 1974 and constituted itself as the independent government of Mozambique in 1975.[5] In contrast with the policy of continuity followed by several ex-colonial states in Sub-Saharan Africa, FRELIMO sought to break away from the colonial structures it had inherited from Portugal. This included traditional authorities, who were seen as collaborators of the colonial regime and were therefore banned. The first National Constitution of 1975 established a one party presidential regime based on socialist revolutionary ideology. FRELIMO sought to modernise rural areas by providing free education, health and basic services. At the level of local justice, a comprehensive reform took place with the abolition of customary courts and their replacement by 'popular courts' that formed part of a unitary socialist legal system as the lowest tier in the court hierarchy.[6] Popular courts were composed of lay judges who were elected by a local assembly and approved by the community. Their main task was to mediate and seek reconciliation rather than to apply formal or customary law. Procedures were informal and emphasised public participation (Sachs and Welch, 1990). However, the spread of the new system proved difficult to implement, especially in the countryside where traditional authorities continued to exercise public authority. As FRELIMO's failure in rural areas became more evident, the

---

2 *'Assimilados'* were African and mulatos who could gain this status if they proved that they could read and write Portuguese, that they had abandoned their customs, and were gainfully employed.

3 Those traditional authorities who refused to cooperate with the colonial regime were imprisoned and replaced (O'Laughlin, 2000).

4 See T.H. Henriksen, *Revolution and Counterrevolution: Mozambique's War of Independence 1964–1974* (Westport, CT: Greewood, 1983).

5 FRELIMO's ascension to power in 1975 was not legitimated by popular elections but was rationalised by its revolutionary nature. This changed with the National Constitution of 1990, the signature of the Peace Agreement in 1992 and the introduction of multi-party democracy with the elections of 1994.

6 At the socio-economic level, FRELIMO's revolutionary programme was based on the promotion of 'villagisation' and collective production. According to this policy, rural populations would move into communal villages and would become either workers on state farms or members of cooperatives. This contradicted long established patterns of disperse rural settlement and family production. To a large extent, these policies eventually failed. (O'Laughlin, 2000: 27).

party increasingly resorted to repression as a means to advance its programme (O'Laughlin, 2000).

From 1976 to 1992, Mozambique went through a bloody civil war. The Cold War and the ongoing liberation struggles in neighbouring countries provided for the backdrop where regional and international opposition to FRELIMO's revolutionary programme would arise. By the late 1970s, a counter-revolutionary movement arose across the border in Rhodesia, RENAMO.[7] Despite RENAMO's brutal massacres and abductions of child soldiers, voluntary support, or at least neutrality for the movement, arose in central provinces, such as Manica, Sofala, Zambezia and Nampula, where the failure of FRELIMO's programme grew with the years and where RENAMO found the support of excluded representatives of traditional society.[8] Throughout the 1980s, war zones arose along the lines of FRELIMO and RENAMO strongholds. Civilians living in these areas were targeted by the opposing fraction, causing the death of thousands and the displacement of hundreds of thousands. By the late 1980s, internal conditions in Mozambique, such as droughts and famines and the changing international and regional political landscape facilitated that FRELIMO and RENAMO would move towards peace negotiations. In 1990, a second National Constitution based on multiparty democracy was adopted, paving the way for the General Peace Agreement, which was signed in Rome in 1992.[9]

As foreseen in the Constitution of 1990, the post-civil war period was marked by the transition towards multiparty democracy and the introduction of liberal market economy. The departure from the socialist model included the adoption of neoliberal measures, such as the liberalisation of prices, the privatisation of state companies and drastic cuts in public and social expenses (Hanlon and Smart 2008). At a political level, RENAMO got formal recognition as a legitimate political party and FRELIMO obtained formal recognition as the legitimate government of Mozambique, winning the first multiparty general elections in 1994. At a judicial level, Law 4/92 was passed making provision for the separation of the popular courts from the formal justice system, which from then onwards were renamed 'community courts' (Trindade, 2003). In practice, community courts were not that different from their predecessors, the local courts. In most cases the same courts, with the same lay judges and in the same localities continued to work under the new name, with the difference that they stopped receiving any governmental support. In addition, this period saw the introduction of decentralisation policies, including Decree 15/2000, which led to

7 Initially, RENAMO was formed mainly by ex-black Portuguese troops in exile across the border in Rhodesia which were supported by white Rhodesian intelligence (Newitt, 2002: 209).

8 See C. Geffray, *La Cause des Armes au Mozambique* (Paris: Karthala, 1990).

9 The Peace Agreement made no provision for the implementation of any mechanism to review the crimes committed during the war. Law 15/92 provided for an amnesty for crimes committed during 1979 and 1992. According to Newitt, the UN and the international community gave great support to securing peace in Mozambique due to potentially destabilising effects that could otherwise affect the peace process in South Africa (2000).

the formal recognition of traditional authorities. This decree delegates traditional authorities several state functions, including policing, taxation, population registration, enforcement of justice, land allocation, and rural development.[10] The third and current National Constitution of 2004 built further on the liberal principles established in 1990 and introduced a series of changes touching on the organisation of the judiciary. Amongst the most important ones, we find the formal recognition of legal pluralism in article 4.

3. THE JUSTICE LANDSCAPE

As a result of these processes, the provision of justice in Mozambique is highly polycentric and channelled through what in Mozambique is often called the 'formal' and 'informal' justice systems. Formal justice comprises the Supreme Court, the High Court of Appeal, the Provincial Courts and the District Courts. Access to these tribunals is limited for the majority of the population due to several factors, such as lack of knowledge, lack of physical access, lack of trust and the high costs involved.[11] These institutions were inherited from the Portuguese colonial administration but were never fully deployed throughout the country due to a lack of financial and human resources. As a result, they are mainly used by middle classes and business people in urban centres (Lubkemann et al., 2011: 37). These courts present major operational challenges, such as poor physical infrastructure, lack of access to legislation and jurisprudence and charges of corruption and political interference (OSISA, 2006). In addition, lack of capacity results in serious case backlogs and breaches of fair trial guarantees, such as exceedingly long pre-trial detention periods and lack of legal counsel (OSISA, 2006). Overcrowded prisons lack minimal safety and health conditions (OSISA, 2006). On top of this, the police are reported to handle a significant proportion of crimes out of court leading to many abuses (Lubkemann et al., 2011: 39) All of this contributes to a general distrust of formal state justice institutions, which are perceived as inefficient and illegitimate (Lubkemann et al., 2011: 39).

As in many parts of Sub-Saharan Africa, most people recur to a wide array of local justice providers, which are frequently grouped under the umbrella term 'informal justice'. According to a recent study, 'customary law and the traditional authorities who administer it constitute the primary form of justice for the overwhelming majority of Mozambique's population' (Lubkemann et al., 2011:

---

10 For an analysis of this process see L. Buur and H.M. Kyed, 'Traditional Authority in Mozambique: The Legible Space between State and Community', in L. Buur and H.M. Kyed (eds.) *State Recognition and Democratization in Sub-Saharan Africa, A New Dawn for Traditional Authorities?* (New York: Palgrave MacMillan, 2007).

11 According to the Organic Law on the Organization of the Tribunals, each district should have at least one district court, but this is not the case. See Open Society Initiative for South Africa (2006).

24). This covers familial and marital disputes, adultery, petty theft, drunkenness and disorderly behaviour, land and resource disputes, cases of sorcery and physical aggression (Lubkemann et al., 2011: 26). Customary law processes are oral and their main objective is the restoration of community harmony taking account of corporate rather than individual interests. For this purpose, traditional authorities, assisted by elders, lead community discussions that seek to arrive at consensual decisions on how to settle disputes, provide compensation and, if possible, achieve reconciliation (Lubkemann et al., 2011: 24, 25). Depending on the locality, traditional authorities collaborate or compete with other justice providers, such as religious authorities, spirit mediums, community courts, local administrative authorities, the police, community policing councils and paralegal organisations (Santos, 2006; Meneses, 2007; Lubkemann et al., 2011). That some of these instances represent a state authority does not necessarily mean that they always apply state law. For example, local administrative authorities and the police perform dispute-processing functions where they combine state and non-state normative orders (Araujo, 2010). Jacobs (2010: 132) documents how police officers in Gorongosa district accept spirit mediums' accusations of crime as valid and punish perpetrators on the basis of it. Though not always associated with judicial functions, traditional healers and spirit mediums act both as a forum where the parties resort to for truth seeking and spirit problems and as expert witnesses within disputing processes officiated by other justice providers when a spiritual dimension is at stake (Jacobs, 2010: 122). Their intervention is often required in order to identify individuals who induce evil powers, mostly women. Christian and Muslim religious leaders also play a role as advisers and mediators within their faith group, particularly in the context of familial conflicts (Jacobs, 2010; Casimiro and Fonseca, 2009).

Next to these justice forums, we find the community courts. According to the last national mapping, in total 1694 community courts exist in the country (GoM, 2008). As explained above, during the post-independence socialist period (1975–1994), FRELIMO followed a policy of abolition of traditional authority, which were considered collaborators of the Portuguese colonial regime, and installed the popular tribunals in order to replace them (Sachs and Welch, 1990). However, these tribunals were not evenly implemented throughout the territory and traditional authorities continued to have a de facto role in the administration of justice (O'Laughlin, 2000). At present, the community courts that replaced the popular tribunals are not part of the official legal system and their regional coverage and levels of popularity vary from region to region (Santos, 2006: 58). Though the law that created the community courts (Law 4/92) foresees that the provincial governments will remunerate community court judges and be responsible for these courts (arts. 11, 12), they receive no financial, material or human resource support from the government or the formal courts. Moreover, they are often suspected of political affiliation to the ruling party (OSISA, 2006; Santos, 2006).

In recent years, legal plurality has been further compounded by the creation of Community Policing Councils (Meneses, 2007). Created by the Ministry of the Interior in 2000 to involve citizens in crime prevention, the Community Policing Councils were left to function by themselves and started to compete with the official police by solving cases on their own, including illegal recourse to the use of force (Meneses, 2007: 35). Finally, many NGOs and paralegal organisations not only offer legal advice but also settle disputes out of court, thereby performing quasi-judicial functions.

Overall, there is an enormous diversity in the legal landscapes of Mozambique, which is not only found in the different kinds of dispute resolution instances that are locally available, but also within one same type, e.g. some community courts operate in a building, others under a tree, some resort to procedural formalities and take registers, others do not, etc. Great variation also exists in the customs that are followed in different regions and the customary laws that traditional authorities rely on. In addition, there are important differences in the way in which these actors interact with one another. Depending on the locality, they may collaborate, compete or simply ignore each other (Santos, 2006). The following figure provides an overview of the justice providers that are recurrently found throughout this polycentric legal landscape:

Figure 3. Main justice providers in Mozambique

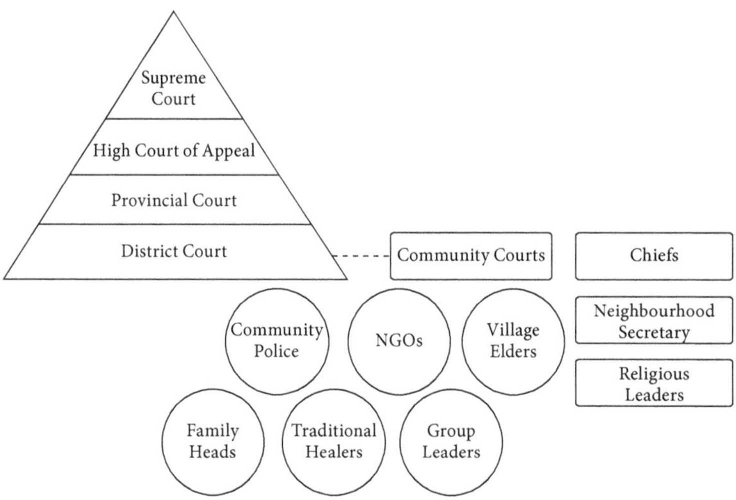

4. THE INSTITUTIONAL FRAMEWORK FOR LEGAL PLURALISM

The current institutional framework for legal pluralism in Mozambique gives official status to a number of the above-mentioned informal justice providers without defining how these relate to each other and to the formal courts. The National Constitution (2004) recognises 'the various normative orders and mechanisms of dispute resolution that exist in the Mozambican society as long as they do not contravene the values and fundamental principles of the Constitution' (art. 4). Additional legislation would render this provision operational (art. 212.3) but so far the existing laws on the topic are silent on many issues. Law 4/92 creates the community courts but does not foresee any form of articulation between them and the formal courts. The Organic Law of the Judicial Courts (Law 24/2007) states that the judicial courts 'may articulate with other existing conflict resolution instances' without stipulating which ones or how (art. 6). Article 86, 1-a, 2 states that the district courts will hear appeals from the community courts 'in accordance with the principles established by the legislation on community courts', which is not specific. Decree 15/2000 defining the articulation between local state bodies and community authorities limits itself to recognising the role of village secretaries, traditional authorities and other local leaders (art. 1-1) in maintaining peace, justice and social harmony (art. 4-a), but it does not mention any concrete implementation plan. Regarding the status of customary laws, the Family Law (Law 10/2004) grants official status to traditional marriages that are registered (arts. 16, 17, 18, 25, 51) and the Land Law (Law 19/97) recognises land held according to customary forms of land tenure (arts. 12, 24). In other words, these customary laws are applicable in so far as they respect the National Constitution but there exists no legislation or jurisprudence indicating how conflicts between both should be assessed.

This means that in practice there is no official connection between the formal and informal spheres of justice. In this context, justice seekers have multiple options for navigating between different informal and formal forums. For example, a family dispute may first be mediated between the families, sometimes with the intervention of a third party, such as a women group's leader or a local administrative authority. If no solution is reached at this point, the case may be taken to the traditional court, or to the community court, or first to one and then to the other if both are present in the same locality. At times, the intervention of a traditional healer can be requested if the case involves a supernatural dimension. If no solution is reached within the informal instances and the parties have enough means, they may recur to a district court.[12] The parties may also decide to resort immediately to a district court without passing through any informal forum. However, some district courts require that 'minor cases' be first handled by a community court, meaning that in some cases, the lack of clarity in the

12 Or when it is a 'family case', the parties may be advised to go to a special unit of the police, the 'unit for women and children'. These units were created to deal with domestic violence, but in practice they mediate in more general 'family cases'. Personal interviews and observations, Maputo, Pemba, August–September 2009.

institutional framework for legal pluralism leads to varying forms of de facto division of legal labour.[13]

There exist at present two law reform proposals that would modify the current institutional framework for legal pluralism. On the one hand, there is a draft law to replace Law 4/92 on the community courts. Next to its lack of clarity as regards articulation with the formal courts, different stakeholders consider it necessary to replace Law 4/92 since it is outdated and has never been regulated on several points.[14] For example, the amounts that community court judges can request as penalties and taxes were never updated (art. 3.2 and art. 5) and the form of remuneration of community court judges was never specified (art. 11). Moreover, many community courts have seen no re-election of their judges since 1987 as the government still has to devise mechanisms to this end (art. 13). However, the existing draft has been retained at the Council of Ministers for several years and seems not to advance since certain issues remain controversial. For example, the budgetary impact of the law, the procedure for the re-election of judges and whether regulation of community courts will result in an unwanted formalisation of their practices.[15] In addition, the Criminal Code and the Code of Criminal Proceedings are currently under revision. The draft that is up for legislative consideration contains a number of provisions that modify Law 4/92. For example, all criminal summary proceedings are foreseen to fall under the jurisdiction of the community courts. This includes corporal injuries that prevent a person from working up to 20 days, robbery up to 60,000 MZN (about USD 2,000) and damages up to 60,000 MZN (about USD 2,000), except for traffic accidents (art. 115). In these cases, community courts are to administer alternative penalties short of imprisonment, such as community work and fines (art. 117). The Ministry of Justice launched this initiative as it is expected that it will relieve the formal courts from case backlogs and contribute to solving the problem of overcrowded prisons, while at the same time reflecting the Mozambican tradition of reconciliation.[16]

5. THE HUMAN RIGHTS LANDSCAPE

Mozambique has ratified most of the main international human rights instruments, and fundamental rights are guaranteed under the National Constitution, but in practice, both formal and informal instances present

[13] This does not mean that community courts deal only with minor cases. In spite of their limited jurisdiction, in practice they deal with more serious offenses such as rape, domestic violence, etc. Personal interviews, Mozambique 2009.

[14] Personal interviews, Maputo, August–September 2009 and February–March 2012.

[15] Ibid.

[16] Ibid.

challenges for their implementation.[17] Human rights concerns at the level of formal justice relate mainly to poor access to formal courts and overcrowded detention facilities, as well as incidents of extra-legal executions and torture by police officers. Widespread poverty and limited resources to realise basic rights form the backdrop to these challenges.[18] In addition, a pervasive patriarchal ethos tends to undermine the realisation of women's rights. Even though official legislation conforms to international standards, in practice state officials do not always know or enforce this legislation (Arthur and Mejia, 2006). This is reflected in the frequent unequal treatment of men and women and the failure to protect women and girls from domestic violence.[19]

In the case of informal justice, these mechanisms enjoy considerable social legitimacy as they are embedded in the symbolic orders that inform life in the communities where they operate. As highlighted by several authors, there is an important connection between the different ontological orders co-existing in Mozambique and the way conflict is defined and resolved (Lubkemann et al., 2011; Jacobs, 2010; West, 2005). Nevertheless, informal justice processes tend to reflect and reproduce social hierarchies and inequality. As in the case of the formal courts, this is remarkable in the area of gender. For example, women are often dispossessed of their property upon divorce, their inheritance rights are seriously curtailed and they are discriminated against in the areas of reproductive rights, education and public decision-making (Andrade et al., 2001). However, this varies depending on the forum. Some of them deny gender equality altogether, whereas other adopt a conciliatory stance, where traditional gender roles are not fully questioned, but they incorporate some elements of gender equality (Arthur and Mejia, 2006). Corporal punishments are also reported to be a problem within some informal forums, such as in the case of traditional healers, which may inflict severe physical violence on a supposed witch to make her confess or punish her (Meneses, 2007: 28; Jacobs, 2010: 129) as well as in the case of some customary and community courts.[20]

---

17 At the time of writing, Mozambique had not adhered to the International Covenant on Economic, Social and Cultural Rights. Chapter 5 of the National Constitution (2004) provides for socio-economic and cultural rights.

18 See Danish Institute for Human Rights, Mozambique and Human Rights at http://www.humanrights.dk/international/geographical+regions/africa/countries/mozambique/mozambique+and+human+rights.

19 See Arthur and Mejia, 2006.

20 Personal interviews, Maputo, August–September 2009.

6. INTERNATIONAL ACTORS AND LOCAL LEGAL ORDERS

In Mozambique, justice is amongst the national sectors receiving the smallest budgets.[21] As analysts point out, the government of Mozambique resists reform in areas that are politically sensitive, though it maintains an appearance of cooperation (Di Renzio and Hanlon, 2007). For their part, donors are lenient on these issues as long as Mozambique remains politically and economically stable and displays satisfactory levels of spending on social indicators, such as health and education, which are more readily associated with poverty reduction, even if they remain aid dependant (De Tollenaere, 2006; Di Renzio and Hanlon, 2007; Castel-Branco, 2008). In this context, most donors providing support for the justice sector concentrate on formal justice. Amongst the few donors who fund initiatives regarding informal justice we find the Danish bilateral cooperation, which at the moment the research was conducted, provided support for the community courts as part of its access to justice strategy. Aid was mainly channelled through the Ministry of Justice for mapping the existing community courts, building new ones and training their judges.[22] This training consisted in providing community court judges with basic knowledge of statutory laws concerning areas they frequently deal with, such as family and criminal matters, including which cases fall under the jurisdiction of community courts and which ones do not.[23] In addition, some support was given to civil society organisations for research on informal justice.

UNDP and the EU also provided some support for informal justice providers in the context of a project to improve access to state courts at the district level by building three 'Citizen's Forums of Justice', i.e. district courts that house the main justice and public order actors in one same building (the police, investigating and judging magistrates, legal and paralegal defenders, prison officers, etc).[24] These activities included a component on legal education for community leaders and community court judges, which consisted in two-day seminars on justice and human rights, preceding the inauguration of the 'Citizens' Forums for Justice'. During the seminars, community authorities were given information on how a district court functions, when cases should be referred to these courts and a general introduction to human rights.[25] This project also included a component on human rights awareness raising in community theatres in a number of districts neighbouring the 'Citizens' Forums for Justice'. Drawing on examples of concrete daily practices and conflicts, the theatre pieces illustrated with humour how these

21 Personal interviews, Maputo, 2009.
22 Interview with an official of the Danish bilateral cooperation, Maputo 13/08/09.
23 Personal interview with a trainer, Maputo, 17/08/09.
24 'Support to the Citizen in Access to Justice' EU and UNDP (2005–2009).
25 Personal observations, Morrumbene, October 2009.

situations could be approached in a way that respects human rights.[26] Finally, the World Bank supported similar initiatives under its 'Access to Justice sub-grants' for civil society organisations to pilot activities, which raise awareness of citizens' rights and disseminate legal and judicial information as part of a multi-donor programme 'Public Sector Reform Project' (2003–2009).

In addition, a number of international NGOs, such as Action Aid, HIVOS and Oxfam International, as well as some bilateral donors, such as the embassies of the Netherlands, Sweden and Norway, provided support to civil society organisations working in the area of gender so that they disseminate simplified versions of the family law adopted in 2004 and of the law on domestic violence adopted in 2009.[27] Most of these organisations did not have a specific focus on informal justice, but their activities interplayed with this domain. For example, according to a local representative of Action Aid, their work aimed at generating a demand for the protection of these rights so that changes are brought about 'from within', including at informal justice forums. As she explained, discussing the new legislation at community level opens the eyes of many women and gives them a tool to improve their situation so that when they seek justice, they know their rights, independently from the forum they resort to.[28] Other organisations, such as MULEIDE, were supported to give free legal advice to women or to mediate in family-related conflicts, such as in the case of the Gabinete Juridico of Pemba. Finally, Oxfam UK launched research into the relationship between traditional culture and domestic violence. The aim of this research was to understand how the community courts can contribute to the elimination of domestic violence. It is the intention to employ this knowledge base in the elaboration of future projects in this area.[29]

Another area in which international actors indirectly engaged with legal pluralism is children's rights. In 2008, a new children's law was adopted and UNICEF supported the distribution of simplified versions of this piece of legislation at grassroots level. The rationale for this was that by knowing the law, people would modify certain practices that are at odds with children's rights, such as early marriages and physical punishments.[30] However, these activities were carried out without engaging in a dialogue on how the law relates to local practices and ideas. As a local school authority explained, 'these laws are perceived to weaken adults' authority to discipline children'.[31] Acknowledging this tension, a member of Save the Children reported that they were still looking

---

26 In the case of the project in the province of Inhambane, the topics dealt with included domestic violence, land conflicts, family conflicts, early marriages and noise pollution. Personal interviews with activists of the local organisation AJUDINHA and observations, Morrumbene and Massinga, August–September 2009.

27 Personal interviews, Maputo, October 2009.

28 Personal interview with a representative of Action Aid, Maputo, 20/08/09.

29 Telephone interview with a representative of Oxfam UK, October 2009.

30 Personal interview with a representative of UNICEF, 19/08/09.

31 Personal interview with a local school authority at Malaia, 01/09/09.

for the right strategies to deal with the uneasy relationship between the principles and ideas enshrined in international children's rights and national laws and local practices and ideas about children and childhood, being the gradual persuasion and collaboration with local leaders the path that so far gave them best results.[32]

Finally, customary land tenure was another area where international actors engaged with legal pluralism and informal justice. The Land Law of 1997 recognises customary land rights and gives them full equivalence to state issued land rights. In this context, FAO in partnership with the national Legal and Judicial Training Centre (CFJJ) gave support for policy development, awareness raising of the new law, capacity building to the formal judiciary for oversight tasks and legal empowerment of local communities through a paralegal programme. The Embassy of Norway funded the FAO and the CFJJ in a similar paralegal project focusing specifically on women's customary land rights (2009–2011). The following table maps these interventions according to the typology developed in Chapter 8:

Type of interventions	At state level	At local level
Law reform interventions	- Adoption of the land law recognising customary land tenure (supported by FAO)	- Dialogue with local leaders about children's rights and local customs (Save the Children)
Institutional support and reform interventions	- Mapping community courts (DANIDA) - Building new community courts (DANIDA)	- Draft law on the regulation of community courts (government initiative, no involvement of international actors)
Strengthening of the legal community (justice providers)	- Training formal judges on their oversight functions regarding customary land tenure (FAO)	- Training community court judges on statutory laws (DANIDA) - Legal education seminaries for community authorities (UNDP/EU)
Empowering justice users	- Community theatre regarding human rights (UNDP/EU) - Human rights awareness raising (the World Bank) - Dissemination of simplified versions of the family law, the law on domestic violence, the law on children and the land law (Embassy of the Netherlands, Embassy of Norway, Embassy of Sweden, Action Aid, HIVOS, Oxfam, UNICEF, FAO) - Provision of paralegal services with a focus on gender (Embassy of the Netherlands, HIVOS, Oxfam) - Provision of paralegal services with a focus on land issues (FAO)/land issues with a focus on gender (FAO/Embassy of Norway)	

32 Personal interview with a representative of Save the Children, 24/08/09.

7. CONCLUSION

When analysing these interventions in the light of the socio-legal insights presented in Chapter 10, we find considerable variation depending on the type of organisation providing aid and the kind of actor they partner up with at national and grassroots level. As mentioned earlier, most multilateral and bilateral donors active in the justice sector adopted a state centric approach to justice sector aid.[33] For its part, the government, their main partner, had no policy on how to implement the principle of legal pluralism enshrined in the National Constitution with regard to other informal justice providers apart from the community courts. In this context, the Danish bilateral cooperation, the only donor that provided support for informal justice, concentrated exclusively on the community courts, while the vast array of other local justice providers remained invisible.

While there is nothing wrong in supporting state justice institutions, a legally plural approach implies that the relationship of state institutions and other regulatory forces present in a certain locality is empirically studied and taken as the point of departure for devising interventions. In this regard, the problem is not so much a lack of studies, but rather that little is done with them. An example of this is the project financed by the EU and UNDP for improving access to justice at local level by building district courts that house all state justice actors. These 'Citizen's Forums of Justice' were built in three pilot districts and informal justice providers were instructed in seminaries when to transfer cases to these courts, assuming that they will automatically do so and that local justice seekers have nothing to say in this. Socio-legal studies demonstrate that the provision of justice is highly influenced by political stakes leading forums to 'shop' for disputes and justice seekers to 'shop' for forums (Von Benda-Beckmann, 1981). Existing studies show clearly that this applies to Mozambique (Kyed, 2009; Lubkemann et al., 2011). This project could have incorporated a component on research about local justice provision in the districts were these courts were built in order to assess informal justice providers' and justice seekers' expectations and stakes. This kind of knowledge could have served as the basis for the organisation of discussions between locally available justice providers, formal and informal on equal footing, in collaboration with NGOs and other local stakeholders, about existing views on how to improve access to justice and how to negotiate competing interests in this domain. Moreover, it is not only informal justice providers who need training about formal justice. State court judges could also benefit from trainings about informal justice and legal pluralism. With the exception of the CFJJ/FAO, who train formal judges on their oversight function in cases of customary land tenure, no international actor provided support for capacity building of formal justice providers in the area of legal pluralism or for exchange and dialogue between

[33] Personal interviews with donors providing aid to the justice sector, Maputo, August–September 2009.

formal and informal justice providers. In other words, interventions should acknowledge that state law is not hegemonic and that it is more in tune with reality to generate legitimate spaces for building trust and addressing contested issues (Sage et al., 2010). Mozambique has already experienced such a participatory process at a much broader scale when it adopted the Land Law in the mid-1990s, with the support of the FAO (Tanner, 2002). This experience could serve as an example of how donors can promote inclusive negotiations in politically sensitive arenas.

In a similar vein, the initiatives financed by DANIDA in the area of community courts do not reflect an engagement with empirical realities of legal pluralism, but rather with legal pluralism as it is defined by state laws and policies. Though there is no doubt that community courts need support, what is questioned here is the exclusive focus on these forums, whereas the reality on the ground shows that local justice provision is much more polycentric. This is surprising since DANIDA has financed important research projects that document this.[34] But even in the case of the community courts engagement seems to be weak, as it is evidenced by the lack of interest donors show on existing law reform proposals to regulate the community courts.

At the level of international NGOs and their domestic partners, most organisations consulted for this research seemed to adopt a more empirical approach to legal pluralism and collaborate with a broader range of informal justice providers, or even create new layers of local justice provision as it is the case of paralegal organisations. However, such activities were undertaken with a focus on specific 'themes', such as the promotion of women's and children's rights and access to land, rather than from the perspective of how multiple forms of justice provision co-exist at local level and the impact thereof.

In terms of the strategies supported for the promotion of human rights within local justice processes, here again we find a tendency towards more state centric approaches supported by donors in partnership with the government, as compared to the kind of initiatives supported and implemented by NGOs. As the previous section shows, most of the interventions to promote human rights entailed education for informal justice providers about state law and the dissemination of national laws at grassroots level. While community authorities may welcome any form of capacity building, a legally plural approach would incorporate a discussion on how state laws relate to local norms and practices, and would open spaces for dialogue and inputs 'from below' on the extent to which this legislation responds to local realities. Similarly, the dissemination of national laws at grassroots level without reference to local experiences implies that local actors are left alone in the task of 'mediating' between competing normative repertoires. As exemplified by the comments of the teacher who considered that

34 B. de Sousa Santos and C. Trindade, *Conflito e Transformação Social: Uma Paisagem das Justiças em Moçambique*, 2003.

children's rights undermine the authority of adults, not taking seriously these local perspectives implies a risk that human rights are seen as illegitimate and are therefore not respected. Dialogic approaches hold better promise as they take such concerns seriously and engage in a process of arriving together at solutions that combine local and transnational forms of knowledge.

Finally, the provision of paralegal services adds a new layer of justice provision to an already highly populated justice landscape. The fact that these initiatives often adopt a gender perspective means that they can potentially empower disadvantaged groups, such as women, by making available knowledge and mediating capacities that resonate with their stakes. However, this entails a shift in power relations that is likely to meet resistance. Therefore, though in principle these initiatives have the potential to promote women's rights, it is necessary to monitor the extent to which their promise is realised and to understand the factors that interplay with their results.

BIBLIOGRAPHY

Araújo, S. (2010) Por uma Ecologia de Justiças: Um Estudo a Partir do Pluralismo Juridico Moçambicano. Paper presented at the International Conference on State and Non-State Public Safety and Justice Provision: The Dynamics of Legal Pluralism in Mozambique, Maputo, 28–30 April.

Arthur, M.J. and Mejia, M. (2006) Instâncias locais de resolução de conflitos e o reforço dos papéis de género. A resolução de casos de violencia doméstica, 47–69. In Arthur, M.J. (ed.) *Memórias do Activismo, pelos direitos humanos das mulheres*. Mozambique: WLSA.

De Tollenaere, M. (2006) Democracy Assistance to Post-Conflict Mozambique: Intentions and Outcomes. Working Paper No. 37, Netherlands Institute of International Relations 'Clingedael'.

Di Renzio, P. and Hanlon, J. (2007) Contested Sovereignty in Mozambique: The Dilemmas of Aid Dependence. GEG Working Paper 2007/25, University of Oxford.

Casimiro, I. and Fonseca, F. (2009) Baseline Study Regarding the Impact of the Mozambican Family Law [online] http://issuu.com/oa-padare/docs/glr_baseline_policy_report__eng._tran___oct._2009_ (08/05/2012).

Castel-Branco, C. (2008) Aid Dependency and Development: A Question of Ownership? A Critical View. Working Paper No. 1/2008, Instituto de Estudos Sociais e Economicos.

Government of Mozambique (2008) Tribunais Comunitarios, Mapeamento de Julho de 2008. Not published. On file with author.

Hanlon, J. and Smart, T. (2008) *Há mais bicicletas mas há desenvolvimento?* Maputo: Kapicua Libros e Multimédia.

Jacobs, C. (2010) Plurality of Religion, Plurality of Justice. Exploring the Role of Religion in Disputing Processes in Gorongosa, Central Mozambique. PhD Thesis, Wageningen University, the Netherlands.

Kyed, H.M. (2009) The Politics of Legal Pluralism: State Policies on Legal Pluralism and Their Local Dynamics in Mozambique, *Journal of Legal Pluralism and Unofficial Law*, 59, 87–121.

Lubkemann, S., Kyed, H.M. and Garvey, J. (2011) Dilemmas of Articulation in Mozambique: Customary Justice in Transition. In Isser, D. (ed.) *Customary Justice and the Rule of Law in War-Torn Societies*, 13–76. Washington, DC: United States Institute of Peace Press.

Meneses, M.P. (2007) *Pluralism, Law and Citizenship in Mozambique: Mapping the Complexity*, Oficina 291. Coimbra: Centro de Estudos Sociais.

O'Laughlin, B. (2000) Class and the customary: the ambiguous legacy of the Indigenato in Mozambique, *African Affairs*, 99/394, 5–42.

Open Society Initiative for South Africa (2006) Moçambique, O Sector da Justiça e O Estado de Direito [online] www.afrimap.org.

Sachs, A. and Welch, H. (1990) *Liberating the Law*. London: Zed Books.

Sage, C., Menzies, N. and Woolcock, M. (2010) Taking the Rules of the Game Seriously: Mainstreaming Justice in Development. The World Bank Justice for the Poor Program. In Golub, S. (ed.) *Legal Empowerment: Practitioners' Perspectives*. Rome: International Legal Development Office.

Santos, B. de Sousa (2006) The Heterogeneous State and Legal Pluralism in Mozambique, *Law & Society Review*, 40(1), 39–76.

Tanner, C. (2002) Law Making in an African Context: The 1997 Mozambican Land Law, FAO Legal Papers online 26 [online] http://www.fao.org/fileadmin/user_upload/legal/docs/lpo26.pdf (06/05/2013).

Trindade, C. (2003). Rupturas e Continuidades nos Processos Politicos e Juridicos. In de Sousa Santos, B. and Trindade, C. (eds.) *Conflito e Transformação Social: Uma Paissagem das Justiças em Moçambique*, 97–128. Oporto: Afrontamento.

Von Benda-Beckman, K. (1981) Forum Shopping and Shopping Forums: Dispute Processing in a Minangkabau Village in West Sumatra, *Journal of Legal Pluralism*, 19, 117–160.

CHAPTER 13
BEYOND DICHOTOMIES: A CASE STUDY ON SIERRA LEONE

Giselle Corradi

1. INTRODUCTION

This chapter discusses how international development actors providing aid to the justice sector in Sierra Leone position themselves in view of legal pluralism and the promotion of human rights in local justice processes. The chapter begins with an overview of the main colonial and post-colonial developments that led to the current justice landscape and institutional framework for legal pluralism. After describing the main features of the latter and their main challenges in terms of human rights, the chapter depicts how international development actors engage with these realities and maps their interventions. The concluding discussion analyses the latter in the light of the socio-legal insights presented in Chapter 10 and argues that these interventions tend to reflect a dichotomous view of legal pluralism, in terms of the dual system that is established by law, in contrast to a legally plural perspective that considers the interaction amongst multiple co-existing legal actors and normative orders.

2. COLONIAL AND POST-COLONIAL BACKGROUND OF LEGAL PLURALISM

As described in Chapter 4, Sierra Leone gained independency from the British in 1961. Before then, the territory of modern Freetown and the Western peninsula became a British Crown Colony in 1808 and was governed by English law. In 1896, a Protectorate was further established to govern the provincial areas by indirect rule (Alie, 1990: 112–164). Under this system, the British colonial administration ruled over rural Sierra Leone by co-opting and subordinating traditional authorities to their power, while at the same time enhancing these authorities' power over their populations (Maru, 2006; Alie, 1990). As a result, chiefdoms were created as administrative units, paramount chiefs were designated as their rulers and the Native Courts Act was passed, giving chiefs authority to adjudicate customary law in their chiefdoms (Maru, 2005: 18, 19; Alie, 1990: 134–135, 152–153). After independence in 1961, the Local Courts Act was passed (1963), replacing native courts by local courts and the power of chiefs to administer justice was passed onto local court chairmen. In this way, a recognised version of customary law continued to be part of the formal legal system of Sierra Leone to date, albeit with the many changes introduced during colonial and post colonial administrations.[1]

With the end of the civil war in 2002, new opportunities opened up for reviewing the organisation of justice in Sierra Leone.[2] In part, this results from the fact that the weaknesses found in the administration of justice after the conflict were not only associated to the legacy of the war itself, but went back to pre-war times (Thompson, 2002: 5). During the conflict, the judiciary was severely affected at all levels (Keen, 2003: 74). State institutions, including magistrate courts, were systematically targeted, bringing the activities of formal courts in the provinces to almost a complete halt (Thompson, 2002: 10). In those regions where local courts were not attacked, they continued to function but without any government support, the – often arbitrary – fines being their only source of income (Thompson, 2002: 11). The role of chiefs in the administration of justice was also affected during wartime, since they were specifically targeted during the conflict (Archibald and Richards, 2002: 344). All these processes led to a complex justice landscape, which is described in the next section.

3. THE JUSTICE LANDSCAPE AND INSTITUTIONAL FRAMEWORK FOR LEGAL PLURALISM

Sierra Leone has a dual legal system, where two types of official law operate concurrently. On the one hand there is general law, which is often called 'the formal system', including the Constitution, laws made by Parliament and common law. On the other hand there is an institutionalised customary law system, often called 'semi-formal', which is recognised by the Constitution as part of common law and which is defined as 'the rules of law', which by custom are applicable to particular communities in Sierra Leone.[3] The formal legal system comprises the Supreme Court, the appeals courts, the high courts and the magistrate courts.[4] These

---

1 For a discussion of the changes brought about in customary law by the colonial rule see Kent, 2007; Manning, 2008a: footnote 27; Archibald and Richards, 2002: 343.

2 For a description of the causes and development of the civil war in Sierra Leone, as well as the transitional justice process see chapter.

3 The Constitution of Sierra Leone, 1991, Section 170.

4 Magistrate courts are courts of first instance for civil disputes below Le 250,000 (about USD 68) or criminal offences where the punishment is a prison sentence of less than three years, or up to seven years if the accused consents. A magistrate court can also be constituted by

courts have jurisdiction to adjudicate serious crimes, civil claims in Freetown and some civil and claims throughout the provinces.[5] However, different studies on the legal systems in Sierra Leone point to the fact that the formal system is not the dominant mode of dispute resolution for the larger majority of Sierra Leoneans (Manning, 2008a; Dale, 2008, 2007; Baker, 2005; Alterman et al., 2002). One of the reasons for this is the inaccessibility of these courts in terms of distance, costs – including direct costs for filing a case – any possible fines, time and transportation (Dale, 2007: 1–2). Moreover, there exist a number of social and cultural barriers, such as language, formality, lack of information and lack of trust (Dale, 2007: 1–2). 'Local courts' are formally and legally empowered to hear and determine cases of customary law issues in the provinces.[6] They have jurisdiction within their chiefdom over all civil cases governed by customary law, all civil cases governed by general law where the claim does not exceed 250,000 Leones, and all criminal cases, where the sentence does not exceed six months or the fine does not exceed 50,000 Leones, though in practice these limits are not always respected (Kent, 2007: 523).[7] This customary system is linked to the formal one by means of an appeal procedure that places the former below the hierarchy of the latter. In theory, a party unsatisfied with the decision of a local court can appeal to the districts appeal courts, which consists of a district magistrate sitting with two assessors who are experts in customary law. Appeals to this court are to the local appeals division of the high court, which is constituted by a high court judge sitting with two assessors. Appeals from decisions of the high court lie to the court of appeal and finally to the Supreme Court. In practice though, the appeals procedure is rarely used.[8] In addition, the law foresees regional customary law officers, who are appointed by the Ministry of Justice and whose functions are to advice on matters related to customary law and revise local courts' decisions, but there are only three officers for the whole country.[9]

---

two 'justices of the peace' or lay magistrates. High courts have original jurisdiction for cases exceeding that.

5 Sierra Leone is divided into three provincial areas: Southern province, Eastern province and Northern province and the Western area, which comprises Freetown, the capital. Each province is divided into districts (12 in total), which are further divided into Chiefdoms (149 in total) and these are divided into sections. Magistrate courts can be found in the provinces up to the district level.

6 According to Sierra Leone's senior customary law officer, there are 300 local courts spread evenly in the country at chiefdom level, except for the Western area. Personal interview, Bo, 14/04/09.

7 Criminal cases, such as murder or armed robbery are mainly reported to the Sierra Leonean police, personal interviews, Bo, April 2009; See also Archibald and Richards, 2002: 343.

8 Personal interviews, Freetown, April 2009; See also Manning, 2008a: 5.

9 Interview with customary law officer, Bo, 14/04/09.

This dual system can be illustrated with the following graphic:

Figure 4. The institutional framework for legal pluralism in Sierra Leone

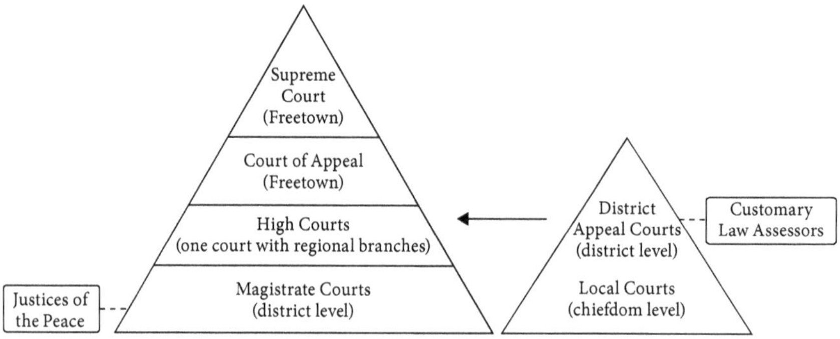

Alongside these official legal actors, there operate a range of traditional justice instances and authorities, such as paramount chiefs', section chiefs' and village chiefs' courts, religious leaders, professional circle leaders, gender and youth leaders, village elders and family heads, secret societies, and sorcerers (Sawyer, 2008; Manning, 2008a; Manning et al., 2006; Baker, 2005; Kane et al., 2005; Alterman et al., 2002; Archibald and Richards, 2002). Chiefs are present in each human settlement in Sierra Leone and they are legally empowered to mediate or arbitrate but not to adjudicate, though in practice they often do (Manning, 2008a: 6; Manning et al., 2006: 13). They play an important role in solving disputes and providing more affordable and speedy solutions to conflicts (Sawyer, 2008), but their popularity varies from chiefdom to chiefdom (Manning et al., 2006). Religious leaders also play a role in mediation, as do women, youth and professional circle leaders regarding intra group disputes (Alterman, et al., 2002: 30–31; Manning, 2008a: 7).[10] In addition, paralegals and peace monitors are often approached for advice and mediation, where modern and traditional laws and views of justice are combined in the treatment of cases with high rates of satisfaction (Sawyer, 2008; Maru, 2006: 427–476; Baker, 2005: 381). Sorcerers and supernatural forces are part of the informal legal landscape too (Manning, 2008a; Sawyer, 2008; Alie, 2008; Fanthorpe, 2007; Kane et al., 2005; Alterman et al., 2002). Belief in the supernatural seems to be quite strong in some communities and infractions of certain rules are feared to bring illness and misfortune, not only to the person in question but also to the community (Alie, 2008: 136). Diviners are often relied upon for the identification of culprits or for planting curses (Sawyer, 2008; Kane, 2005: 15; Alterman et al., 2002: 33). In addition, certain matters are

[10] According to the 2004 National Census, 77% of Sierra Leoneans are Muslim, 21% are Christian and 2% follow no religion, but the majority combine the latter with traditional beliefs (Manning, 2008a: footnote 43).

handled by sodality groups called secret societies (Fanthorpe, 2007: 4; Kane, 2005: 15; Alterman et al., 2002: 31–32). These are single sex communities, the purpose of which is to regulate sexual identity and social conduct, while canalising and controlling powers of the spirit world (Fanthorpe, 2007: ii, 1). They prepare men and women for adult life by means of initiation ceremonies, forming solidarity networks amongst age groups who are initiated in the same event (Fanthorpe, 2007).[11] Their activities include meetings that are only open to society members and where decisions are taken affecting many aspects of open communal life. These institutions are deeply rooted in Sierra Leonean culture (Fanthorpe, 2007), though according to some reports their importance is in decline in some communities (Manning, 2008a: 7). However, because of their very nature, their actual role and functioning in terms of justice administration remains difficult for outsiders to assess.

4. THE HUMAN RIGHTS LANDSCAPE

Several aspects of the social organisation in Sierra Leone have been identified as marginalising and unfair. In human rights terms, this comes down to the exclusion of many Sierra Leoneans, and in particular certain categories of persons, such as women, children, 'youth' and 'strangers', from civil and political rights, as well as social and economic rights.[12] In varying degrees, this is reflected at all layers of the administration of justice, and it would be inaccurate to regard this problem as one of customary justice. At a formal level, Sierra Leone is signatory to the main international and regional human rights conventions. Treaty provisions have to be domesticated into national laws, which according to the Sierra Leonean Human Rights Commission, has not been satisfactorily done.[13] For example, the National Constitution is contradictory in that some sections grant the protection of the rights of women and discourage discrimination – section 6(2), whereas other sections allow discrimination under laws of adoption, marriage, divorce, burial, property and aspects of personal law – section 27. In 2007, the government of Sierra Leone enacted the Gender Acts, i.e. the Domestic Violence Act, the Devolution of Estates Act and the Registration of Customary Marriage Act, as well as the Child Act in order to domesticate the Convention on the Elimination of all forms of Discrimination against Women and the Convention on the Rights of the Child. This legislation represents an advancement in the protection of

11 In rural Sierra Leone, initiation is a requisite for full integration of the individual as a community member. In the case of women, this includes circumcision (Fanthorpe, 2007).

12 The term 'stranger' refers to a migrant from another region of the country, whereas 'youth' is not necessarily defined by age, but rather socially as a person that is unmarried, landless and without economic and political power (Manning, 2008b: 2).

13 Human Rights Commission of Sierra Leone, The State of Human Rights in Sierra Leone 2007, p. ix.

women's and children's rights, though certain areas still fall short of international standards, such as the silence regarding the prohibition of female circumcision (Mannah, 2007).

The discrimination of women in customary law and justice is one of the most problematic human rights issues throughout the entire country (Human Rights Commission of Sierra Leone, 2007: 22; CEDAW Report Sierra Leone, 2006; Amnesty International, 2006). At present, customary justice in its various forms tends to be male-dominated and patriarchal, which is reflected in traditional laws related to land tenure and inheritance, where women are not allowed to own or inherit property, in customary marriages, where women fulfil a subservient role towards their partners, in the husband's right to punish his wife, and in the exclusion of women from participation in many spheres of political life, amongst other issues. These discriminatory customs result in widespread violations of women's most basic human rights, including lack of access to a fair hearing, unlawful imprisonments and punishments, a lack of respect for their physical integrity, disrespect for their property rights, as in the case of forceful evictions from their homes and land, as well as high levels of domestic and sexual violence, which represents a significant obstacle to reducing poverty.[14]

Children are also subject to discrimination, particularly in the case of the girls. Clear examples of discriminatory practices are the forced betrothal of girls and early marriage, which are often related to dowry transactions. Moreover, only local 'citizens' have access to local courts, whereas 'strangers' can only access a local court through a local citizen protector (Archibald and Richards, 2002: 344).[15] Another salient feature of customary law is its oral character, which in many cases has resulted in manipulation, abusive fines and arbitrary trials (Archibald and Richards, 2002). Corporal punishments were reported to be in decline, though this is probably the case at local courts and adjudication by chiefs, whereas it remains unclear if it is also the case within secret societies.[16]

5. INTERNATIONAL ACTORS AND LOCAL LEGAL ORDERS

The interviewed development actors reported not to follow a specific or official policy regarding legal pluralism as such. Concerning the institutions associated with customary justice and traditional authority in particular, most international

---

14 For instance, according to the testimony of a woman from Kenema town, local court officials put her in a box in public all day to humiliate her as a punishment for not signing divorce papers that would deprive her and her children of any maintenance rights (Amnesty International, 2006: 5, 6).

15 'Local citizens' are persons from the town, whereas 'strangers' are migrants from other regions of the country.

16 Personal interviews, April 2009. According to some authors, human sacrifices are carried out within the secret societies in order to assuage the spirits. Bellman, 1975, in Fanthorpe, 2007.

development actors acknowledged the need to engage with these structures. In most cases, the main rationale was access to justice, i.e. in the absence of state justice these institutions perform an important role (DFID, UNDP, UNIPSIL), but some actors also emphasised the intrinsic value of these institutions, in the sense that they are less adversarial and contain a dimension related to social harmony and cohesion that is missing within state justice (UNDP, UNIPSIL, UNFPA). In addition, there was a general perception that it was necessary to make traditional authorities and local level justice institutions more downwardly accountable in order to avoid a repetition of the circumstances that led to the violence. In this regard, a recurrent discourse amongst development actors was that it is necessary to do away with the negative features of customary justice, while preserving the good ones. Amongst the negative features that development actors associated with customary justice we found are its unwritten character, which would result in legal uncertainty and abusive practices, and the fact that customary justice is male-dominated, resulting in discrimination of the basis of gender. Other challenges included the local character of customary law, i.e. that it varies from community to community.

Regarding the kind of interventions that development actors supported in order to address these challenges, we found four main strategies, each dealing with customary justice at a different level: first, the enactment of legislation at a national level regulating problematic aspects of customary law; second, interventions at the level of local courts, such as the restatement of customary law and capacity building, including human rights education for local court personnel; third, sensitisation and human rights training for traditional authorities, and fourth, human rights awareness raising activities at grassroots level. In addition, we found a series of initiatives, the main objective of which was not to address the tension between customary justice and human rights as such, but which in practice deliver a significant contribution to this end. This is the case of paralegal services and peace monitoring schemes, which create new local layers of justice.

At a national level, the above-mentioned Gender and Child Acts were adopted in 2007 with the support of UNIFEM. This legislation introduced a new framework for the regulation of several aspects of customary law. The Registration of Customary Marriage and Divorce Act provides for the registration of customary marriages and divorces so that marital status can be proved. In addition, it forbids marriage below the age of 18 and it requires the consent of both parties. It also confers on women the right to acquire and dispose of property in their own right, and it abolishes the return of dowry in case of divorce or separation. The Devolution of Estates Act modifies customary law by introducing a principle that both husband and wife have the right to inherit property from each other. In addition, male and female children are given the same inheritance rights. Further, it prohibits involuntary wife inheritance. Finally, the Domestic Violence Act introduced a new offence of domestic violence, which should modify the stance of customary justice towards condoning certain forms of conduct, such as wife battering. The Child Act refers to the prohibition of forced marriage and dowry transactions and it provides for the right to inherit from parents, whether or not a child was born in wedlock. However, these steps are seriously undermined by the fact that section 27(4)(d) of the Constitution, which takes precedence over these laws, tolerates discrimination with respect to 'adoption, marriage, divorce, burial, devolution of property on death or other interests of personal law' (Kamara, 2008).

The Ministry of Social Welfare, Gender and Children's Affairs (MSWGCA) was the lead agency in the implementation of this legislation through a three year (2009–2011) 'Strategic Roll Out Plan', which included a series of initiatives related to primary justice (MSWGCA, n.d.). This plan was developed with the technical support of the Human Rights Commission for Sierra Leone, the International Rescue Committee, UNIOSIL and Action Aid, and with the financial support of UNIFEM and Irish Aid. However, the implementation of this plan was seriously undermined by a lack of funding and capacity. The MSWGCA had one of the smallest budgets, with current government priorities lying elsewhere. As a result, by the time of our visit to Sierra Leone, the Ministry had not been able to attract the necessary funding and these activities could not yet be properly undertaken.[17]

In addition, a 'Local Courts Bill' was in the process of being drafted with the support of the Justice Sector Development Programme (JSDP).[18] This law reform aimed at depoliticising the local courts and reviewing aspects of their functioning that interfere with the right to a fair trial, such as the appointment of local court chairmen on the recommendation of chiefs. In the proposed Bill such appointments are transferred to the Chief Justice, on the recommendation of a 'local court service committee'.[19]

Local courts were targeted by different initiatives, the 'restatement' of customary law and human rights education being amongst the main ones. Under a pilot project of JSDP in Moyamba district, a 'restatement' of the customary law of the local courts of the 14 chiefdoms of the district was completed. The exercise was carried out by the senior customary law officer of Sierra Leone assisted by local court clerks, who by means of consultation with the communities and traditional authorities arrived at a first written version in English of the customary laws in place. The purpose of this intervention was to register the customary laws at the level of local courts in order to identify the areas that contravene human rights and modify them. Once approved by the Ministry of Justice and the local traditional authorities, this would serve as a model to be scaled up to eventually

17 Interview with an official from the MSWGCA, Freetown, 17/04/09.

18 JSDP was a five-year programme (2005–2010) of the Government of Sierra Leone for the justice sector funded by the UK Department for International Development and managed by the British Council. This programme was followed by the programme 'Improved Access to Security and Justice Programme in Sierra Leone' (IASJP, 2010–2013).

19 Paramount chiefs would continue to form part of these committees, but their influence would be limited by the presence of other members. Interview at Court Monitoring Programme, 07/04/09; Interview at JSDP, 09/04/09.

arrive at a national codification of customary laws.[20] Even though codification has been generally rejected by most scholars on the basis that it 'freezes' tradition, in Sierra Leone the dominant view amongst most national and international actors was that the unwritten character of customary law led to uncertainty and abuse, which can be remedied by writing it down and making it publicly known.[21] In this sense, it is worth noticing that the customary law that would be registered is the one used at the level of the local courts, leaving aside the norms that guide disputing processes within the many other local forums that exist in Sierra Leone.

In addition, research on the functioning of local courts led JSDP to conclude that there was a need for capacity building, so a training manual was developed for this purpose, including a module on procedures and jurisdiction of the local courts, a module on human rights, and a module on records management, which was used to train the local courts' staff. Support to the capacity of local courts extended to infrastructure as well, with the provision of material for record keeping, which would be used in case of appeals. Further, the United Nations Integrated Peacebuilding Office in Sierra Leone (UNIPSIL) and UNDP supported human rights monitoring and training at local courts in collaboration with the customary law officer.[22]

Chiefs and traditional authorities were mainly targeted for sensitisation about human rights. Such was the case of UNICEF's initiative 'Chiefs Champions for Children', which aimed at getting traditional chiefs to promote girl child education, and denounce early marriages and female circumcision, amongst other acts.[23] The United Nations Population Fund supported the formation of community leaders' networks, with the purpose of reinforcing their capacity to promote human rights and the Pilot Project of JSDP in Moyamba district has also involved traditional authorities in their 'task force', including a paramount chief who is a member of the human rights committee.[24] All these initiatives aimed at generating the collaboration of traditional authorities in the promotion of human rights, which would eventually be reflected in the incorporation of human rights ideas in the way they deal with conflict resolution.

At the same time, chiefs were sensitised to devolve adjudication to the local courts, which would result in fairer trials.[25] The World Bank's 'Justice for the Poor' programme in Sierra Leone conducted research on processes of justice delivery

---

20 Interview with an official from the JSDP, Freetown, 09/04/09; Interview with Customary Law Officer, Bo, 14/04/09; Interview with an official from the JSDP, Moyamba, 15/04/09.

21 Personal interviews, April 2009. See also Kane et al., 2005: 24, 25.

22 Interview with an official from UNIPSIL, Freetown, 08/04/09. See also UNDP, 2009.

23 Interview with an official from UNICEF local office, Freetown, 08/04/09.

24 Interview with officials from United Nations Population Fund (UNFPA) local office, Freetown, 06/04/09 and Interview with Paramount Chief Joseph Ali-Kavura Kongomah II, Fakunya Chiefdom, 15/04/09.

25 All national and international organisations that were interviewed coincided in agreeing that the role of chiefs should be to mediate or arbitrate but not to adjudicate. Personal interviews, April 2009.

and decision-making at grassroots level and concluded that chiefs should be empowered to mediate and arbitrate on disputes, but not to adjudicate, as a means to assure their social legitimacy and downwards accountability. This was taken up by the JSDP, which foresaw the sensitisation of chiefs so that they would focus on mediation and derive cases that need to be adjudicated to the local courts.[26] This was complemented by informing communities about the official role of the chiefs in the justice sector and by encouraging people to reconcile rather than resorting to chiefs' courts for adjudication.

In addition, different awareness raising campaigns were organised with the goal of promoting a better understanding of the justice sector and an internalisation of human rights at the grassroots. For example, JSDP and the Lawyers Centre for Legal Assistance (LAWCLA) supported the dissemination of the Gender and Child Acts at community level and UNICEF supported the incorporation of new curricula at schools, where children learn about their rights and more progressive gender roles.[27] In addition, illiterate people were targeted by radio programmes, community drama and storytelling, community cinema projections and music. The use of theatre, social drama, storytelling and songs for the promotion of community discussions on traditional values and human rights were reported to be popular techniques for opening up discussions on human rights issues by building on the African oral tradition.[28] In doing this, some actors tried to identify local practices and ideas that reinforced those values that can be found in human rights, so that the concept would not be perceived as strange or as coming from outside.[29]

Finally, paralegals and 'peace monitors' were also expected to raise human rights awareness at the grassroots. These organisations did not address the tension between customary justice and human rights directly, but they provided different services at community level, such as mediation, education, advocacy and free legal services, thereby constituting an alternative to other local channels to seek justice.[30] Working with local respected people facilitated the acceptance of these schemes that, in principle, constitute some form of 'competition' with local traditional authorities. This was mitigated by a search for cooperation and mutual involvement, and by seeking to reinterpret local customs in line with human rights, rather than challenging them altogether. Amongst the main paralegal organisations engaging in these activities we found Timap for Justice, who was supported by OSISA. In addition, the British NGO 'Conciliation Resources' provided support for community mediation schemes and 'peace monitors', which

---

26 Interview with an officer of J4P, Freetown, 09/04/09.

27 Interview with an official from UNICEF local office, Freetown, 08/04/09.

28 Interview with an activist from 'Community Organization for Mobilization and Empowerment' (COME) Sierra Leone, Bo, 14/04/09. These activities have been financed by JSDP. See also Jalloh and Braima, 2008.

29 Interview with officials from UNFPA local office, Freetown, 06/04/09.

30 Interview with a member of 'Timap for Justice', Freetown 09/04/09, Interview with a member of 'Timap for Justice', Bo 14/04/09.

are respected individuals in their communities, including sometimes the chiefs. The peace monitors received training on conflict management techniques and human rights, which was linked to local traditional methods of compromise and conflict settlement. The aim of this project was that during meetings and dialogues, the peace facilitators, the conflicting parties and community members analyse the causes, consequences and solutions to their problems.[31] The following chart presents a mapping of these interventions according to the typology developed in Chapter 8:

Type of interventions	At state level	At customary level
Law reform interventions	- Enactment of legislation regulating the content of customary law (the 'Gender Laws' and the 'Child Act' of 2005) (UNIFEM)	- Ascertainment of customary laws applied by local courts (DFID) - Theatre, storytelling and songs for the promotion of community discussions on traditional values and human rights (DFID)
Institutional support/reform interventions		- Modification of appointment procedures for local court chairmen (DFID) - Infrastructural support for local court buildings (DFID) - Provision of record keeping material for local courts (DFID) - Ad hoc monitoring of local courts (UNIPSIL)
Strengthening of the legal community (justice providers)		- Training on human rights for local court personnel (DFID) - Training on record keeping (DFID) - Sensitisation on human rights for chiefs (UNICEF, UNFPA, DFID)
Empowering justice users	- Provision of paralegals and community mediation schemes (Open Society Justice Initiative; Conciliation Resources) - Awareness raising on human rights (DFID) and Education on national laws (LAWCLA) - Incorporation of new curricula at school where children learn about human rights (UNICEF, UNFPA)	

[31] Interview with a member of 'Conciliation Resources', Freetown, 08/04/09; interview with members of 'Conciliation Resources' Bo, 14/04/09; interview with members of 'Peace and Reconciliation Movement', Bo, 14/04/09.

6. CONCLUSION

Even though in Sierra Leone the bulk of aid remains channelled towards state justice institutions, we see a relatively high awareness of the importance of customary justice amongst the discourses of most development actors active in the justice sector.[32] In practice, we see that the majority of interventions targeting customary justice in the context of justice sector aid focused on the local courts, whereas other customary justice forums, such as chiefs, elders, group leaders, etc. occupied a less prominent place.[33] This reflects a dichotomous view of legal pluralism that mirrors the way in which legal pluralism is established by law, i.e. 'formal courts' vs. 'local courts', in contrast to more empirical perspectives on legal pluralism, based on how justice seekers relate to the vast array of local justice providers that co-exist at local level. The Justice for the Poor programme of the World Bank seemed to adopt a more empirical perspective by exploring how disputes are handled locally and how grassroots actors experience justice. This programme, which mainly consisted in research, has the potential to deliver critical insights for the design of future justice sector interventions.

As described above, the local courts were the target of most initiatives addressing customary justice, such as the restatement of customary laws, infrastructural support, and training on record keeping and human rights. Chiefs on the other hand were targeted more marginally as justice actors, the main initiative being their sensitisation so that they would only mediate but not adjudicate disputes and so that they would respect and promote human rights. Given the political nature of justice provision (Von Benda Beckmann, 1981; Kyed, 2009), the power of chiefs in rural areas in Sierra Leone (Jackson, 2011), the problematic way in which local courts operate in terms of delivering equitable justice (Castillejo, 2009), and the limited power of formal courts and state authorities to regulate the conduct of chiefs (Albrecht, 2010), it is questionable whether this strategy is realistic and likely to deliver any improvement in terms of access to justice and human rights for marginalised groups. The 'Local Courts Bill' could counterbalance this situation since the procedures for the appointment of local court chairmen would be modified by increasing the number of local stakeholders that are involved in the selection, making it more transparent.

As regards the strategies supported for the promotion of human rights within local justice processes, we see that efforts were made to 'localise' international standards. This is exemplified by those initiatives that sought to build alliances with internal actors of change, such as progressive chiefs and local leaders, and by those initiatives that tried to find local equivalents to the values found in

[32] According to Albrecht, the 'Improved Access to Security and Justice Programme (IASJP) that was designed in 2010 to follow up the JSDP pays more attention to 'non-state justice and security actors' (Albrecht, 2010).

[33] This contrasts with the prominent role that chiefs occupied within post-war interventions that aimed at restoring governance and security structures in the countryside (Jackson et al., 2011).

human rights so that the latter are not perceived as alien, what Merry calls the 'vernacularisation' or 'indigenisation' of human rights (Merry, 2006). Moreover, the initiatives that incorporated storytelling and drama as a means to promote community debates seemed to reflect a dynamic view of culture and customary justice. Attention for the role of education on progressive gender roles at school also reflected a holistic view of how to achieve results in this area by generating broader processes of social change, rather than focusing on 'fixing a justice system in isolation' (Isser and Chopra, 2010). However, these interventions were seldom linked to an analysis of how power and resources are distributed at local level and how these issues affect access to human rights. Similarly, the pilot initiative to restate the customary laws in Moyamba district, which would eventually bring customary laws in line with human rights, shows little consideration for the 'negotiated' characteristics of customary justice provision, in which power relations are central, and overemphasises the role of 'rules' in determining the outcome of disputes.

The provision of paralegal services and mediation schemes at grassroots level, which create a new 'layer' of locally available justice, did reflect a more 'power informed' perspective as these actors constitute an alternative for marginalised justice seekers that may counterbalance the power of other local justice providers. However, the extent to which these actors are actually contributing to a redistribution of resources and more equitable power relations at local level is something that deserves more study.

All in all, we can conclude that in Sierra Leone there seems to be a considerable degree of awareness amongst development actors of the importance of considering changing local level justice processes into policies and interventions in the justice sector. During interviews and focus group discussions, donor representatives pointed out that one of the crucial factors in this regard was the openness of the government of Sierra Leone to discuss these issues. The recommendation of the Truth and Reconciliation Commission of Sierra Leone to revise oppressive features of customary structures in order to avoid a repetition of violence seems to play an important role in this. However, the interventions examined in this chapter show that this concern with 'justice at a local level' does not always imply a concern with 'legal pluralism' and the way in which different justice providers interact and influence each other. Future interventions could benefit from incorporating such a perspective as this impacts on access to justice and human rights.

BIBLIOGRAPHY

Albrecht, P. (2010) Betwixt and between: chiefs and reform of Sierra Leone's justice sector. DIIS Working Paper 2010:33.

Alie, J. (2008) Reconciliation and traditional justice: tradition based practices of the Kpaa Mende in Sierra Leone. In Huyse, L. and Salter, M. (eds.) *Traditional Justice and*

Reconciliation After Violent Conflict, Learning from African Experiences, 123–146. Stockholm, Sweden: IDEA.

Alie, J. (1990) *A New History of Sierra Leone*. Oxford: Macmillan Education

Alterman, O., Binienda, A., Rodella, S. and Varzi, K. (2002) *The Law People See. The Status of Dispute Resolution in the Provinces of Sierra Leone in 2002*. Freetown: National Forum for Human Rights.

Amnesty International (2006) Sierra Leone, Women Face Human Rights Abuses in the Informal Legal Sector. Amnesty International.

Archibald, S. and Richards, P. (2002) Converts to human rights? Popular debate about war and justice in rural central Sierra Leone, *Africa: Journal of the International African Institute*, 72/3, 339–367.

Baker, B. (2005) Who do people turn to for policing in Sierra Leone?, *Journal of Contemporary African Studies*, 23/3, 371–390.

British Council (2004) Sierra Leone Justice Sector Development Programme, Project Memorandum.

British Council (2005) National Policy Framework for the Justice Sector in Sierra Leone.

Castillejo, C. (2009) Building Accountable Justice in Sierra Leone, Working Paper 76, FRIDE.

Chopra, T. and Isser, D. (2010) From 'fixing' systems to supporting processes of change: rethinking women's access to justice in fragile states. Paper presented at the International Conference on Access to Justice and Security, Non-State Actors and the Local Dynamics of Ordering, Copenhagen, 1–3 November 2010.

Dale, P. (2007) Barriers to justice in Sierra Leone, *Justice for the Poor*, 1, 4.

Dale, P. (2008) *Access to Justice in Sierra Leone: A Review of the Literature*. The World Bank Group.

Daramy, I. (2008) Undermining the powers of local courts in Northern Sierra Leone: a case of the chiefs. Official Newsletter of the Sierra Leone Court Monitoring Programme, 27: 15–16.

Fanthorpe, R. (2001) Neither citizen nor subject? 'Lumpen' agency and the legacy of native administration in Sierra Leone, *African Affairs*, 100/400, 363–386.

Fanthorpe, R. (2005) On the limits of liberal peace: chiefs and democratic decentralization in post-war Sierra Leone, *African Affairs*, 105/418, 27–49.

Fanthorpe, R. (2007) Sierra Leone: The Influence of the Secret Societies, with Special Reference to Female Genital Mutilation. A Writenet Report commissioned by the United Nations High Commissioner for Refugees, Status Determination and Protection Information Section (DIPS).

Government of Sierra Leone (2004) Justice Sector Development Programme: Project Memorandum.

Government of Sierra Leone (2005) Poverty Reduction Strategy Paper, A National Programme for Food Security, Job Creation and Good Governance, 2005–2007.

Government of Sierra Leone (2007) Justice Sector Reform Strategy and Investment Plan 2008–2010.

Human Rights Commission of Sierra Leone (2007) The State of Human Rights in Sierra Leone.

Human Rights Commission of Sierra Leone (2009) Report on Knowledge, Attitudes and Perceptions of Human Rights in Sierra Leone.

Jackson, P. (2006) Reshuffling an old deck of cards? The politics of local government reform in Sierra Leone, *African Affairs*, 106/422, 95–111.

Jackson, P. (2011) Decentralised power and traditional authorities: How power determines access to justice in Sierra Leone, *Journal of Legal Pluralism*, 63, 207–230.

Jalloh, G. and Braima, L. (2008) 'Leh Wi Tok for Change Wi Village': Community dissemination of research findings, *Justice for the Poor*, 2, 3.

Kamara, H. (2008) A look at the major changes in the three Gender Acts. Official Newsletter of the Sierra Leone Court Monitoring Programme 28, 9–10.

Kane, M.J., Onyango, O. and Tejan-Cole, A. (2005) Reassessing Customary Law Systems as a Vehicle for Providing Equitable Access to Justice for the Poor. Conference Paper: New Frontiers of Social Policy: Development in a Globalizing World.

Keen, D. (2003) Greedy elites, dwindling resources, alienated youths. The anatomy of protracted violence in Sierra Leone, Internationale Politiek und Gesellschaft, 2, 67–94.

Kent, D. (2007) Custody, maintenance, and succession: the internalization of women's and children's rights under customary law in Africa, *Michigan Journal of International Law*, 28/507, 507–538.

Koroma, B. (2007) *Local Courts Record Analysis Survey in Sierra Leone*. Freetown: Institute of Geography and Development Studies, Njala University.

Kyed, H.M. (2009) The Politics of Legal Pluralism: State Policies on Legal Pluralism and Their Local Dynamics in Mozambique, *Journal of Legal Pluralism and Unofficial Law*, 59, 87–121.

Mannah, M. (2007) The Child Rights Bill, A Discussion part II. Official Newsletter of the Sierra Leone Court Monitoring Programme 24, 8–11.

Manning, R. (2008a) The landscape of local authority in Sierra Leone, how 'traditional' and 'modern' justice and governance systems interact. The World Bank Group.

Manning, R. (2008b) Challenging generations, youths and elders in rural and peri-urban Sierra Leone. The World Bank Group.

Manning, R., Foster, E. and Dale, P. (2006) Crime and Conflict Statistics from Baseline GoBifo/ENCISS/ Decentralization Surveys. Preliminary Analysis. The World Bank Group.

Maru, V. (2005) The challenges of African legal dualism: an experiment in Sierra Leone. In Open Society Justice Initiative (ed.) *Human Rights and Justice Sector Reform in Africa: Contemporary Issues and Responses*, 18–22. Governance and Social Development Resource Centre.

Maru, V. (2006) *Between Law and Society, Paralegals and the Provision of Primary Justice Services in Sierra Leone*. Open Society Justice Initiative.

Merry, S. (2006) *Human Rights and Gender Violence: Translating International Law into Local Justice*. Chicago: University of Chicago Press.

MSWGCA (Ministry of Social Welfare, Gender and Children's Affairs Sierra Leone) n.d. Strategic Roll Out Plan for Implementation of the Three Gender Acts: The Domestic Violence Act 2007, The Devolution of Estates Act 2007, and the Registration of Customary Marriage and Divorce Act 2007.

Sawyer, E. (2008) Remove or reform? A Case for (Restructuring) Chiefdom Governance in Post-Conflict Sierra Leone, *African Affairs*, 107/428, 387–403.

Thompson, N. (2002) *In Pursuit of Justice, A Report on the Judiciary in Sierra Leone.* Commonwealth Human Rights Initiative and Sierra Leone Bar Association.

Truth and Reconciliation Commission, Sierra Leone (2004) *Witness to Truth: Report of the Sierra Leone Truth and Reconciliation Commission.* Freetown: Truth and Reconciliation Commission.

UNDP – United Nations Development Programme (2009) Improving Access to Justice Programme in Sierra Leone. Project Document 2009–2011.

United Nations Committee on the Elimination of Discrimination Against Women (2006) Consideration of Reports Submitted by States Parties Under Article 18 of the Convention on the Elimination of All Forms of Discrimination Against Women. Combined Initial, Second, Third, Fourth and Fifth Periodic Reports of State Parties, Sierra Leone. United Nations [online] http://daccess-dds-ny.un.org/doc/UNDOC/GEN/N06/687/70/PDF/N0668770.pdf?OpenElement.

Von Benda-Beckman, K. (1981) Forum Shopping and Shopping Forums: Dispute Processing in a Minangkabau Village in West Sumatra, *Journal of Legal Pluralism*, 19, 117–160.

CHAPTER 14

TRADITIONAL LAW THROUGH A STATE LENS: A CASE STUDY ON ZAMBIA

Lia Nijzink

1. INTRODUCTION

This chapter discusses how international development actors providing aid to the justice sector in Zambia position themselves regarding legal pluralism and the promotion of human rights within traditional law. The chapter begins with an overview of the main colonial and post-colonial developments in the field of law and justice. After describing the main features of the justice landscapes of Zambia and their main challenges in terms of human rights, the chapter depicts how international development actors engage with these realities and provides a mapping of their interventions. As in the case of Malawi (see Chapter 9), the conclusion shows that because most interventions in the justice sector were aimed at the formal legal system, the way in which the state approaches the justice sector and the role of traditional law in it plays a crucial role in development actors' position vis-à-vis legal pluralism and local legal orders.

2. HISTORICAL BACKGROUND

Northern Rhodesia, now known as Zambia, came under British colonial rule in 1899. The British colonial government introduced common law and a Western legal system, while at the same time recognising customary law and traditional forms of dispute settlement, especially in private law matters. This created a bifurcated or dual legal system in which certain courts mainly applied imported Western law, while other courts applied traditional law (Chanock, 1985).

Traditional leaders took seat in the so-called Native Courts and paramount chiefs took part in the Native Courts of Appeal. The district and provincial commissioners functioned as appellate courts for these traditional courts. Members of the Native Courts were appointed by the Governor, who also decided which private and criminal cases fell under their authority. It was the task of the

Native Courts to apply customary law as long as this did not conflict with morality and natural law. There was a clerk in every Native Court, meaning that cases were documented and presented to the district commissioner for revisions. The commissioner could, if he deemed it necessary, revise the ruling or the penalty, refer the case back to the Native Court or take on the case again himself.

When Zambia became independent in 1964, the two justice systems were integrated: the Native Courts were incorporated in the judiciary and obtained, with certain limitation, jurisdiction both over cases that fell under Western law and customary law cases. Their authority no longer depended on the ethnicity of the law user, which is why the Native Courts were replaced by the so-called local courts through the Local Courts Act in 1966. To realise a separation of judicial and executive powers, traditional leaders were not allowed to be part of these new courts. This element may have been inspired by complaints concerning corruption among traditional leaders and dissatisfaction about the functioning of traditional leaders within the Native Courts. The new local courts were intended to have a national character, as opposed to the geographically limited authority of the Native Courts. This development can be seen as a first attempt to promote the uniformity of customary law of the diverse ethnic groups. Another important step towards that goal was taken in 1989, when legislation, which introduced a uniform customary law system of succession, took effect (Zambia Law Development Commission, 2006).

At the moment there seems to be a general conviction, reflected by a report from the Zambia Law Development Commission (2006), which states the integration as aimed at in 1966 did not have the intended effect. Traditional forums for dispute settlement are still operational, meaning that they have not been replaced by the local courts, as the plan originally was. Instead there are presently two parallel systems for the application of traditional law – the traditional and the local courts – which leads to friction and quarrels over authority. An additional problem is that appeals for customary law cases treated by the local courts are hardly treated by the higher courts. These courts' legal experts are poorly equipped to apply traditional law.

There are furthermore several problems specifically related to the functioning of local courts. Since they were established little attention has been paid to the quality of justice and the staff, or the physical infrastructure of the local courts. Although 80% of the population depends on the local courts for the settlements of their customary law conflicts, these courts are marginalised within the judiciary. At the same time there are complaints which describe the state of affairs within the local courts as chaotic, threatening and insensitive to gender and human rights.

The Zambia Law Development Commission has consequently proposed several quite extensive recommendations, which will be discussed in more detail below.

3. THE JUSTICE LANDSCAPE

Traditional law is constitutionally recognised in Zambia. The Constitution determines that traditional law is applied by the local courts that are part of the formal legal system. The local courts have jurisdiction over private law cases that fall under traditional law and over certain criminal offenses. They are connected to the rest of the formal legal system through a system of appeals (Coldham, 1990; Himonga, 2008). However, daily practice shows that this appeal system and the so-called repugnancy clause function poorly.

Appealing to a higher court is a rare occurrence in customary law cases. Moreover, the parallel system of no-longer-recognised traditional law forums is still operational. In practice it seems that large parts of the population even prefer these unofficial forums for dispute settlement (ISS, 2009). There is, therefore, a large gap in the legal framework when it comes to the functioning of these traditional courts and their relation to the officially recognised local courts.

4. THE INSTITUTIONAL FRAMEWORK FOR LEGAL PLURALISM AND PROPOSED REFORMS

The Zambia Law Development Commission (2006) developed a proposal for reforming the current legal framework for legal pluralism in Zambia. This proposal consists of several elements. Firstly, the Commission suggests the constitutional recognition of customary law, making it subject to human rights as included in the Constitution. This would make the so-called repugnancy clause void. The second element is the proposal to recognise the current unofficial forums of dispute settlement and to grant them exclusive authority in the application of traditional law. This would also entail the establishment of traditional appeal bodies, such as the House of Chiefs, although the Supreme Court is in this proposal still identified as the highest court of appeal for customary law cases. The proposal to recognise traditional law forums would mean that the current local courts would merge in the so-called magistrates' courts and would no longer have any jurisdiction over customary law cases.

According to the Zambia Law Development Commission, this proposal aims to introduce a modern and flexible system of traditional law. The Commission's study preceding the proposal brought several complaints about the local courts system to light. The fact that many women prefer unofficial traditional forums for dispute settlement over the local courts indicates, the Commission says, that the people experience the unofficial traditional forums to be more sensitive to gender issues and human rights. The study shows that in some cases the unofficial traditional forums have displayed more flexibility in accepting modern approaches and changes in traditional values and practices. It still remains to be seen whether state recognition of the informal system as proposed by the

Commission will reinforce these advantages, or whether the system of traditional law is more flexible and appeals more to the expectations of the law user precisely because it lacks state recognition or support.

Figure 5. The current legal framework for legal pluralism in Zambia

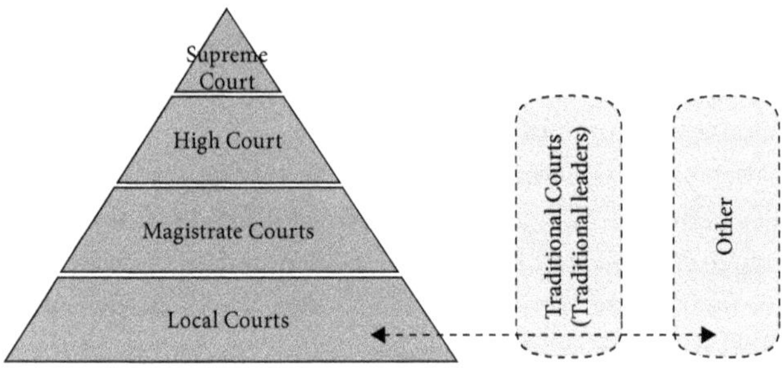

Figure 6. Proposed reforms in Zambia

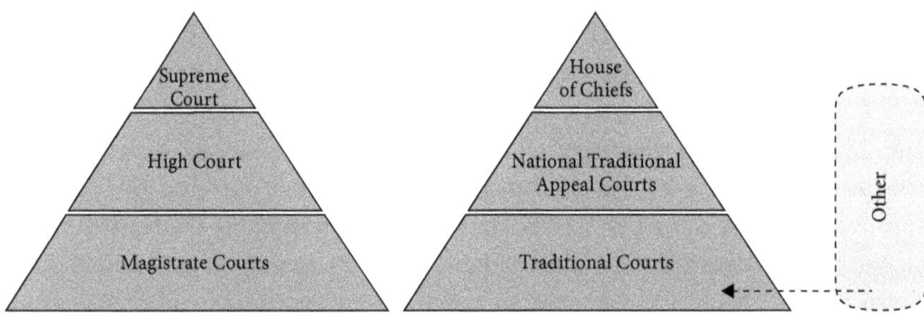

These figures are a graphical representation of the institutional framework for legal pluralism as exists in Zambia at the moment and of the reforms proposed by the Zambia Law Development Commission. The dotted lines and the lighter colour indicate traditional bodies and actors who are not officially recognised by the state and therefore are not part of state-recognised legal pluralism.

5. THE HUMAN RIGHTS LANDSCAPE

In Zambia, traditional norms and practices are widespread and despite the existence of local courts, the traditional leaders still play an important role as guardians of traditional law. In some cases, chiefs and village chiefs even take the lead in the public debate on the tensions between human rights and traditional norms and practices. The most important areas in which such tensions are part of the public debate in Zambia are inheritance law, the problem of 'property grabbing' (the unlawful appropriation of someone else's property), women's rights, children's rights and the issues with arranged marriages and sexual relations with young girls.

The current debate shows that there is no strong lobby in Zambia that rejects human rights on grounds of tradition. There are, in fact, interesting examples of traditional leaders actively trying to accomplish a change in traditional values and practices. The sexual cleansing of widows, for example, is a traditional practice, which is heavily criticised because it unnecessarily exposes people to the dangers of infection with HIV/AIDS. Traditional leaders are closely involved in attempts to abolish these practises or to change them to such an extent that they no longer pose a health risk to the involved parties. Another example is adultery, which according to traditional law can only be committed by women. Under pressure from women, women's organisations and communities some traditional leaders have started to treat cases, under the name of marriage interference, in which men have committed adultery.[1]

6. INTERNATIONAL ACTORS AND LOCAL LEGAL ORDERS

At the moment the research was conducted, DANIDA was the most important development actor active in the Zambia justice sector because of its Access to Justice programme (DANIDA, 2009). This programme intended to take the shape of a so-called 'basket fund' in which support from DANIDA, the EU and the German GTZ was assembled. The Access to Justice programme was coordinated by the Zambia Ministry of Justice and DANIDA provided technical support through a unit, which was installed in the judiciary for this purpose. The programme was exclusively aimed at the formal legal system and collaborates with a large number of actors in the justice sector. Within the programme there was little special attention for traditional law other than the immediate support to the judiciary for the improvement of local courts, both for the physical infrastructure and for the education of judges and staff.

DANIDA's Access to Justice programme had a study carried out to investigate the access to justice in Zambia, so that they would be better able to oversee and evaluate their programme. It is still too early to assess whether this study will have an effect on the place traditional law has in the justice sector. For now, DANIDA's involvement in traditional law seems limited to the support for local courts, and they oppose the proposal to abolish these and recognise the unofficial traditional law forums.

UNICEF had a programme aimed at improving the access to justice for children and to guarantee the rights of children in the criminal law process. The programme was coordinated by the co-called Child Justice Forum, which was

---

1 Personal interviews with stakeholders, Lusaka (Zambia), November–December 2009.

established within the judiciary. Components of the programme were education for judges of local courts and general awareness campaigns concerning children's rights (Muntingh, 2005).

Women for Change (see www.wfc.org.zm) is an organisation from the civil society which receives support from several donors and international organisations and performs gender-related development work in Zambia's rural areas, where they work with women, men and children in the communities. Its programmes are awareness programmes, which strive to increase knowledge concerning human rights and good governance, and to boost citizens' participation in local, regional and national governance issues. An important part of the work, however, is aimed at the economic empowerment of communities in a gender-sensitive way, by developing practical skills and facilitating cooperations for trade, keeping livestock and commercial ways of growing crops.

Women for Change also carried out a programme for Zambia's traditional leaders, both on a district and on a national level. These leaders received education about gender analysis and awareness, matters regarding HIV/AIDS and human and children's rights. One of the goals of this work with traditional leaders was to engage them in the battle against HIV/AIDS, for example by ensuring that traditional practices that entail a contamination risk, such as the sexual cleansing of women after their husbands' death, are abolished or changed. Finally, Women for Change brought traditional leaders of the Southern Africa Development Community (SADC) together for education and workshops.[2] The following mapping provides an overview of these interventions according to the typology presented in Chapter 8:

Type of interventions	At state level	At customary level
Law reform interventions	– Research-related activities; proposal to abolish repugnancy clause and to make traditional law subject to human rights as recorded in the Constitution (Zambia Law Development Commission – no involvement of development actors)	– Research and so-called restatement of customary law norms regarding marriage with codification as long-term objective (Zambia Law Development Commission – no involvement of development actors) – Stimulating the debate in communities about procedural and substantial traditional law norms (Women for Change – several development actors)

[2] Personal interviews with representatives of van Women for Change, Lusaka (Zambia), November–December 2009.

Type of interventions	At state level	At customary level
Institutional support and reform interventions	- Infrastructural and organisational support for local courts; revision of procedures for the appointment of members of local courts; improving case documentation in local courts (Judiciary/Ministry of Justice – DANIDA/EU)	- Proposal to recognise traditional justice forums (Zambia Law Development Commission – no involvement of development actors)
Strengthening of the legal community (justice providers)	- Education for judges and staff of local courts regarding justice, documentation and procedures (Judiciary/Ministry of Justice – DANIDA/EU) and regarding children's rights (UNICEF – several development actors)	- Education for traditional leaders regarding human rights and national legislation (Women for Change – several development actors)
Empowering justice users	- Human rights education and awareness programmes (several civil society organisations – several development actors) - Awareness programmes aimed at children (UNICEF – several development actors)	

The above table is an overview of interventions regarding traditional justice as these were executed in Zambia. The table follows the division into kinds of interventions as presented in section 3.1.3.3. of this book. The table also includes several interventions of the Zambia Law Development Commission: first of all the proposal to abolish the so-called repugnancy clause and to make traditional law subject to human rights as recorded in the Constitution. Secondly, the study that was performed for the Commission and that investigated the customary law norms and practices regarding marriage and the proposals resulting from this study for a restatement and, in the long term, codification of traditional marriage law. This is aimed at increasing uniformity and alleviating the tensions with human rights. Thirdly, the Commission's proposal for the abolishment of the local courts and the recognition of the unofficial traditional law forums. In is noteworthy that, as far as we could tell, the development actors working in the Zambia justice sector have not been involved in the creation of these proposals and have hardly involved themselves in this process either. During our field study, we found that these actors were barely aware of the details of said proposals and that they especially rejected the abolishment of the local courts.

7. CONCLUSION

The description of the situation in Zambia that was offered above allows us to draw the following conclusions regarding the question how international actors that are active in the field of development aid to the Zambian justice sector handle traditional law and legal pluralism.

Firstly, it is clear that the development actors in Zambia were exclusively aimed at the formal legal system and that they take their lead from the Zambian government regarding their position vis-à-vis traditional law. The legal framework for legal pluralism as it existed in Zambia led development actors to focus any attention for traditional law on the officially recognised local courts. Development actors were also hardly aware of existing proposals to adjust this legal framework.

Secondly, it is clear that in cases where interventions of development actors did specifically relate to unofficial traditional law, these interventions were executed by organisations from the civil society. These organisations were generally sensitive to the local contexts where traditional law applies and opted for an intercultural approach to the advancement of human rights. The extent of these programmes, however, was limited and did not seem to result in more influence for justice users in determining policy within the justice sector.

Development actors therefore hardly seem to be aware of legal pluralism approaches to justice. Development aid to the Zambia justice sector seemed to pay little attention to the existence of several legal orders that are interrelated and influence each other. Where there was any attention for legal pluralism, it was aimed at reforms to the institutional framework for legal pluralism, and this by national actors.

As it was the case in the case study on Malawi, the case study on Zambia shows that, since most interventions in the justice sector were aimed at the formal legal system, the way that the state approaches the justice sector and the role of traditional law is of the utmost importance. As yet, the Zambian state does not consider the development of the unofficial traditional justice sector a priority. It is unclear how much support the proposal of the Zambian Law Development Commission can count on. The attention of both the state and the development partners is concentrated on strengthening the official local courts and their role in the current formal legal system. This reflects a certain conception of traditional law that does not primarily take the views, experiences and expectations of the law users into account. This may change if the proposal to abolish the local courts and to recognise the traditional law forums gains momentum. The introduction of the new system could in principle lead to a proper division of tasks between the customary law and the formal law system, and to relieving the tension between traditional law and human rights. However, it remains to be seen whether this will actually happen in practice.

Development actors in Zambia have not concerned themselves with the proposal to recognise the traditional law forums, which are still unofficial. This could change in the future. Much will depend on the position the Zambian government takes regarding the reform proposals. If the proposal to abolish local courts and to recognise traditional law forums gains momentum, this could generate renewed interest in legal pluralism and traditional justice in the development aid to the Zambian justice sector. It is, however, far too early to be able to determine whether this will also result in improved access to and better quality of justice in Zambia.

BIBLIOGRAPHY

Chanock, M. (1985) *Law, Custom and Social Order, The Colonial Experience in Malawi and Zambia*. Portsmouth: Heinemann

Coldham, S. (1990) Customary marriage and the urban Local Courts in Zambia, *Journal of African Law*, 34(1), 67–75.

DANIDA (2009) Support to Good Governance Zambia, Programme Document June 2009–December 2012.

Himonga, C. (2008) Zambia: General Introduction. In Blanpain, R. (ed.) *International Encyclopaedia for Family and Succession Law*, 14–69. The Netherlands: Kluwer Law International.

Institute for Security Studies (2009) The Criminal Justice System in Zambia: Enhancing the Delivery of Security in Africa African Human Security Initiative [online] http://www.africanreview.org/docs/zambia/mono159.PDF (27/05/2011).

Muntingh, L. (2005) Report on Child Justice in Zambia with reference to UNICEF supported projects, commissioned by UNICEF [online] http://www.unicef.org/evaldatabase/files/Zambia_2005_002_Child_Justice.pdf (27/05/2011).

Zambia Law Development Commission (2006) Report on the Local Courts System.

CHAPTER 15

FROM ADDRESSING LOCAL LEGAL ORDERS TO EMBRACING LEGAL PLURALISM

Giselle CORRADI and Lia NIJZINK

1. INTRODUCTION

In Chapter 8, four types of possible interventions dealing with local legal orders and legal pluralism were identified: legislative reforms, institutional support and reforms, capacity building for justice providers and empowerment of justice seekers. In addition, Chapter 8 provided examples of how the first three can be deployed at the level of state justice and/or at the level of local legal orders. Based on the case studies presented in Chapters 11, 12, 13 and 14 on Malawi, Mozambique, Sierra Leone and Zambia respectively, this chapter pinpoints salient trends regarding the sort of interventions that international development actors are supporting in this domain. Subsequently, it analyses how these trends relate to the socio-legal theories sketched out in Chapter 10 and explores how current strategies can be improved by incorporating these insights. The chapter argues that the emerging will amongst some development actors to address local legal orders is a step in the right direction, but in most cases strategies remain state centred instead of embracing a legally plural perspective.

2. THE CONTEXT OF INTERVENTIONS

Despite the growing international attention for local legal orders, as reflected in various guidelines issued by development agencies, this topic was not yet systematically considered within justice sector aid in the countries included in this study. Most interventions in the justice sector were directed at formal state justice and tended to ignore other legal orders and how the state relates to them. The emerging interest in local legal orders seems to be counter-balanced by a number of factors that contribute to the perpetuation of a narrow focus on state law and justice. Current aid modalities, such as direct budget support and sector-wide approaches (SWAPS), are crafted upon a template in which international development actors' main partner is the recipient state, thus working according to a logic that reinforces the lack of attention to other sources of authority and justice provision. The research in Malawi, Mozambique, Sierra Leone and Zambia clearly showed that state driven interventions tended to privilege state justice. When they were directed at local legal orders, this was limited to officially recognised local legal orders that in some cases were created by the state itself, such as the community courts in Mozambique. Interventions directed at unofficial local legal orders were mainly supported by NGOs. At the same time, there was little consideration for legal pluralism as such, i.e. how to deal with the co-existence between different legal orders and sources of justice provision in a same socio-political space, how non-state normative fields interplay with state law and vice versa.

Given this context, it is not surprising that most interventions that targeted local legal orders took the form of capacity building for local justice providers and justice seekers regarding state law. As the case studies show, international development actors tend to support the provision of trainings for local justice providers and justice seekers on human rights principles, national legislation embodying human rights and civic education in general. In a few cases, interventions were aimed at providing information about the jurisdictional boundaries between state and local legal orders as established by state law. This demonstrates that engagement with local legal orders does not necessarily imply engagement with legal pluralism. These interventions remained centred on state law without questioning the extent to which the state is actually in a position to implement and enforce this legislation. In some cases, support for the provision of paralegal and mediation services at grassroots level constituted an exception to this trend. On the one hand, some paralegal organisations combined state and non-state norms when giving advice and mediating disputes, rather than relying on state law exclusively. On the other hand, these organisations constituted another layer of justice provision, contributing to the existence of legal pluralism. However, we did not come across any independent evaluation considering how this has an impact on access to justice and human rights.[1] Finally, the participation of local justice providers within policy development in the justice sector was quite limited in the cases that were studied. Even if this involves considerable challenges in the countries considered, international actors were seldom proactive in facilitating the views of local justice providers and the experiences of justice seekers with local legal orders and legal pluralism to be represented in decision-making processes.

[1] For example, the Sierra Leonean Paralegal Organisations 'Timap for Justice' produced a number of positive narratives about their work, but we did not find any systematic and independent evaluation about the impact of 'vernacularisation' initiatives (Merry, 2006) by paralegal organisations in the countries considered for this study.

3. TRENDS IN THE TYPE OF INTERVENTIONS SUPPORTED

3.1. LAW REFORM

Law reform initiatives addressing local legal orders were mostly executed at the level of state law, i.e. legislation was adopted at state level modifying local legal orders. These processes were often supported by international development actors who seemed to expect that the adopting such legislation would facilitate modification of local practices in order to comply with human rights standards. These reforms tended to focus on specific topics or practices, rather than on the mechanisms available to demand compliance with human rights in legally plural contexts. For example, in Sierra Leone, UNIFEM supported the adoption of the 'Gender Laws' (2007) and the 'Child Act' (2007), which domesticated CEDAW and CRC. This legislation modified customary practices that discriminate on the basis of gender. However, there was no attention for the fact that there are only three customary law officers in the entire country to monitor whether this legislation was implemented by the local courts, let alone other local forums. Another example can be found in Zambia, where international actors were involved in the process of legislative reform regarding the minimum age of marriage, while they showed no interest in the Law Commission's proposal to replace the repugnancy clause with a model of compliance with the Bill of Rights.

Regarding interventions that aimed at modifying local norms and practices directly, i.e. not by means of state laws regulating them, three types of interventions were supported. First, international development actors gave support to civil society organisations to promote discussions within communities on the content of local norms and practices, and their relationship with human rights. Second, international development actors financed research on local norms and practices and the extent to which these respect human rights. For example, the research projects conducted by the 'Justice for the Poor' programme in Sierra Leone and the Malawi Human Rights Commission. Finally, international development actors gave support for writing down customary laws and modifying them if they contradicted human rights, i.e. the pilot project for ascertaining the customary laws of Sierra Leone in Moyamba district.

3.2. INSTITUTIONAL SUPPORT AND REFORM

The institutional framework for legal pluralism, i.e. how state law accommodates and regulates local legal orders is a topic of much study, debate and concrete reform proposals. However, international development actors generally do not to take a position or intervene regarding these proposals. For example, in Zambia international actors showed little interest in a proposal by the Law Commission to recognise the currently unofficial traditional courts, while a proposal by the Malawi Law Commission to reintroduce a system of local courts has so far also attracted little attention. Similarly, international actors in Mozambique were positive about the intention to introduce legislation to regulate the community courts but adopted a 'wait and see' approach with regards to the two reform proposals that were on the table. International actors seemed to be more active in interventions involving institutional support or reform of local legal orders, such as providing infrastructural support and promoting more female inclusion within local forums, although most of these initiatives related only to officially recognised local legal orders. For example, in Mozambique, the Danish bilateral cooperation supported the creation of new community courts. In Sierra Leone, the British bilateral cooperation provided training for local court functionaries, while in Zambia, the Danish bilateral cooperation and the EU-supported institutional reform and infrastructural support for the local courts. Malawi seemed to be the exception with the British bilateral cooperation supporting the Commission for Justice and Peace to assist the unofficial traditional justice system with training on record keeping and other means to strengthen its procedures.

3.3. STRENGTHENING THE CAPACITY OF JUSTICE PROVIDERS

Most interventions aiming at strengthening the capacity of justice providers targeted local legal orders. On the one hand, state bodies were supported to provide training to local justice providers that are officially recognised by state law. For example, in Mozambique and Zambia international actors supported the Ministry of Justice to provide training for community courts and local courts respectively. These training programmes adopted a state-centred approach, their main goal being that local justice providers know better how to respect state law. On the other hand, international development actors supported a number of civil society organisations that worked with unofficial local justice providers. These tended to take a more participatory approach in their training activities. A case in point is the organisation Women for Change in Zambia, which directly worked with communities and traditional leaders to support ongoing local processes of change in the area of gender relations. Another example is Save the Children in Mozambique, which cooperated with traditional authorities in devising solutions for the social exclusion faced by orphan children.

In contrast we found virtually no training for formal justice providers in matters related to local legal orders and legal pluralism. With the exception of Mozambique, where the Danish bilateral cooperation gave support to the Centre for Legal and Juridical Training to provide courses on legal pluralism to state court judges, international actors paid no attention to the need to strengthen the awareness of legal pluralism within formal justice institutions.

3.4. EMPOWERING JUSTICE SEEKERS

Most interventions targeting justice seekers consisted in civic education and awareness raising campaigns on human rights, where information was disseminated about mainly civil and political rights, as well as specific legislation in the area of gender, e.g. the family law, legislation pertaining to children and laws on domestic violence. In addition, development actors supported paralegal and mediation services provided by NGOs and civil society organisations. In a few cases, international actors also assisted the state in providing free legal assistance, e.g. in Mozambique. All these interventions were conducted with the aim of improving access to justice for the poor. However, besides supporting some research, international actors were not active in empowering justice seekers to participate in public debates on legal pluralism and the justice sector in general. Nor did they support the participation of local justice providers in decision-making processes within the justice sector, despite the move towards a sector-wide approach and the emphasis on ownership.

4. ANALYSING AND IMPROVING STRATEGIES

Overall, the fact that in Sub-Saharan Africa development actors at various levels start to show a will to look beyond state justice and consider local legal orders constitutes a window of opportunity to engage with important realities that have often been neglected. However, the empirical findings presented in Part III of this book support the critique previously articulated by other authors working on this topic: several interventions tend to deal with the issues in a superficial way.[2] The next paragraphs pinpoint four areas where this is the case, i.e. the kind of actors targeted by interventions, the way in which human rights are promoted within forums that rely on mediation, the minimal engagement with local knowledge and the rare critical approach to human rights' cross-contextual implementation. In addition, this chapter argues that development actors' engagement with local legal orders needs to move beyond a state-centric approach and embrace a legally plural perspective.

4.1. ADDRESSING THE ACTORS 'AT THE TIP OF THE ICEBERG'

The tendency to address local legal orders superficially is visible at the level of the actors that most interventions target. Chapters 11 to 14 demonstrate that interventions tend to deal with 'official' legal actors mainly, which only constitute

[2] Introduction, pp. 10, 11.

the tip of the iceberg as compared to the multiplicity of actors that are actually implicated in local justice processes. While a number of non-governmental organisations go beyond this top-down approach to legal pluralism and identify and collaborate with 'less visible' local actors, such as traditional healers and spirit mediums, these organisations tend to work around specific topics, often related to human rights, such as domestic violence and widow's inheritance rights, but they are not in a position to articulate an integrated 'legal pluralism and human rights' strategy. A hypothesis that deserves further exploration is that this tendency arises from the paradoxical situation in which, on the one hand, international aid has become more focused on the state due to new aid modalities such as budget support, while on the other hand, international development actors seek to improve access to justice by supporting local legal orders which tend to be either overlooked by the state or only partially recognised in state managed development programmes. In other words, the emphasis currently placed by the international aid architecture on country ownership may result in the official framework for legal pluralism and the recipient government's priorities in this regard becoming central to the way in which justice sector aid engages local legal orders. This is problematic for several reasons. For one, it only considers legal pluralism from a normative standpoint while ignoring it empirically and from the perspective of the justice seekers whose capacity to access justice is supposed to improve as a result of interventions. Moreover, this approach fails to identify local actors that, despite not displaying typically legal characteristics, may nevertheless play a vital role in the regulation of behaviour and the protection of human rights within local justice processes.

4.2. HUMAN RIGHTS WITHIN DIFFERENT MODES OF DISPUTE PROCESSING

Another area in which some development actors have tended to understand local legal orders superficially in the reviewed case studies involves the implications of different modes of dispute processing for the implementation of human rights. As explained in Chapter 2, this is crucial in various regards. On the one hand, norms play a relative role in defining the outcome of disputes that are processed within forums that rely on mediation, which is often the case of local justice forums in Sub-Saharan Africa. On the other hand, enforcement of decisions made by these forums depends heavily on social pressure, meaning that a widespread consensus on the appropriateness of the outcome is needed. Many of the interventions described above fail to grasp these issues. In addition, donors are willing to provide support for law reform initiatives that domesticate international human rights law, but they fail to make available the necessary funding for implementing this legislation. Considering the legal and socio-cultural landscapes of Sub-

Saharan Africa, this should be considered as important as the adoption of the right laws by the legal orders of the state.

Interventions that aim at training local justice providers on human rights also tend to overlook the difficulties of implementing these standards within forums that rely on mediation. The purpose of these interventions is that the decisions made by local justice providers respect and protect human rights. However, local justice providers who rely on mediation need to arrive at decisions that are considered appropriate by those involved in the dispute, not the least because otherwise it will be difficult to enforce them and the effectiveness of the forum may decline. The same line of reasoning applies to those interventions that provide mediation services by 'human rights minded' actors at grassroots level, such as paralegals. For the services of mediators to be effective, compliance with decisions is necessary. This is difficult to achieve when mediators deviate too much from what is locally enforceable by consensus and the state is not available to enforce decisions by coercive means or cast 'the shadow of the law'. As a result, these interventions can only produce gradual changes that need to be accompanied by sustained efforts at other levels, such as grassroots dialogue on human rights and the implementation of national policies in education, health, land, etc. that are conducive to broader social changes in line with human rights. A hypothesis that needs further exploration is that these constraints may be mitigated by improving the collaboration between local and state justice providers. As illustrated by Chapters 11, 12 and 14, these strategies have not always been consistently pursued.

4.3. MINIMAL ENGAGEMENT WITH LOCAL KNOWLEDGE

In addition, most of the studied interventions seem to ignore local knowledge. This is mainly the case of state sponsored interventions seeking to disseminate national legislation embodying human rights by means of one-off, unidirectional legal education campaigns at grassroots level. But even certain awareness raising campaigns that target problems identified by means of participatory methodologies and that rely on an accessible language to bring the message, such as community theatre, seem to fail to appreciate local knowledge when they refer to state laws as the only solution. It seems that research on how local normative orders relate to the problems at hand and may contribute to providing local answers constitutes a strategy that only a few organisations follow.

4.4. APPROACHING HUMAN RIGHTS IN A CRITICAL WAY

Viewed from another perspective, this may reflect a tendency to take issue with the problem of lack of knowledge about human rights at local level, without looking at human rights in a critical way and acknowledging the challenge of cross-cultural and cross-contextual implementation. For example, more research is needed on the extent to which human rights, in their current form or mainstream interpretation, are equipped to contain non-state forms of power involved in the administration of justice within local forums, such as traditional authorities and spirit mediums. Moreover, development actors tend to support interventions that take the form of capacity building for local justice providers and local justice users by means of training and awareness raising on human rights but only a few NGO-led initiatives seem to embark on truly dialogical processes that make room for bottom-up inputs that explore how local narratives of human dignity may contribute to enriching human rights.

Finally, interventions rarely focus on building the capacity of state justice providers to apply human rights cross-culturally and in relation to local legal orders, or on how national policies and legislation may need to be adapted in order to respect human rights embodied in local norms.

4.5. EMBRACING A LEGALLY PLURAL PERSPECTIVE

Finally, most interventions show little awareness of the semi-autonomous nature of normative orders, including state law. For example, interventions aiming at improving access to justice by building state courts at lower administrative levels often neglect how these courts' operation interplays with that of local justice forums. Similarly, legal education campaigns tend to overlook how state laws relate to local social institutions and normative repertoires, as well as how the latter may enable or constrain the implementation of state laws. In the case studies examined in this book, this was mainly a shortcoming within those interventions designed by governmental bodies, whereas a number of non-governmental and civil society organisations did explore this issue (e.g. Save the Children in Mozambique with respect to orphan children and their inheritance rights). In other words, justice sector aid should not only address local legal orders, but should also do so from a legally plural perspective.

5. THE WAY FORWARD

These general findings and the insights presented throughout Part III of this book clearly show that socio-legal theory may feed into the practices of development actors and improve them. A question that follows is how development actors at different levels may capitalise on these insights and how they may take account of these five findings within the different types of intervention they support.

Considering that international development actors generally participate in these processes as donors, technical advisors and stakeholders in policy dialogue, and that their main goal is 'state building', these actors are likely to intervene mainly at the level of strengthening the capacity of governmental actors, as duty bearers, to deal with local legal orders, legal pluralism and human rights. At the same time, donors also provide funding and technical advice for non-governmental actors, such as international and national NGOs and civil society organisations so they also play an important role in supporting right holders indirectly. In this context, donors may lobby, provide funds and technical advice for legal and institutional reform, where they can facilitate empirical studies to inform the discussions and policy options on how legal pluralism and human rights work on the ground. As well as providing funding for studies that uncover the extent to which local legal orders contravene and/or reinforce human rights, donors may provide support to domestic governmental and non-governmental actors for the organisation of inclusive discussions that are informed by these studies and make room for bottom-up contributions. In addition, it is equally important that they provide funding to the ministries that are supposed to implement reforms and that they make available technical advice regarding how to deal with the interplay between state and local normative orders. At the level of building the capacity of justice providers, donors may support trainings for state magistrates on legal pluralism, local normative orders and the cross-contextual implementation of national laws embodying international standards, as well as dialogic encounters between state and local justice providers. They may also offer technical assistance to governmental actors for devising trainings for local justice providers so that the determination of which actors get involved and the issues that are discussed are grounded on local experiences. Finally, donors may support local civil society organisations by means of funding and technical advice so that they are in a position to engage in political dialogue with governmental actors and formulate internal demands on these issues.

In turn, governmental actors need to acknowledge that their policies and interventions need to go beyond support for officially recognised local legal orders. Ensuring that officially recognised local justice providers operate in a fair manner is a huge task in and of itself and requires important efforts, but it can only yield sustainable results when unofficial justice providers are also involved. Furthermore, governmental actors need to consider how attempts to improve access to justice by expanding the reach of state courts may become more effective by establishing better forms of cooperation with local justice providers. This requires an open but critical mind set where local normative orders are neither a priori condemned as inferior nor simply embraced. Local and international experts can collaborate with policymakers and state authorities in order to improve their knowledge base in this domain. At the level of support for right holders to know their rights, governmental actors may want to invest more efforts in adapting their message to local realities, concerns and demands while looking at how interventions can capitalise on local norms and practices that reinforce human rights. In addition, these interventions need to generate dialogic spaces in order to discuss how national legislation relates to local practices and norms and vice versa.

International non-governmental organisations are prone to work with national non-governmental actors, who in turn support justice users. Depending on the capacity of these local organisations, international non-governmental partners may support them in generating a domestic demand for addressing the challenges posed by legal pluralism. Both international and national non-governmental actors may also provide technical advice within national policies and state-sponsored interventions. National civil society organisations also collaborate with domestic governments in the implementation of certain strategies, such as the dissemination of state laws. In this regard, these organisations may generate valuable knowledge on local realities and adapt their strategies accordingly, as well as promote that local contributions feed back into national processes of policymaking and law reform.

These recommendations reflect the view that justice sector aid in legally plural Africa requires that interventions at different levels reinforce each other and address both sides of the coin, i.e. provision and demand. Moreover, making state justice more responsive to local realities by taking account of the legally plural medium in which state justice institutions are immersed may indirectly contribute to improving the operation of local justice processes in general. A number of factors may nonetheless constrain development actors' implementation of the above suggested recommendations. First, one of the issues that was raised by policymakers during the field research and at the international forum in Cape Town is that the resources allocated to the justice sector are limited as compared to other sectors such as health, education, and infrastructure. That said, some of these recommendations require more a change in mind sets than big changes in fund allocation. Second, the justice sector tends to be fragmented so that generating participatory policy dialogues may be a complex undertaking. Nevertheless, some experiences from other countries in the region suggest that the exercise is worth trying.[3] Finally, there are a series of constraints related to the availability of local capacity, such as a limited choice of appropriate local partners, and a low knowledge base on the extent to which human rights, in their current form, are able to contain abuses of power by authorities other than the state. These issues require a constant effort to generate new knowledge and test its applicability.

---

[3] See Rawls, 2011.

However, one might question whether the issue is confined to improving the strategies that underpin the practice of development actors? According to Stephens (2009), the issue that bedevils development practice in all fields of endeavour is how to bring about policy and institutional change in an environment that is hostile to reform. According to him, there are three pre-conditions for advancing a policy agenda: political support, resources and a coherent strategy. The main contribution of Part III of this book lies with the third element. In other words, this analysis may hopefully contribute to overcoming relatively 'benign' though not to be underestimated constraints, such as the lack of coherent theories of social change or epistemological bias in justice sector aid and human rights assistance. However, how to generate political support and a genuine commitment to the implementation of coherent strategies, while making enough resources available to achieve this end, are amongst the topics that researchers in this field may want to investigate further.

Complementary research may explore how the internal organisational logic and political interests of different development actors may enable or constrain the implementation of these strategies. Studies may examine the interplay between donors' policies at headquarters level and their implementation at country level. They may also elucidate what international actors are able to influence within justice sector national policies in this domain. At another level, additional research may deepen the findings presented here by documenting the impact of specific interventions that incorporate any of the above suggested recommendations. In particular, researchers may want to focus on the extent to which development practice in this area contributes to more inclusive interpretations and definitions of human rights as well as the factors that influence this. More generally, further research is needed on how the paradigms of justice that underpin the operation of local legal orders relate to specific human rights standards in their current form. On the one hand, this may yield valuable insights into whether human rights standards need to be revisited in order to contain abuses of power by authorities administering justice outside the realm of the state. On the other, it may uncover alternative ways of protecting human dignity, which may enrich our global possibilities to claim and enjoy human rights.

BIBLIOGRAPHY

Rawls, A. (2011) Policy Proposals for Justice Reform in Liberia: Opportunities under the Current Legal Framework to Expand Access to Justice. In Ubink, J. (ed.) *Customary Justice: Perspectives on Legal Empowerment*. Rome: International Legal Development Organisation.

Stephens, M. (2009) The Commission on Legal Empowerment of the Poor: An Opportunity Missed, *Hague Journal on the Rule of Law*, 1, 132–157.

PART IV

GENERAL CONCLUSION

CHAPTER 16
EMBRACING LEGAL PLURALISM: GENERAL CONCLUSION

Giselle CORRADI, Lia NIJZINK and Martien SCHOTSMANS

1. INTRODUCTION

Due to a number of important differences between transitional justice and justice sector aid, this book explored how international actors address 'traditional justice' in these fields in two distinct parts, which has led to separate analyses. Justice sector aid is often part of broader development cooperation programmes, which may or may not take place in a post-conflict country. Transitional justice processes are part of conflict-related international interventions, such as peacebuilding programmes, which are often implemented before the wheels of more long-term development cooperation programmes are set in motion. Chronologically speaking, both kinds of programmes – support for transitional justice and justice sector aid – often do not run parallel, although there can be overlaps. It also turns out that the international actors are not necessarily the same. Although in principle the same donor countries are involved, justice sector aid is often provided by bilateral or multilateral development organisations, while transitional justice interventions are more often – but certainly not exclusively – initiatives of specific agencies aimed at post-conflict reconstruction, which are established by several donor countries. Although respect for human rights is heavily emphasised in both domains, policy and interventions regarding transitional justice also need to take international norms regarding the criminal prosecution of international crimes into account. In spite of these differences, this concluding chapter formulates a number of mutual findings and recommendations. First, it discusses common elements at the level of policies, then it identifies a number of trends regarding interventions, and finally it examines the way in which international actors handle the tension between traditional justice and human rights.

2. POLICIES IN THE FIELD OF TRADITIONAL JUSTICE

Both parts of this book show that international actors rely on a discourse of respect for the guidelines of the Paris Declaration regarding ownership in order to justify that their support is aligned with the policy of the recipient government. In other words, if the government proposes a certain approach towards traditional justice, international actors are inclined to follow this approach without being too critical about it.

In the field of justice sector aid, support for traditional justice is justified by rhetoric of improved access to justice for the poor, but at the same time this seems to be optional. The cases considered in Part III of this book demonstrate that when recipient governments pay marginal attention to this topic, international actors do not question this. Despite the guidelines that were produced by several international actors regarding the relevance of traditional justice and legal pluralism in the context of justice sector aid, country representatives of these organisations tend to look at these issues as a matter of choice. In the field of transitional justice an evolution occurred from internationally imposed standard models towards more attention for strategies adapted to the local context and based more on local ownership. If tradition-based mechanisms are part of the official transitional justice policy, international actors will support it. If they are not, the funding of any possible unofficial initiatives is mostly left to international NGOs or foundations. If traditional mechanisms are part of the official policy but are not yet operational, actors take an attitude of wait and see, and they will mainly support preparatory actions.

This implies that the perspectives and experiences of justice seekers in both fields are not always considered. Moreover, justice seekers' perspectives seem to have little influence if they run against state policy or the preferences of international actors. Especially in cases of transitional justice, this leaves gaps on the level of accountability mechanisms at the local level. As mentioned earlier, ownership is one of the principles of the Paris Declaration that international policies rely on. While ownership was initially understood exclusively as state ownership, attention has more recently shifted towards the importance of participation of the civil society. But which civil society organisations are in a position to represent the multiple experiences and stakes of justice seekers? This book shows that international actors are too quickly satisfied with participation from actors of civil society, without answering these questions in depth. And even when civil society participates, the question remains to what extent this opinion is taken into account when policy is made. Recently, the field of transitional justice started to attach great importance to consulting the population, but the instruments used to do so do not always take the evolving nature of public opinion into account, nor the complexity of the world views on justice and reconciliation that people have. Often, consultative instruments only ask about the opinion of justice seekers concerning a certain conflict resolution mechanism or a certain legal order, without inquiring after their view on broader issues. Within justice sector aid, international actors are increasingly financing studies on justice seekers' experiences in legally plural contexts, but these studies are seldom considered the cornerstone of policy development.

3. TRENDS IN INTERVENTIONS ADDRESSING TRADITIONAL JUSTICE

Another common finding is that international actors supporting transitional justice and justice sector aid do not adopt a legally plural perspective. In the case of justice sector aid, international actors may support interventions addressing local legal orders, but as explained in Chapter 15, this is not the same as engaging with the dynamics and challenges that exist due to the co-existence of multiple normative sources in a same social field. Moreover, in most cases this involves support for officially recognised traditional justice, which is only one amongst the many layers of local justice provision. Although to date legal pluralism is hardly referred to in transitional justice, the trend is the same. Since traditional mechanisms as such are rarely suited for dealing with international crimes, they are usually adjusted and mixed with international norms, creating tradition-based, hybrid mechanisms. International actors often base their decision to support such mechanisms on the extent to which they are part of the official policy ('official legal pluralism'), and – due to concerns with criminal accountability for international crimes – on the extent to which they differ from international norms. There is little room for supporting tradition-based views on accountability for crimes that heavily deviate from international norms as an alternative for retributive prosecutions.

In addition, both parts of this book indicate that most interventions related to traditional justice opt for a top-down approach, which is characterised by a lack of dialogue. Only in a few cases was a more bottom-up approach advanced and supported. Even if the outcome of bottom-up approaches is unpredictable, mutual openness and the creation of dialogic spaces are essential in order to attain an integrated approach to justice that takes peoples' 'hybrid' experiences into account. The investigated interventions show that international actors would be wise to increase their awareness of 'interlegality', i.e. the fact that people rely and combine several legal orders (Santos, 2002). Traditional justice, its values and its mechanisms for dispute processing, occupy an important position in the legal landscapes of all the countries considered in this book. It is therefore important that interventions take into account how these interplay with state legal orders. In other words, more important than considering legal pluralism as a matter of policy choice, development actors need to understand it as an empirical reality that impacts interventions one way or the other. Hence, the need to engage with it.

4. STRATEGIES REGARDING THE TENSION BETWEEN TRADITIONAL JUSTICE AND HUMAN RIGHTS

Concerning the tension between traditional justice and human rights, Parts II and III of this book show that international actors deploy a range of strategies to advance human rights within tradition-based legal orders and mechanisms of dispute processing. These strategies are mainly 'legal'. However, the extent to which human rights are respected and protected is linked to broader societal preconditions leading to their institutionalisation (Rask Madsen et al., 2013). These issues are often overlooked and left unaddressed by interventions. In addition, most interventions tend to look at legal orders in isolation, i.e. they examine whether a certain legal order respects human rights or not. By contrast, a legally plural perspective points to the need to assess which actors rely on which normative orders and for which purposes. Such perspective demonstrates that justice seekers combine legal orders and contest them, sometimes by relying on human rights. By understanding how different actors relate to multiple normative orders in their quest for justice and the role of human rights therein, interventions can build on ongoing dynamics of social change. In the field of transitional justice in particular, the international community is one of these actors, either through its interest to end conflicts and bring about sustainable peace, or because the nature of international crimes forces the community to take action following internationally agreed upon norms. This is why its values and objectives – next to those of the locally involved individuals and those of the national authorities of the country concerned – are also important. Mutual acknowledgement and acceptance of each other's values, stakes and interpretations of human rights can lead to hybrid strategies to deal with past crimes that are legitimate and acceptable to the different stakeholders involved. This requires, every time and in each country, a dialogical process. This can consume a lot of time and go against the already time-bound nature of the interventions of international actors. This might be uncomfortable for international actors, but it is essential nonetheless.

5. RECOMMENDATIONS

One of the main objectives of this book is to orientate future strategies of international actors regarding traditional justice in the fields of transitional justice and justice sector aid. To this end, this section formulates a number of concrete recommendations based on the analyses presented in Parts II and III.

5.1. RECOMMENDATIONS REGARDING TRANSITIONAL JUSTICE

5.1.1. Refine the Concept of Local Ownership

- First of all, policymakers, who in application of the Paris Declaration rightfully align their policy with the policy of the partner country, are encouraged to understand local ownership not as merely state ownership but as national ownership.
- This means that the views of non-state stakeholders should be taken into account in developing and implementing the official transitional justice policy, through dialogue with civil society and popular consultations.
- The needs for transitional justice existing at the local level should be assessed, especially if victims and offenders need to coexist after the conflict. Since it turns out that there is not just a need for reintegration or reconciliation at this level, but also a need for mechanisms to establish (non-criminal) accountability for crimes, and that the lack thereof can lead to tensions and stigmatisation with the potential to threaten sustainable peace, it is important to examine the potential of local, tradition-based mechanisms.
- Even if certain activities or initiatives do not feature in the official transitional justice policy but are still identified as being important by civil society and/or the population, donors should consider to support these, and should not leave this to non-state donors or international NGOs, so that systematic and coherent support, including the necessary guarantees and oversight, can be developed.
- When searching for local views, one should make sure to consult a broad range of representative stakeholders and not automatically assume that representatives of civil society effectively reflect the population's opinions.
- There should also be consideration of the evolution of opinions and needs over time, depending on the country's security situation and other aspects of the post-conflict situation, meaning that local views should regularly be inquired after and that the developed policy should be sufficiently flexible to take this evolution into account.
- It is important to realise that local views on justice and reconciliation are part of a cosmovision, which may be unfamiliar to the West, as certain questions in surveys show. If international actors wish to encourage local ownership they should keep an open mind for the complex, sometimes divergent or conflicting views that may come to the fore, and which may also deserve support.

5.1.2. *Understand Transitional Justice Holistically*

- Human rights tensions identified in transitional justice are often not limited to traditional justice, since this is part of a wider social, political context and the power relations in that context, which may be conservative, discriminatory or even conflict-generating, meaning that an isolated approach to traditional mechanisms and practices is useless.
- This is best illustrated by the ways both offenders and victims of sexual violence are treated, since the importance of restoring social harmony is taken into account more than the interests and views of the individuals involved. If the use of tradition-based mechanisms is considered for addressing sexual violence, the context needs to be carefully considered.
- It is furthermore important not to understand tradition as something from which certain fragmentary elements can be isolated to increase legitimacy or ownership of activities in the eyes of the population. 'Localising' an already existing mechanism by selectively adding a few traditional elements, such as ritual cleansing, can – depending on the context – lead to unexpected and even harmful results, which conflict with the 'do no harm' principle. International actors have a responsibility for the choices they make, also with respect to the local population that bears the consequences.
- Donors also need to be aware of the impact that the choices they make in the context of peacebuilding (such as empowering traditional leaders to take part in peace negotiations or supporting traditional ceremonies during demobilisation) can eventually have on choices to be made in transitional justice, since their support can reinforce or decrease the legitimacy of certain mechanisms.
- Both exchanges with civil society and consultations with the population should therefore be supplemented with more in-depth research, on the one hand of a legal-anthropological nature (a combination of already conducted studies from the pre-conflict period and new research in light of the conflict), on the other hand of a political nature. Only a careful analysis of the specific context, combined with legal anthropological and political studies, can bring the complex combination of divergent views, values and power relations to light.
- There should also be sufficient attention for the interdependence between the local, national and international levels. A one-sided emphasis on tradition-based solutions entails a risk of limiting responsibility for the conflict and the response to it, exclusively to the local level. This could imply that both the responsibility and legitimate interest of the national and international level can be underappreciated, and the impact of the (in)action at one level on the results at the other level could be underestimated.
- Every donor intervention regarding transitional justice should therefore involve a preliminary analysis and research phase lasting several months.

This would allow for a more holistic approach to transitional justice, which acknowledges the interconnectedness and equal importance of the local, national and international levels, which would allow for the formulation and implementation of a coherent strategy, allowing interventions to be planned and checks and balances to be included accordingly.

5.1.3. Support Transitional Justice as a Hybridisation Process

- Checks and balances, however, cannot be imposed from a hierarchal top-down position. Clauses in peace agreements or funding contracts that subject the use of tradition-based mechanisms to the integration of international standards and human rights are not effective in themselves, since they only strive to transplant norms from one normative order to another.
- Donors should be aware that clashes between various, overlapping normative orders can occur in all societies and at any moment, and are therefore a reality that is not limited to post-conflict countries, though they can be more pronounced in post-conflict countries because of the fundamental choices that are necessary in the framework of transitional justice.
- Hence, donors should, besides automatically integrating a preliminary research phase, be prepared to invest in preliminary, dialectical, time-consuming processes to create legitimate, hybrid transitional justice mechanisms, orders and standards, by combining a particular society's underlying, traditional values with international human rights and criminal law norms (such as the processes donors have been supporting in Uganda and Burundi).
- If donors engage in the above, they should be aware that this will require long-term, enduring efforts, together with diplomatic interventions to maintain the transitional justice momentum. They should also be aware that stakeholders who are involved in the process do not only expect (financial and diplomatic) support to the process itself, but also to its outcome (i.e. the transitional justice mechanisms).
- The new, hybrid mechanisms created by such processes will be unique to the country involved and cannot be transplanted to other post-conflict countries, nor can one hope that this will lead to a new standard model for tradition-based justice and reconciliation mechanisms. Nevertheless, the experience with several of these processes could lead to a new transitional justice paradigm, based on 'strong' legal pluralism.
- Donors should therefore be aware of their crucial position in this process, even if it is uncomfortable.

5.2. RECOMMENDATIONS REGARDING JUSTICE SECTOR AID

5.2.1. *Adopt a Dynamic Perspective on Local Legal Orders and Human Rights*

- All legal orders are contested and change, including so-called 'traditional' ones. The same applies to human rights. Diverse views may be embedded in conflicting interests and power differentials. This often determines whose version prevails. Development actors can take account of these issues by providing support for inclusive processes of dialogue and decision-making. This could take the form of capacity building for marginalised stakeholders at local level to participate in grassroots debates about human rights and access to justice or lobbying so that local views and experiences are considered within national policies.
- Local legal orders should not be seen as isolated normative frameworks, nor as alternatives to state justice. Justice seekers rely on and combine both. Moreover, the extent to which local normative orders uphold human rights is often influenced by the availability of state justice and the knowledge of state law. Therefore, support for local legal orders should not be seen as a replacement for support to state justice.
- Regarding the promotion of human rights within local justice processes, international actors should provide training to governmental and civil society actors on dialogical and intercultural methodologies (see Chapter 10). This means that education on state law and human rights at grassroots level should include a discussion of how these relate to locally existing normative orders.

5.2.2. *Adopt a Legally Plural Perspective*

- International actors should understand the difference between normative and empirical legal pluralism, since these two aspects of the phenomenon may lead to different types of intervention (see Chapter 10).
- Engaging local legal orders is not the same as addressing legal pluralism. A legally plural perspective entails understanding which normative repertoires and justice forums are available in a certain locality, how they interact with each other and how this affects access to justice and human rights. Development actors can finance research on these issues and lobby so that these insights are taken into account within justice sector policies.
- Development actors should also support initiatives that contribute to a better collaboration between state and local justice providers, such as encounters where both share their views and experiences, observation of each others' work, etc. This should be accompanied by training on legal pluralism and

cross-cultural approaches to human rights in order to avoid state justice providers adopting a superior position.

5.2.3. *Adopt a Power-Informed Perspective*

- Development actors should be aware of the fact that norms and justice forums constitute 'resources' that justice seekers mobilise in order to advance their interests. Legal education about human rights and state laws, especially when these activities include discussions on how these relate to local normative orders, can therefore empower marginalised populations. The same applies to initiatives that improve marginalised groups' access to forums that uphold these laws.
- However, state law and state justice are not always the best or only resource. In some cases, justice seekers may find better protection in local norms and forums. Development actors can provide support for legal anthropological studies producing knowledge on which normative orders deserve which kind of protection and to whom, particularly in the area of gender and natural resource management. This knowledge should form the basis of further interventions.

BIBLIOGRAPHY

Rask Madsen, M. and Verschraegen, G. (2013) Making human rights intelligible: An introduction to a sociology of human rights. In Rask Madsen, M. and Verschraegen, G. (eds.) *Making human rights intelligible. Towards a sociology of human rights.* Oxford/Portland, OR: Hart Publishing.

www.ingramcontent.com/pod-product-compliance
Ingram Content Group UK Ltd.
Pitfield, Milton Keynes, MK11 3LW, UK
UKHW051922100926
8556IPUK00021B/1320

9 781780 682877